The Big Band Days: A Memoir and Source Book

By

John "Jack" Behrens

ISBN: 1-4033-6857-0 (e-book)
ISBN: 1-4033-6858-9 (Paperback)

This book is printed on acid free paper.

Cover photos: Harry James and his Chesterfield Music Makers, Jimmy Dorsey, Tony Pastor and Bunny Berigan. Photos courtesy of Lou DiSario.

1stBooks - rev. 10/24/02

CONTENTS

Foreword

I am an unabashed fan of the good old days, specifically, the good old days of the age of swing. Unfortunately, I missed that era by a generation. As fond as I am of rock'n'roll, I wish the garage bands I played in had been struggling to play stock arrangements of "In The Mood" or "Take the A Train" instead of the top ten of 1965. I fantasize at times about growing up when my father did, when swing was the thing.

The concept of "swing" is almost impossible to define. In musical terms, it has something to do with the way musicians play eighth notes, with the interaction between the bassist and the drummer, with the pitting of the brass section against the reed section and, of course, it has everything to do with the era in which it was conceived. This was an era where music was precious, not omnipresent. I can't imagine young people thought it was low tech to wait until the Saturday night radio broadcast to hear their favorite groups or that it was bothersome to flip their 78's after two and a half minutes. It was a time when fans were allowed to use their imaginations. The desire to see and hear your favorite band was not fulfilled in your living room with a three minute MTV video but in a live show at the local ballroom. And it was a time when parental advisory stickers were not required.

Luckily for musicians, it was an era when the problem of creating more sound for larger venues was solved by adding people, not amplifiers. Bands numbering up to eighteen players were everywhere. A young musician might find work with a territory band, playing dance halls and gin mills in a specific area of the country. After the on-the-job training, he might catch a break and land in one of the *big*, big bands, crisscrossing the country in a bus or a Pullman railroad car. While singers were an important element, we had yet to arrive at a time when vocalists were backed by nameless orchestras. Each band had its fans and they knew who sat in the drum chair, who blew hot trumpet, lead alto and jazz tenor. Downbeat kept track of personnel in the top bands and broke the news if one band raided another (When Johnny Hodges left Ellington it would have been as if Paul McCartney had abandoned the Beatles!).

I know it was not all great, as does author Jack Behrens. Life on the road was rough and very few musicians got rich or even close to it. Trumpeter Wendell Brunious told me: "yes, Lionel Hampton paid weekly…very weakly." The more creative sidemen grew frustrated sitting in their sections waiting for those sixteen measures where they might play licks of their own invention instead of the arrangers. Personal relationships were bound to ebb and flow. Imagine sixteen men on a bus day after day where laundry might be done in a backstage sink and a "bathroom stop" could mean leaning out the door with the vehicle still in motion.

Still, I wish the time machine was a reality, because *The Big Band Days* reminds me that I arrived after the songs had pretty much ended. Jack writes from a double perspective, as a fan and as a swing musician himself. He weaves stories and anecdotes from his extensive interviews that illuminate the role of the well known and the hardly known. His own experiences as a young drummer were shared by countless sidemen whose names never made it to the back of an album cover. I am pleased to see him draw attention to the musicians of Upstate New York, underscoring the fact that swing and jazz are not the sole property of the big cities. Importantly, Jack recognizes the fact that music cannot survive as a museum piece and his nostalgic documentation of big band leaders, movies and ballroom segues into a detailed listing of current jazz festivals, swing organization web sites and educational resources. And the big band trivia test is a hoot.

As director of the Hamilton College Jazz Archive, I have had my own opportunities to meet and interview musicians from the swing era. Variations on the phrase "I'm glad I was a part of it" were spoken over and over. Jack was a part of it. Fortunately, he can write about it, too, both with deep insight and humorous perspective. As his first chapter states, "It Was Too Much Fun To Call It Work."

After all, why do you think they call it *playing*?

Monk Rowe
www.monkrowe.com
Director
Hamilton College Jazz Archive

Introduction

God works in mysterious ways my grandmother used to say. It didn't matter what the problem or crisis. Grades. Something I hadn't done. Something I did...What ever it was, she said, God had the answer.

Years later, like most of us, I realized how right she was. Regrettably, I never had the chance to tell her. Yet, I know she's smiling right now. She knew she was right all along.

It was God who made sure that I didn't become a professional musician. God knew what I didn't; as a drummer I didn't have the confidence and perseverance to *really* make it. Sure, I had the enthusiasm, the huge Slingerland set complete with floor toms and an array of Zildjian cymbals. Some believed I had the talent, too. I even had two years where most of my annual earnings came from playing gigs. But He intervened. He saw to it I met this girl from a nearby community and she was ambitious, determined and wanted no part of a life as a band roadie's wife. When I got back from military service one of the first things that greeted me in our one-bedroom apartment was my dust-covered bass and drum case with assorted stands. Without too many words between us, I got the message. The drums were sold within a couple of weeks.

Yes, grandmother's words have always been with me. They've brought me through life and death matters, career decisions and, now, at a time when I can really understand what my parents and grandparents meant about getting old...doing things like writing this book.

But music has been my life since I was old enough to know the sounds I heard coming from a varnished wood shell Philco in a corner of the room. My six years as a territorial band musician and membership in James C. Petrillo's American Federation of Musicians were icing on my musical cake. It started with the violin that had been handed down from family member to family member (and still sits forlornly in my basement closet) and took a controversial turn to crashing cymbals and crisp rim shots on a snare when I determined I wanted to be a drummer. The family wasn't keen on my instrument of choice. At times I felt like Bix Beiderbecke, the great trumpet player a generation ahead of me. He tried everything to get his Iowa parents to respect his work as a jazz musician only to discover at a vulnerable time in his life—28 and near death, in fact—they had stashed every record he ever sent to them in the hallway closet...unopened.

My parents thought it was a phase that would end if they ignored it...and me. No, I absolutely couldn't major in music at college, they said. No, I couldn't make a living as a musician (they knew more than I did on that score!) and no, don't count on bopping in and out of the house to have the laundry done like Rolly Bundock, the bass player with Glenn Miller and Les Brown who used to drop in unannounced on his parents when he was close to Boston and leave the same day...with clean clothes.

My "big" band work (my father used to fume when I said I worked as a drummer and was paid) began with a well-respected territory band directed by Dick Trimble. A long time school friend, Jim Booker, who would go on to play in some other territorial bands and service groups, urged me to give Dick a call when his popular drummer and vocalist, Kenny Carpenter, decided to step out after years of weekends and holidays away from his family. There was a catch: all I owned was a snare drum and a battered hi-hat that might have been around since the first one was manufactured in 1927. I talked to the leader...but I apparently ignored that part of the discussion. He assumed I had all the necessary equipment.

When I arrived at his music store to rehearse with the band with a snare and a hi-hat...he wasn't exactly ready to offer much hope. Fortunately, he let me use a new drum set he had in his display window...but his warning was quick and clear: "You aren't the piano player, you know. Drummers are expected to have their own drums! No drums...no work!," he said with enough exasperation to send me on my way with no hope.

When I got home my mom sensed my depression. I didn't expect much sympathy. In fact, I thought my parents would be thrilled. Dick had innocently let slip to me that "I know your old man and he doesn't think much of this idea."

After telling her I had no future...my life was over and I was canceling all weekend plans (remember in the 1940s we had no television set to help us rehabilitate), I retired to a basement hideaway.

Some time later, I found out that my mom had confronted my father about my dire circumstances and to ensure family harmony my father had sought out Dick's drummer, then an advertising person with the local newspaper. My father bought the set without knowing what he had purchased aside from the fact that it was what Kenny used to play. The next day my mother calmly told me at breakfast that I had a set of drums at Dick's store "just DON'T bring them home. Leave them at the store." I learned something about parenting that day, too.

I got the job, played that weekend without a rehearsal, got some backhanded praise from a very critical trumpet player who kept mumbling that since I couldn't sing "what good are you to us?" Later, I found Webb Ricketts, longtime lead trumpet with the band, a great guy when it came to sound balance and my loudness, softness and solos. Together with people like Dick, Jimmy Claar, a soft-spoken Hoagy Carmichael on the piano; a beefy bassman from the farm, Dano Estell, a gentle giant who made it possible for me to sneak two and four-beat rhythm in when I wanted to, and Jim, who became my wheels since my father wouldn't let me drive (my father sold insurance and in those days children of insurance men were like those who were minister's sons) life for me started every weekend.

Dick knew what it meant to be a professional musician. He believed if he could just catch a break in the band business like nearby Circleville, OH entertainer Ted Lewis of "Is Everybody Happy?" fame, he could be on his way.

Lewis, he remembered, was a real showman who took a "sobbing clarinet," a battered top hat and some hackneyed clichés during an economic depression when few faces were smiling and made a name for himself in music, stage, radio, screen and, later on, television.

Dick Trimble, like Lewis, saw stardom and wanted to be a part of it. He was born of the era of Cab Calloway, Carmichael, Benny Carter, Big Sid Catlett, the Crosby boys, Bing and Bob, as well as Lewis.

He agreed with other more hip musicians that Lewis, who hired top sidemen and made popular the song "When My Baby Smiles at Me," played corny music. Yet he also knew that Ted's style was extremely popular.

The big hurdle, consequently, was being discovered. But Dick sometimes overlooked the strength of his own regional popularity.

Stan Kenton, a bandleader who during his lifetime was always on the fringe of musical popularity and became resigned to it, told a radio interviewer late in his life that the most important thing he ever did in the business "was getting bookings for my band. We worked regularly. George Shearing said the same thing," Stan confessed.

Certainly no one who played with Dick Trimble could say he didn't give it his best in the very competitive band business of the 1940s and 1950s. The Trimble band, which started in the mid-1930s, played throughout Central Ohio in high school gyms, armories, country clubs, wedding receptions, hotels, service club events, fraternity and sorority parties, lakeside ballrooms and community programs.

It was a band that also loved to please dancers as well as listeners. And to many who heard it, Dick succeeded. "I love to go to the lake on a warm weekend evening with whoever I was going with at the time, walk up the wooden steps to the ballroom, find a booth usually filled with friends and wait for the music. What a thrill, dancing to music in an open air pavilion. Besides a Coke, you couldn't ask for more when Trimble played because there was no cover charge," said one of the thousands of Trimble band fans from the early 1950s.

I couldn't have asked for a better teacher and a more comfortable group of weekend and holiday friends. I couldn't have asked for a better way to break into an industry.

Later, I played college fraternity and sorority smokers (remember when packs of Chesterfields were handed out like candy?), night club openers, those lavish college and university proms and holiday dances where I didn't know I was playing until I'd get a call several hours before the gig to tell me a drummer was needed...be there. Sometimes, I didn't know anyone else in the group, mostly collegians and territory musicians, and sometimes...we didn't get paid either. I started to see the dark side of a business that could take a toll on your health (more alcoholics than I had ever met and a few marijuana smokers who gave our bandstand a blue halo and got us fired once or twice too).

Such experiences came back in chunks of long term memory and became a motivating factor in writing this book. I wanted to give back in some small way what I felt about musical acquaintances, events and circumstances and, at the same time, provide a compendium that gives a reader more than just a memoir. Over more than two years of research and reviewing my collection of nearly 2,000 recordings dating back to 45s, I interviewed more than 80 musicians, leaders, ballroom people, sons and daughters of former big bandleaders and others, like me, who were somewhere on the fringe of something we felt inside every night we played, sang or performed. I didn't find one who considered it was merely a "job" even though many talked less fondly of the travel and living accommodations they had to endure. Most said money was important to survive but it didn't prevent them from spending endless hours of voluntary individual practice and rehearsals. They dreamed about the lucky day "the call" would come. Unfortunately, it rarely did.

And I never forgot grandmother's words when it came time to make choices.

I hope your life has had the kind of musical interludes that make this book so special to me.

Jack Behrens
Clinton, NY

Typical Wildroot Cream-Oil ad in a weekly Life Magazine promoting the Woody Herman Show on the ABC (blue) Network, circa 1946

Every Community has an Elks Club and had held dances on the weekend. Here's where I started in the late 1940s at the Lancaster (OH) Elks Club.

Tommy Reynolds was a popular clarinetist and bandleader in the 1930s and 1940s.
Photo courtesy Louis DiSario

Two teenagers destined for the band business with or without "axes".
The tenor saxophonist is Jim Booker. The drummer with a makeshift set is the author.

I. It Was Too Much Fun To Call It Work

It was the worst of times yet it was likely the best of musical times for the big band business.

It was 1940...War spilled from country to country in Europe and a threatening Japanese empire churned through Asia destroying nations, murdering civilians and menacing the world.

America, meanwhile, was mesmerized by music makers out of the '30s swinging and swaying in ballrooms, nightclubs, high school gyms and college fraternity houses. The swing era—some believe it started with Benny Goodman's tour that came screaming East from hundreds of bobbysoxers and teens at the Palomar Ballroom the night of Aug. 21, 1935—was riding a crest of popularity for bandleaders, soloists, thrushes (remember who they were?) and boy (that's what they were called) singers.

Benny played his first gig at 16 in a day without child labor laws with the Ben Pollack band. He'd been heard mimicking popular clarinetist Ted Lewis. Others started early, too. Talented composer/arranger/trombonist Neal Hefti needed to help his family with income and at 17 went on the road with Nat Towles' band writing ballads. A year later he was on tour with Dick Berry Band when he was let go after the second gig. Stranded in New Jersey with no money to get back to his Midwest home, he was able to join the Bob Astor Band. He never forgot what it meant to lose a job during hard times and get back up and find his way.

Trombone player and leader, Urbane Clifford "Urbie" Green had a similar story. Born in Mobile, AL, he began his big band appearances at 16 shortly after his father died. He had to support his mother and sister when the family moved to California and he spent his teenage years with the bands of Tommy Reynolds, Bob Strong and Frankie Carle.

Les Brown started in the music business when he was 6 with his musician father in a community band. Buddy Rich was traps the boy drumming wonder at 2. At 8, singer/composer/drummer Mel Torme was doing vocals as a solo and in groups. Talented people rarely had childhoods in those days.

Goodman, of course, became a popular New York City studio musician in 1929 and started his first band three years later. Although his only competition during the difficult days of the Depression was the Casa Loma band, it took a second Goodman band two years later to really set the stage for the man crowned the King of Swing. He was chosen one of three bands on a coast-to-coast "Let's Dance" party night on NBC. Most swing fans probably remembered Benny's band not those of Xavier Cugat, the ex-cartoonist Latin bandleader, and Kel Murray who shared the five hour program. It was packaged perfectly for bands seeking exposure. Each time zone was covered with lots of music; there were three hours in the Eastern and Central time zones while the Mountain sector got two hours as did the West Coast.

Not everyone thought Benny was necessarily swing's godfather, however. Said Gunther Schuller in his intellectual examination of the age called "The Swing Era,": "The Goodman band (in 1938) here was not much more creative than the Jan Garbers, Dick Jurgens, Kay Kysers and so on."

But survival was clearly what any musician had to worry about in those foreboding days. The Depression had cost popular bandleaders Louis Armstrong and Duke Ellington engagements and they decided to journey to Europe to seek places to play. Every East Coast musician was mindful of how tough it was to just pay the rent and not succumb to the Bix Beiderbecke tragedy. A legend among musician friends for his phrasing, friendliness and his recording—considered a jazz classic—"In A Mist," he died broke in a boarding house at 28 years old, an alcoholic. Stories about Bix abound but one of the best, his friends say, had to do with keeping his low rent boarding house room and not offending the landlord with the many jam sessions he and the Dorsey brothers held. After the first complaints brought warnings, Bix and friends muffled the piano in his bathroom with every kind of paper they could find so they could keep the music going all night.

Leo Walker, a legendary big band historian and music businessman, says the first fulltime dance band leader was probably Wilber Sweatman who played regularly in Chicago in 1911. He called himself a "ragtime clarinetist" who could play three instruments at the same time and, consequently, was considered more a vaudeville act than a band leader.

Walker had his own candidate for the title of the first big band leader, however. His name was Art Hickman, a musician whose love of baseball possibly produced the big touring band era as we know it. Hickman followed the San Francisco Seals, a professional baseball team, and when the club went to Spring Training in Sonoma County, CA, he approached Seals' manager Del Howard in 1913 with an idea: why not sponsor a series of dances to relieve the boring evenings at camp?

Howard liked the idea, Walker remembered, and Hickman found a spring home for his band.

It was the celebrated Florenz Ziegfeld of the Follies' fame, who heard the band and invited Hickman and company East where they played the Biltmore and the Ziegfeld Roof. Big bands had come of age.

Of course, some want to believe the credit goes to a roly poly violinist with a handle bar mustache named Paul "Pops" Whiteman. He also started on the West Coast playing his first set in the Fairmont Hotel in his hometown, San Francisco. Whiteman, it had been said, was an ambitious bandsman who ended up with the baton by accident. The story was that trumpeter Henry "Hot Lips" Busse started a band but found difficulty making announcements because of his heavy German accent. Whiteman was asked to lead the band. The rest was history…and marketing.

To his credit, Whiteman added more flavor to the big band period and possibly created his own legacy at the same time. He was considered the first white band leader to use complete arrangements to fit his orchestra of more than 40 musicians. He flavored his charts with a European sound created by Ferde Grofe and he hired him to add symphonic jazz to harmonize themes using saxophones, a first for an instrument previously used only in vaudeville. Whiteman's first recordings sold over 3 million copies and helped establish the title "King of Jazz" that was set aside a few years later when Benny Goodman was dubbed "King of Swing."

Few of Tom Brokaw's Greatest Generation could forget the excitement of Goodman's controversial but very successful Carnegie Hall concert, January 16, 1938. Carnegie was a high brow institution and had been since Peter Ilyich Tchaikowsky, the Russian composer, played to an opening audience in May, 1891. Even Goodman was nervous about how his music would be accepted. He wanted a warm up act and suggested comedienne Beatrice Lillie. Promoter Sol Hurok refused, saying it would make matters even worse to have humorous antics before an audience of critics and people totally unfamiliar with Goodman's new music. Carnegie officials were so concerned about the screeching and the decibel level they thought would be produced they had employees conduct a thorough search of the place to check seats, chandeliers, the walls and even the roof.

Smoking, of course, had become a national pastime worrying fire marshals about crowds in large halls. The sale of cigarettes virtually doubled in little more than a decade. Consequently, the American Tobacco Company saw the growth of radio and music as natural avenues for its audiences. In 1935, the Lucky Strike Hit Parade radio program was launched. At the same time, Max Gordon, considered by some a bohemian intellectual, who had a good eye for talent, launched the first Village Vanguard in the city. It has been called "The Carnegie Hall of Jazz Clubs" and later "cats" gave it the title "The Mecca of the Hip." Meanwhile in the Midwest, an East Coast musician who had learned how to play the organ while watching a theater organist finger and foot pedal the pipe organ, had organized his own group shortly after the death of his bandleader, Benny Moten. Bill Basie, called the "Count," had assembled some of the Moten sidemen and found a gig playing in the Reno Club, Kansas City. Swing was gathering momentum from clubs and bars to ballrooms.

Beer was 5 cents and whiskey was 15 cents a shot and the Count was making $15 a week to play from 8 p.m. until 4 a.m. except Saturday when the music was virtually non-stop from 8 pm. until 8 a.m.

Popular music of the time came hot from a place called Tin Pan Alley. Songs like "I'll Be Seeing You," "In the Mood," "Over the Rainbow," "We'll Meet Again," "How High the Moon," "Bewitched," and loads of other haunting melodies and swinging, toe-tapping numbers riffs that became songs lifted spirits and buoyed hope during the dark days when slogans like "Brother, can you spare a dime?" weren't humorous. But the music was infatuating…infectious.

"I'm a veteran big band listener. Give me 15 seconds of music and I could name the band…that is, if they played in the mid-1930s and early 1940s," the late Harold Whittemore, a longtime Gannett editor, writer and columnist in New York, wrote me. "I'm talking Emery Deutsch, Russ Morgan, Freddy Martin, Henry King, Eddie Duchin, Jan Garber, Johnny Long, Shep Fields, Sammy Kaye and, of course, Lawrence Welk from the Aragon and Trianon in Chicago along with Hal Kemp and Guy Lombardo. We used to catch all these bands on remote broadcasts late at night."

Like Harold, I was drawn by the allure of bandstands, touring musicians, snazzy uniforms, instruments and the suggestion of big money which created dreams and futures only teenagers could concoct. It certainly made an impact upon me in the 1940s.

My father unwittingly caused my fascination with faraway places and rhythmic sounds when he encouraged me to listen to radio remotes of the big bands. At a Central Ohio lake cottage on a Saturday night in the summertime for more years than I can remember, he'd let me stay up past midnight to join him in front of an old Philco radio playing the music of Ben Bernie from the Aragon Ballroom in Chicago, the rippling rhythm of Shep Fields from some club in Cleveland and a newcomer with a fresh sound, Glenn Miller from the Glen Island Casino on the Long Island shoreline.

Later, my dad would do everything possible to discourage me from playing the drums, my instrument of choice. He paid for violin lessons for a year but gave up when I persistently asked for, but was denied, a drum set. I was so determined I fashioned a pair of metal potato chip cans into a Gene Krupa-styled set with a very fragile hi-hat stand and a snare drum I had scrounged from the school.

My friends had horns—later we would call them "axes"—and we jammed whenever a parent would relent and let us use the garage or basement. Thanks to trumpet player John Huddle's mother, Dottie, we had a rehearsal basement site several times a week. My 15-year-old sister, Beverly, became our girl singer in rehearsals. We rehearsed more than we played in those days, frankly.

My summers were spent at an amusement park at Buckeye Lake where I volunteered to help bandleaders and musicians offload instruments from buses at the park's two ballrooms. I sat in on so many rehearsals I knew some scores by heart and listened to the shoptalk among musicians about the business. I devoured Downbeat and Metronome magazines, even submitted my first writing contributions to each. None ever made it in print but I did receive a nice note from the legendary jazz critic George T. Simon once telling me not to be discouraged.

Music would be my life one day, I thought. And bandleader Dick Trimble gave me the chance during my teens. He had a music store and led that typical territory band of high school music teachers, bank employees, utility workers, small business owners and college and high school students that played weekend engagements. You could usually find one in every town and city from New York to California. The Dick Trimble combo of five to eight depending upon the need played YM dances, Elk Clubs, Country Club Christmas and New Year's parties and a variety of other special community, high school and college events in Central Ohio.

Dick played alto sax and clarinet. He was born in the era of Cab Calloway, Hoagy Carmichael, Benny Carter, the Crosby boys, Bing and Bob, and Ted Lewis from nearby Circleville, OH. Robert "Webb" Ricketts, who spent 21 years playing trumpet in the band, told newspaper reporter Dwight Barnes in the 1990s that the Trimble combo "was one of the best around. We played jazz and sang. I'd describe our sound as being like Benny Goodman (which was Dick's favorite) and Glenn Miller. 'Once in A While' was one of my favorite numbers."

Tenor saxophone player Jim Booker, who gave up music for a career in law, believes music played an important part of his life although he didn't pursue it as a career. "Playing in the bands between 1950 and 1955, including the Trimble band, was very important to me. Dick was a fine musician as well as a kind mentor. It was something special that I could do and, of course, I loved the music. Like so many I dreamed about playing with touring big bands like you did. I wasn't a great musician but I am a great lover of the music," he told me.

Paul Kumler, another alto sax/clarinet player, recalls the band during the war years and later.

"I remember I took Dick's place while he was in the service. When he came back I moved over to tenor and we picked up a trombone player."

Trimble had previously played with two territory bands and, like Glenn Miller; he searched for a distinctive sound that gave his group appeal. "I was a sophomore in the high school marching band when I met Dick when he played at a school dance...I asked him if I could sit in some time," drummer/vocalist Kenny Carpenter said in a newspaper interview. He tried out when Dick's drummer left to join a "house" band locally. His voice added another dimension for Trimble and Kenny became another longtime member. "We were known as a university band because we played at places like Ohio Wesleyan. But we also played...the Deshler Wallick Hotel and the Neil House in Columbus, the American Legion and radio station WHOK on Sundays."

Jimmy Sain, a radio announcer at Lancaster's lone radio station, WHOK, remembers what it was like when the band did its shows on Sunday. Dick bought time on the radio to give listeners a chance to hear "Tempos With The Trimble Treatment." Like Miller, the most popular and savvy leader of the period who could cram more music into 15 minutes than any of his peers, Dick squeezed plenty of music into his half hour Sunday afternoon session. He wanted people, especially those who made dance program decisions, to hear the variety the band offered. A typical 4 p.m. Sunday live show at the station's Rt. 33 North studios would feature a mix of Dixie, ballads by vocalists Carpenter and Dottie Dare and current Hit Parade numbers. The band would slow down Les Brown's popular up tempo "I've Got My Love to Keep Me Warm," follow with Carpenter's rendition of "Blue Velvet," and then add more zest with Rosemary Clooney's "Come on to My House" sung by Dottie.

A show might also feature instrumentalists like Bob Bechtol, a high school music teacher and trombonist, who arranged, too. It was Bechtol during the late 1940s that provided the band with a medley of British pianist George Shearing hits. One of my thrilling moments came when we played the medley and I used tom-toms on a chorus and Trimble turned and glared at me. "Behrens!" he said after the number, "this wasn't written as a rumba! I pointed out that I thought it fit. Needless to say, I once more considered my future in the band when a couple strolled to the bandstand and told Dick loud enough for my ears "loved that tom-tom kick to the beat...that was so hep!" I occasionally inserted it after that and Dick said nothing.

"The band would also record at Dick's aunt's house. Back then, of course, there was no such thing as tape. And finding a studio was very expensive. I had to cut acetates once in a while and it took real coordination, believe me. I was watching once but I wasn't paying much attention until I realized that they were repeating something they had just recorded. I pointed out the error and they weren't too happy about it. But they simmered down and, in a few minutes, we had a good laugh," Sain smiled.

While many listeners and dancers took the music for granted, the musicians didn't. "Thanks to Dick, we took our sound seriously," says Kumler. I know that other territory bands I was with merely played gigs without much rehearsal time. Trimble, on the other hand, believed practice time was necessary. "The sax section which consisted of Paul Risor, Paul Smith, and Bob Skiever and, of course, Dick playing lead alto, was absolutely out of sight. They practiced nearly every day for an hour. Dick would mark the sheet music in the sax section so they would all breathe at the same time," Carpenter continued.

"There were enough good musicians around to put together really good bands," Sain remembers. "There were three or four groups or bands that were led by guys like Trimble and Dick McClintock (also of Lancaster). At the time, probably all of the good local musicians played with one or both of these guys and they probably could have worked every night of the week." A radio DJ for more than three decades in Ohio, Sain handled many of the remote dance sites.

The sound was the kind of uniform harmony that was pleasant on the ears at a time when big bands were experimenting with larger brass sections that could make a soft number sound loud.

Bands like Stan Kenton, Woody Herman, Harry James, and Count Basie turned up the volume with arrangements that featured trombones and trumpets for their audiences. What made the Trimble sound different to those who were really interested in the music was the way the saxophone section would give you a full chord of a number and breathe in unison instead of independently.

And it was very popular in an area that enjoyed dancing, remembered Dorothy Dare Moore, the band's girl singer. She exchanged her real name of Sands for "Dare" because she wanted something more exciting and her friends all "dared her to do it. I did everything from carrying band instruments across the street from the music store to the Sherman Armory (where the dances were held) to fixing dents in trumpets. Every place you went was an adventure. Every place was different when it came to the acoustics and the reception you got from the crowd," she told the Lancaster (OH) Eagle-Gazette.

The adventures, I discovered, were what went on before and after the music stopped. There were the early morning hours in the 1950s after a gig at the local Elks Club when I set my large Slingerland bass drum near my car at the top of Main Street hill and went to pick up my drum case by the door. A tipsy lady who was "taken" with my drumming stumbled over to my bass drum and launched it on a roll down the hill. I "caught" up with it near the traffic light at the bottom with only minor damage after a 100 yard dash that could have qualified in any Olympics. Antics and bizarre experiences could become routine, musicians of the era, said. A trumpet player in the Stan Kenton band told of a guy who stole a cow and tried to store it on the Kenton band bus! He also remembered a time when half the band showed up 400 miles away from the other half in a town with the same name.

Tenor man Jim Booker and I were kindred spirits on the Trimble band and saw ourselves striving to get breaks that would put our careers in the major leagues. Like many musicians, artists and writers of the time we thought "15 minutes of fame" like Andy Warhol talked about later would demonstrate our abilities. So it came as a shock to both of us at an engagement that Dick got at a high school dance when we were informed we would play a "square dance." Totally unacceptable to two "cool" musicians we insisted and we vowed not to play the set. In fact, we sat out the music for "squares." Dick calmly asked for my sticks and played drums while we were outside smoking cigarettes. He didn't dock us pay but he let me know that even "hepcat" musicians play what audiences want to hear or they don't work...and if I didn't like it, I could leave. It was a sobering lesson I never forgot...

Like other regions of the United States, there was exceptional talent in Ohio during the 1940 and 50s. I sat in with Bullmoose Jackson one night at the Chief Tecumseh Club outside Toledo and had the time of my life with a genial soul who not only was a good player...he was a totally relaxed, fun-loving person. A Cleveland native, Jackson was known as a boogie tenor saxophonist who could do a nasal but dreamy ballad like "I Love You, Yes I Do" and please women everywhere. When rock'n'roll put traditional musicians out of work, Bullmoose found a job as a janitor. He returned in the 1970s for a final tour with a Pittsburgh group.

Without a doubt, you didn't take your children to hear Bullmoose sing "Ten Inch," "I Want A Bowlegged Woman" or "Big Fat Mamas Are Back In Style Again." He didn't play to family audiences but neither did many musicians of the time. Second hand smoke in most clubs I played could have damaged our lungs for life whether we smoked or didn't His 1991 album said it all: "Badman Jackson, That's Me." He died in 1989 at 70.

There were other Ohioans who gained fame in the business, too. Wild Bill Davidson, a celebrated cornet player who recorded more than 800 numbers in his lifetime, was born in Defiance.

Vocalist Nancy Wilson hailed from Chillicothe. Sammy Kaye was from the Cleveland suburb of Lakewood and bandleaders Freddie Martin, Ray Anthony, Ken Peplowski and Henry Mancini, were also Clevelanders. Tenor player Dave Matthews is a Chagrin Falls native. Bandleader Ralph Flanagan was from nearby Lorain. Walter "PeeWee" Hunt whose "Twelfth Street Rag" put him on the charts was born in Mount Healthy. Trombonist/singer and bandleader Bobby Byrne left Columbus to play with the Dorsey brothers and head his own group. Rahsann Roland Kirk, one of the nation's outstanding reed talents, left Columbus to make his name. Also from the Capital city was one of great trumpet players of the big band era, Harry "Sweets" Edison. One of Count Basie's alto sax men, Earle Ronald Warren, came from Springfield. Trombonist Vic Dickenson was born in Xenia.

Singer Helen O'Connell, who older folks still remember for her popular duet with Bob Eberly doing "Green Eyes" while with Jimmy Dorsey, was a Lima native. Hezekiah Leroy Smith, later called "Stuff", played the violin and led bands after departing Portsmouth. Stuff's popularity, besides his dynamic personality and reputation as a drinker, was heard on Nat King Cole's "After Midnight" sessions.

Another band leader whose compositions and ear for distinctive sounds led to a career as a record producer was Enoch Light of Canton.

Certainly a prominent member of Ohio's popular musical hall of fame was John Carl "Jon" Hendricks, a composer, vocalist and drummer from Newark. His work with Bobby McFerrin on the evolution of the blues was an example of his creativity. Add Myron "Tiny" Bradshaw, a well-known leader from Youngstown right next door to crooner, leader and occasional trombonist, Vaughn Monroe of Akron of "Racing With the Moon" fame. Tenor sax player Frank Foster from Cincinnati can be included as can Duke Ellington's genius arranger who brought us "Take the A Train, "Lush Life" and others, Billy Strayhorn of Dayton. Another well-known Daytonite was J.C. Heard, a drummer whose playing with Jazz at the Philharmonic placed him among the best of the day. And don't forget the granddaddy of all piano players, the great Art Tatum of Toledo.

Finally, there was a brush-cut saxophonist with the largest horn-rimmed glasses I ever saw who you knew had talent when you heard him play. Whether it was a soft melody or a swinging solo or doing section work, Chuz Alfred of Lancaster, was always a reed player leaders could turn to. And they did.

He paid his dues in territory bands and then went on to lead his own group, cutting records and doing a road trip with Ralph Marterie.

For every Ohioan, there were hundreds of big band musicians from New York City, Brooklyn, Chicago, Los Angeles, Philadelphia, New Orleans and even a family of musicians named Brubeck from Concord, CA…

While most people identify New York City as the Big Apple of music, a steady amount of big band music flowed from upstate…from Buffalo to Albany with stops at Rochester, Syracuse and Utica.

Musicians like Sal Alberico Sr, Carmen Caramanica, the Zito family (Ronnie, Torrie and Fred), Jack Palmer, Jack Palmer Jr, Bob Sterling, Rick Montalbano, Don Cantwell, Syracuse's Peanuts Hucko, Sal Nistico, and Stan Collela, Chuck and Gap Mangione of Rochester, J.R. Monterose and Monk Rowe have given the area North of the Empire State's Thruway in Central New York a rich musical history that hasn't been recognized as well as it should.

In a tastefully crafted article in the Life & Times of Utica, NY, March 8-14, 2001, by Vinnie Garco, Sal Alberico offers a familiar story about getting his start in the music business. Married with nine children and a member of the painters' union, he said "I would paint all day with a contractor and then play a gig at night. If I didn't have a music job to play, I would do a small paint job at night." He started his own band in 1955 and he's played every kind of engagement and backed a list of musical attractions that include Nat "King" Cole, Tony Bennett, Sammy Davis Jr, Andy Williams, Al Martino, Jerry Vale and Connie Francis among others. These days he also finds time to serve as president of the Local 51 American Federation of Musicians and vice president of the New York State Musicians' Conference.

Rowe, a teacher by day and performer by night, frequently plays a solo piano or the saxophone with various ensembles. In 1995, he added more duties. He became the director of the Hamilton College Jazz Archive. "The mission of the archive," he says, "is to gather video interviews with renowned jazz personalities, saving their stories and experiences for researchers, authors and interested jazz lovers. To date, dozens of interviews have been conducted at many locations across the country."

The Jazz Archive is a classic example of alumni response to a college's interest in preserving an American art form in a modern day venue. It was 1944 Hamilton alumnus Milt Fillius, an ardent jazz fan, who helped bring about the creation of the repository. The Hamilton College Jazz Archive is one of the few that preserves the words and image of the performer for posterity. "Having videotapes give an interested person a chance to understand the body language and nuances that are possibly missed in audio or print venues," Monk observes. "Musicians aren't always the most articulate to define what they mean in words only and, consequently, by seeing a performer's hand and body gestures you certainly have a better understanding of what they're trying to convey."

Cantwell, meanwhile, mixed fulltime teaching with playing and leading a number of groups in Central New York. He initiated successful jazz festivals at Whitesboro Schools where he taught and brought in such professional talent as trumpeter Clark Terry, Tonight Show drummer Ed Shaughnessy and some of the musicians he mentored while teaching. He formed a group called the Clef Dwellers which participated in a Rotary Club International Exchange with Taiwan in 1995. Thanks to Clef Dweller tuba player, Dana Jerrard, and Mohawk Valley Community College Prof. Don Reese, the group played several "gigs" in Taiwan and took part in an international concert with bands from Germany and the Middle East in a soccer stadium filled with thousands.

I interviewed Monterose a few years before his death when he was an artist-in-residence at Syracuse University's Utica College. He never won a Grammy but his background made other players at the time envious. Despite a "low profile" he had recorded 10 albums and had been a tenor sax sideman with leaders such as Lionel Hampton, Teddy Charles, Kenny Dorham, Gunther Schuller, Buddy Rich and Claude Thornhill. He laughed when he told me it all started when he went for a year's tour with Hot Lips Henry Busse, one of the "sweet" bands of the era and his "shuffling music."

The 1950 tour with Busse at 23 showed JR he desperately needed to find a "progressive" band. "There were some good young fellows in the band and once in a while there was an opportunity for a few solo bars," he remembers, but little chance to play what he loved. He spent six months with the Buddy Rich and he remembered it was tougher than playing on the Busse band. In an interview years later, Buddy gave his view about managing an orchestra. The Rich Band did about 250 one nighters a year. "I don't make any substitutions and I don't change the music whether it's a concert hall or a high school. You buy Buddy Rich and his band and that's what you get," he told USA Today in the 1980s. "His (JR's) style has been likened to that of Sonny Rollins and...after hearing Sonny play in 1949 he went home and threw out all of his Stan Getz records," wrote Mark Gardner in the liner notes for JR's Straight Ahead album.

Typical Monterose. When he started playing he liked Coleman Hawkins and Chu Berry, he told friends but, he said, "my real inspiration that decided me to take up tenor sax seriously rather than clarinet or alto was, believe it or not, Tex Beneke." Even Beneke might have found that surprising! But JR told jazz critic Leonard Feather that the secret to what success he had came from every association that came his way. "I didn't go about it the same way they did, from studying; I got it all from listening but I guess I was doing what they wanted and they seemed to dig it," he said.

Today, some of J.R.'s (short for junior not his name) work sells for upward to $400 a copy.

Like many musicians when they reach career milestones, Monterose loved teaching improvisational techniques to college players. "I was very fortunate to have good teachers growing up in Utica and I figured it was about time to start passing it on," he told me in the mid-1980s. "I teach the kind of theory that trains ears to improvise spontaneously. I use the piano mostly for composing. It is very visual...it's like the slide rule of music." JR died Sept. 16, 1993, at 66 years old. Today, the JR Monterose Scholarship honors his work and assists young musicians in Central New York.

A trumpet playing op ed editor for Gannett's Utica, NY newspaper, Dave Dudajek, became a chronicler of big band musicians who returned to their home communities after their tours of duty on the road. He found himself writing their obituaries.

When Frank Sinatra died, for example, Dave talked to Frank's road roomie from his touring days with James' band, Jack Palmer of Rome, NY. Palmer, one of Harry's original sidemen, remembered Frank's first gig with the band in New Haven, CT.

"Harry told the audience that he (Sinatra) was new to the group and that we didn't have any arrangements for him..." Dudajek wrote. "He asked Frank to sing something anyway and he sang 'Stardust.' That was the first thing he did with us."

Jack and his wife became friends with Frank and his first wife, Nancy. "Frank's mother had gotten him a car, but his first wife, Nancy, didn't drive. So when we left New York for Chicago, my wife went to Hoboken and drove Frank's car with her to meet us. Since we were traveling by bus, this way we had a car when we got there. She later drove it to California."

The James "Music Makers" were the band to play with in the 1940s. Harry's group had caught CBS' attention when airchecks gave the network positive feedback on the West Coast. Unlike the early days, Harry was making money fronting one of the commercially successful orchestras of the day. Variety carried a story that the band got $12,500 for a week at New York's popular Paramount Theater where bands split the bill with first run movies. While the doors opened at 9:45 in the morning, lines began forming at 5 a.m. and extra police had to be called in to prevent a riot. In 1942, the band broke records at both the Palladium on the West Coast and Frank Dailey's Meadowbrook on the East Coast. A few years later, veteran trumpet player and arranger Neal Hefti told Patricia Willard, who wrote the liner notes about the band on a Hindsight album that "I played the Palladium twice with Harry James, twice with Woody Herman, twice with Charlie Spivak and once with Ziggy Elman—all good solid bands—and nobody drew more than Harry."

During the same year, James took the throne away from Glenn Miller, America's number one orchestra, as the band of the year on Martin Block's "Make Believe Ballroom."

I saw the James band at the Pier Ballroom, Buckeye Lake Park in the late 1940s. He had been off the road for more than two years but, regardless, he had a swinging big band that stepped off with his beat and plowed old favorites as well as some new numbers like "Blue and Sentimental," "Lazy River" and "You Turned The Tables On Me." Corky Corcoran and Bob Poland were in the sax section along with a number of younger players who seemed to make James more relaxed. Among the dozens of big bands I saw that summer in the post-World War II years, James filled the place with dancers and listeners.

Palmer, who later played with Red Norvo, Jan Savitt, Tommy Dorsey and Benny Goodman and became well-known to television fans with his trumpet lead on the celebrated "Honeymooners" theme song while a member of the Sammy Spear Orchestra, told Dudajek that Frank had reservations about leaving James shortly after the singer got a call from Tommy Dorsey. Palmer said he remembered the decision was a turning point for Sinatra. The James' band was playing Buffalo, Harry was paying Sinatra $75 a week, Nancy was pregnant and Frank needed the $50 increase Tommy was offering to replace Jack Leonard who had already left the Dorsey band.

"He (Frank) said, 'Jack, I got a call from Tommy to come with him but I don't know how to tell Harry. Harry took me out of Hoboken and he's been good to me. But this is such an opportunity.'

"I told him that he had to do what he thought was best for him. We were a 'baby band' Dorsey was big, well established."

Palmer, who died Jan. 7, 2000, a few years after Sinatra, told the Utica editor that James was notably disappointed but he showed a lot of class when Frank broke the news. "He said he hated to see him go but he wished him good luck."

Dudajek will never forget the moment and the day he sat in with the legendary trumpet player from neighboring Rome.

"Jack was a big man, very friendly and always happy to discuss his career. He got his first trumpet at 13 when his construction worker father came home one day, handed him a horn and suggested he take lessons. He got his first break at Sylvan Beach—then a big band hot spot—when he filled in for another trumpeter. Soon, Palmer was playing with the best in the business. He toured with big bands for five decades," Dave remembers. Sal Alberico Sr, who played with a band Palmer started after returning to Rome and a bandleader well-known throughout Central New York, said what many musicians felt about Jack. "He was just a great guy. I enjoyed every minute that I worked with him. He was a dynamite trumpet player."

Dave remembers playing at the Betsey Ross Nursing Facility where Jack was a resident in his final years. "For several years, I had organized an event called 'Bandfest' for which I recruited area groups to play as a benefit for Operation Sunshine. Since I knew many of the musicians, they all did it for nothing which helped us raise money to send inner city kids to camp. During one gig, Jack came down from Rome and sat in…I sat next to him and I hardly could play through the show because all I could do was thinking 'wow, this guy used to play with Harry James and here I am playing next to him. I believe he took the 2nd trumpet solo to 'In the Mood' that day…and he didn't miss a beat."

Jack's son, Jack Palmer Jr., who recalls his dad as a "wonderful father who was always fair," started out on the trumpet but at an early age he just enjoyed "banging on virtually everything in sight" and the drums became his instrument. He remembers the stories of the road trips when he and his mother would accompany his dad to cities throughout the country. His dad, says Jack Jr., was an excellent reader in a day when a number of musicians played "by ear." It opened doors everywhere. He took up circular breathing, a method of playing later promoted by blind tenor man, Rahsaan Roland Kirk. Circular breathing permits the player to blow uninterrupted sound throughout a number using but not damaging the ear. Kirk advanced the technique to play three horns at a time. Some wind players believe the theory is fiction. "I believe it amounts to good coordination of lungs and cheeks," one said.

Jack used the technique to create a far better sound. And he did. "My father never wasted a note when he played. He coached other players on breathing and creating a better sound. He chose sound over just developing technique and if you consider the work he got in the first chair he demonstrated his ability," Jack Jr. says today. That's how he really got his start with the big bands. As a teen, he filled in for a trumpet player at Russell's Danceland on Oneida Lake near Rome and later, he went to New York City where, by accident, he bumped into Jerry Jerome, a saxophone player who had started his career with Glenn Miller. Jerome told him that James was holding a rehearsal and looking for players. He spent the next three years with James and rooming with Sinatra. Later, Jack Sr. backed such singers as Al Martino, Don Cornell, Lena Horne and entertainers like Foster Brooks and Pat Cooper and a number of entertainers from the Arthur Godfrey Show.

Farther East, a young Lou DiSario was just putting his own act together between giving dance lessons and managing one of the established ballrooms along the coast…A Philadelphian, Lou took the stage name "Lou King," and became the likeable emcee at Hamed's Million Dollar Ballroom at Atlantic City. He remembers introducing the name bands during the latter part of the 1930s.

Charlie Spivak, the trumpet playing leader, "was an extremely warm, a very pleasant guy. We became friends." Randy Brooks, another trumpet player with a band, "was a buddy. He was a Navy band leader and I was an Army band singer and entertainer while I served as a combat MP and handled water safety instruction." Ozzie and Harriet Nelson, the popular bandleader and his singing wife, "were really like brother and sister to the public, I think."

The best of the best at the Hamed Ballroom? "Tommy Reynolds, Tony Pastor and Sam Donahue, were great at showmanship with their bands and they had warm personalities to the public. Harry James, by contrast, was a very down-to-earth guy well liked by his musicians. Certainly an outstanding trumpet player when he played Hamed's and one of our top bands during the 1938-1940 period."

Glenn Miller was a top draw as he became popular during the period. Yet, there was another side to him, too. "I found him unfriendly. Really for a bandleader, he tended to be anti-social at times," Lou remembered. He introduced Glenn and his band several times at the ballroom. Ed Herlihy, a veteran Miller announcer, offered another explanation on a Public Television Glenn Miller Special in 1995:"Glenn was a charming man, very dedicated, yet a reserved man, too, who was difficult to know."

Guy Lombardo? Tops, the ballroom manager, then 20, said. "He was the kind of great guy whose music was really an extension of his personality. He was very friendly." And he recalls how Lombardo's manager made his day once during the band's visit at the dance spot. "He asked me to join the Lombardo crew as an entertainer and go on the road. But I couldn't give up a secure position in the security office of the City of Philadelphia and lose a good pension," he remembers.

After World War II, Lou returned to the road on weekends as an emcee, singer, dancer and comic appearing with groups like Jerry Murad and the Harmonicats of "Peg of My Heart" fame. He has great memories of meeting and socializing with entertainers like Billy Eckstine, Andy Williams, Frankie Laine, Vic Damone and a lanky Italian who bought him a drink and offered him tickets to a performance by the Tommy Dorsey band at Hershey Park, PA. "That's how I met Frank Sinatra," he smiled. Lou, although retired, still carries his American Guild Variety Artists card.

But ballrooms and dancing pavilions were very different in the 1920s and 1930s, old-timers contend. "It was much more sedate. Much more formal. There were many rules of conduct when you went dancing in those days," Lou recalls.

Music was changing rapidly as the Jazz Age became the Swing Era and musicians, who were also adapting to the different moods and musical tastes, had to deal with fickle consumer taste while maintaining patience with dance hall operators and community leaders. In the country's mid-section, for example, the regulations at a typical ballroom could stifle bandleaders, musicians and the public. Worse, the controls could be totally one-sided. "Read a clause taken from a Cleveland, OH ordinance (circa 1925) that was used to regulate couples attempting to dance: Male dancers are not permitted to hold their partners tightly—generally this is the fault of the gentleman's partner. Both dancers should assume a light, graceful position. Partners are not permitted to dance with cheeks close or touching. When dancers put their cheeks together it is simply a case of 'public love-making.'"

Imagine enforcing such rules anywhere today. They were virtually unenforceable in the 1940s and 1950s. By the 1960s, such social monitoring would have been a court case!

The Cleveland ordinance gave wide latitude to ballroom operators in regulating social conduct. No suggestive movements were permitted. And the dancer had to assume proper positions and take certain kinds of steps to be dancing. "The gentleman's arm should encircle his partner's waist, his hand resting lightly at her spine, just above the waist line; the lady's left arm should not encircle the gentleman's shoulder or neck."

Furthermore, no "neck holds" were permitted and no "shimmy" dancing—shaking or jerking of the upper body—while taking short steps or standing still. And dancers were restricted in the steps they took; no long or short steps. Natural steps only. Those rules, I'm told, still exist in the regulations of some ballrooms around the country.

Couples, said the Cleveland ordinance, must dance from the waist down...not the waist up. The Cleveland legislators warned educators about dancing etiquette, too. "Teachers should not teach any steps or movements which cannot be controlled."

Bandleaders, meantime, had other concerns besides making sure dance numbers had the right tempo and the songs that were sung weren't suggestive. "Vulgar, noisy jazz music is prohibited. Such music almost forces dancers to use jerky half-steps and invites immoral variations," the ordinance warned. A number of traveling salesmen of the era remember that dance halls open to the public, not strictly stag parties or private affairs, weren't as some movies portrayed them. "You behaved or you were tossed out," said a Clevelander of the period.

Musicians were moderate to heavy drinkers and smokers and leaders couldn't ignore such behavior by their sidemen in ballrooms, hotels or clubs during the decade. In Cleveland, for example, "carrying intoxicating liquor on their person" would subject you to eviction and arrest. Ironically, at a very early age in US social history ballroom operators were trying to extinguish the heavy emphasis that was placed on smoking and drinking in the movies.

And dance hall owners wouldn't tolerate sloppy dress especially among musicians. Most bands in the 1930s through the 1950s were forced to wear tuxedos or pants, coats, ties regardless of the weather. The Ohio ordinance was typical of the vast majority of written or informal regulations that dictated attire at dancing establishments. "Gentlemen must wear coats while dancing. During the hot summer months, shirtwaist must be worn with full-length sleeves, cuff links fastened and a belt."

While television and videotape convey the image of rock and hip hop stars today, big bands of the earlier era relied on radio, the movies, magazines and newspapers to carry their appeal and promote their appearances.

One of the most influential media messages for me was the release of a March of Time film in 1946 by 20th Century Fox about the night club boom. It featured the very places I'd heard about on the radio at the cottage by the lake. Restaurants and clubs like 21, the Stork Club, El Morocco, the Embassy Room, the Café Society, Café Rouge, the 400 Restaurant, Eddie Condon's, Monte Carlo, the Zanzibar and others. Bands like Eddie Condon's crew and singing groups like the Ink Spots, comedians Danny Thomas and Ed Wynn and my favorite author at the time, John O'Hara, played roles in making this movie one I saw a number of times.

And who could forget Dorothy Lamour, Bob Hope and the Road to Utopia...especially Dorothy in a two piece bathing suit drinking RC Cola! It became my drink right away. More great music came my way when Benny Goodman, along with Dinah Shore, Jerry Colonna and Andy Russell did the music and voice soundtrack for Walt Disney's Make Mine Music. I shelved my dreams of becoming a musician and wanted to become a famed cartoon creator like Walt.

Without a doubt, though, artistic development could clearly be linked for me and lots of others like me to radio rather than movies. Radio allowed us to create our own pictures to the spoken word and envision our own interpretation of what the words and the voices meant. I surprised myself later in life when I looked back at the number of radio scripts I tried to embellish as a teen listening to Jimmy Durante, the Lone Ranger, the Aldrich Family (which I felt very close to), Philip Marlowe, Suspense, Our Miss Brooks,, the Great Gildersleeve, Lights Out!, the Bickersons, Fibber McGee and Molly, Inner Sanctum, Gang Busters and so many others.

There were 17 televisions stations and 136,000 sets in 1947, according to Life Magazine. Twelve months later, there were 700,000 sets and 50 stations but it was 1950 before my parents thought TV was more than a fad. When it did come to my town, it quietly brought the end of social dancing, the need to go out to party with friends and...unfortunately, the beginning of the end of the big band era.

How much fun was it?

Ask former President Bill Clinton, our sax playing chief executive for eight years. He was offered $250,000 reportedly to play at Italy's posh San Remo Song Festival at the even poshier Italian Riveria.

The ex-president, who showed up at one of his inaugural balls in 1993 with a borrowed axe and played some, got us "in the mood" for a musician in the White House. We were forewarned certainly. He donned dark glasses and played "Heartbreak Hotel" on the Arsenio Hall Show during the 1992 campaign.

Just before he left office his sax came out of the case again to blow some riffs to "Louie, Louie" with a high school band in New Hampshire. No question it will continue to find use, too. "If he continues," smiles a New York musician who struggles to find gigs, "he better get a union card."

No question, swing bands were the glue that held America together in the 1930s during times that sapped public morale and drained optimism about the future. While an economy made it virtually impossible for bandleaders and backers to make such a precarious business profitable, the music and dancing continued frequently in speakeasies where you risked your reputation as well as your life to mingle among gangsters, unsavory characters and America's politically correct elite. Prohibition added to the nation's migraine.

"Large ballrooms were common and bands were needed to fill them," said a web site entitled "Between the Wars."

"Such bands produced a much broader, pleasing sound than Dixie Groups. The music was more homophonic in construction. The result was music which sounded more organized, more melodic—less complex and less harsh. Block chords were a primary way to meet homophonic style."

World War II would bring more demand and more bands to the scene.

**A good trumpet player and bandleader, Charlie Spivak.
Photo courtesy Louis DiSario**

A prized ticket to see Buddy Rich and his big band at a club on Hilton Head, South Carolina.

PERSONNAlly
Speaking by
XAVIER
CUGAT
Drawings by Mr. Cugat
The Rhumba King
1—Once ze senoritas would have nuzzing to do with Cugat. Zen a friend gave me advice...
2—"Coogie," say this hombre, "You'll be a satin Latin if you try Personna's close, smooth shaves."
Good
Good
Good
3—I did! And now I'm hot stuff wiz ze pepitas. For sleek, queeck shaves, try ze Personna Blades!
4—Why it makes sense to pay 10¢ for this blade:
Sure, Personna costs more. But Personna is a precision instrument —worth many times 10¢ in shaving ease, in skin health.
Personna is made of premium steel... hollow-ground for extra keenness... rust-resistant for longer use. Spend a little more to get Personna... and get a lot more shaving comfort!
Available also in Canada
PERSONNA
PERSONNA
Precision Blades
10 FOR $1

Connie Friesner sang with the Dick Trimble band in the late 1940s. To her right is leader Trimble playing baritone sax. Beside Trimble is Chuz Alfred playing saxophone and to the far left in the photo is Bob Bechtol playing trombone. On the bass is Dano Estell. Photo courtesy Chuz Alfred

II. World War II Brings Demand For Music Makers

Only those who lived during the 1940s can remember with clarity the fear, the work, the sacrifices and experiences that touched every American family at a time when our world appeared ready to come apart.

Young men either volunteered for military service in the branch of their choice or took their chances with the inevitable physical and induction notices following the Congressional passage of the Selective Service Act, for all males 21 to 35 Oct. 29, 1940. Young married couples with children hoped the family deferment would protect the male provider (most women didn't work) so he could remain on the home front. My 32-year-old father had a wife and two children under 10 and between 1941 and 1945 he received eight classifications from the Selective Service System. The uncertainty was as difficult as the callup.

Those physically disqualified (4-F) for service because of everything from flat feet to bad eyes took jobs with defense plants to avoid the stigma and harsh looks that followed them during the war years as casualties mounted overseas and men in uniform were a common sight everywhere.

I can still hear the great Burns and Allen radio shows with guests like Gene Kelly, Richard Widmark, Gracie as a Girl Scout Leader in training and the Aldrich Family featuring Ezra Stone as Henry. Who could mess up more than that teen? Henry's first date, playing shortstop, buying a class ring, dating a taller woman...all these major decisions being made in one week and all of them real life to me. Along with the broadcasts of the big bands which came on during the weekends, it helped you realize what the war really meant; the freedom to listen and enjoy.

Observers of the period believe that one of the reasons Glenn Miller became Capt. Glenn Miller was his quiet but honest patriotism. It certainly wasn't opportunism. Over the draft age in 1942 (38), riding a crest of popularity that was growing monthly with booming record sales, Miller voluntarily disbanded Sept. 27, 1942,in an emotional final show at Central Theatre, Passaic, NJ., and entered the Army Air Corps. Weeks earlier, he and his band had finished a second movie in two years; this one was called "Orchestra Wives." Critics, who had seen enough films featuring big bands in hokey scripts since the 1920s, called it the best big band black and white movie available.

While some would be astonished that progressive bands like Stan Kenton's would get involved in the patriotism of the moment, they only have to go back to a June 6, 1944 broadcast of the Kenton band on the Bob Hope Show the day of Victory in Europe. Kenton inserted patriotic songs during the pre-broadcast and while Hope read a stirring monologue, the Kenton orchestra played "America the Beautiful," a number not often called during the band's performances. At the end of the program, a chaplain read a prayer and the band finished with the "Battle Hymn of the Republic."

There was pent-up demand for big band music and the ballroom, hotel, supper and night club scene became an overnight sensation during the 1940s as Americans quickly moved away from the Depression and Prohibition to a new way to put the pressures of the world on hold for a night or a weekend. A growing number of young and middle-aged bandleaders saw the opportunities and seized them.

Monk Rowe, a 21st century bandleader, arranger and director of the Hamilton College Jazz Archive, recalls a conversation he had with the late Stanley Dance, critic, jazz historian and book editor of JazzTimes: "He told me that he traveled from England to America in steerage on the Queen Elizabeth in 1937 as a 27-year-old just to hear the great music. In his first three weeks in America, he told me he heard 18 high quality bands. It was the pop music of the day."

There was so much to like about the bands of that period, Rowe continues. "You could like the star soloists that most big bands had; you could like the leader whether he was a fine musician or a showman; you could like the look of the band, the uniforms; you could like the arrangements of the band, the sound the band produced and, of course, you could like the vocalists, too. There was something for everybody. If you were a musician, you could dig it for the music...if you were a fan, you could dig the dancing and the fun of the performance. It was a terrific combination of art and entertainment."

Bands led by trumpeter Harry James and drummer Gene Krupa joined touring veterans like Benny Goodman, Count Basie, Duke Ellington, Glenn Miller and the Dorsey Brothers to usher in Jan. 1, 1940. Within weeks and months, new bands headed by vocalists Russ Carlyle and Vaughn Monroe joined others such as Lionel Hampton, Sonny Dunham, Teddy Powell, Claude Thornhill, Charlie Spivak and Georgie Auld to launch their careers. Just five years earlier, the microphone had been invented permitting singers in front of a big band to style a song with more subtle tones.

George T. Simon in his major work called "The Big Bands" (MacMillan, 1971) said there were approximately 200 big bands on the road at the time. I believe his number was conservative.

They played to packed houses at the Commodore Hotel, the Pennsylvania Hotel and Billy Rose's Music Hall in New York City, The Steel Pier and Marine Ballroom in Atlantic City, NJ; the Palmer House and the Congress Hotel in Chicago; The Carlton in Boston; Frank Dailey's well-known Meadowbrook along the eastern seaboard together with the Glen Island Casino. It was a day when a New York City dweller was called a "Gothamite," a Louisianan a "Creole" and Missouri residents got the dubious nickname "Pukes."

Elsewhere in the country you would find one of the hundreds of big name bands or territory groups playing at the Crystal or Pier Ballrooms on man made Buckeye Lake near Columbus; the Mocambo in San Francisco; Natatorium Park, Spokane, WA and the Lagoon in Salt Lake City.

Writer Frank Tomaino of Utica, NY compiled a partial list of the big bands that visited Central New York in the 1930s and 1940s with the help of readers of the Utica Observer-Dispatch, Jan 1, 1990. His story and list generated the fond memories of people who could remember the band, the girl or boy they were with and the place, but obviously not always in that order. Carole Crimmons of Frankfort, NY, for example, told Frank that Harry James' appearance at the city's Stanley Theatre was a very special occasion for her in a packed house of nearly 3,000 people. She was chosen a guest soloist with the James band at 9 and felt like "cinderella at the ball." She later had a guest appearance with the Louie Prima Band, too.

Among the bands that stopped at various places in addition to the Stanley, Russell's Danceland on Oneida Lake and the Richfield Springs' Canadaraga Park Dance Pavilion in the historic Mohawk Valley were: Sammy Kaye, Tommy Dorsey, Jimmy Dorsey, Woody Herman, Artie Shaw, Duke Ellington, Cab Calloway, Gene Krupa, Les Brown, Lionel Hampton, Maynard Ferguson, Charlie Spivak, Charley Barnet, Ozzie Nelson, Fletcher Henderson, Horace Heidt, Bob Crosby, Jan Garber, Billie Butterfield, Desi Arnaz, Hal MacIntyre, Billy May, Chick Webb, Claude Thornhill, Shep Fields, Jimmy Lunceford, Bunnie Berigan, Ted Weems, Ray McKinley, Dizzy Gillespie, Benny Goodman, Glenn Miller and a leader who had started a career in the field but discovered zany antics would be more popular than just fronting another big band; Spike Jones and his famous City Slickers.

Virtually every section of the country could boast a similar roster. And whether it was a ballroom, a supper club or high school gym on prom night...young and old enjoyed a special evening, a chance to dance or merely listen to a band they had heard on the radio the night before from New York City, Long Island, the Windy City or the shoreline of mythical places on the West Coast like the Claremont Hotel in Oakland.

Herman's band was probably the most respected by audiences and musicians as it criss-crossed the nation from the mid-1930s until the late 1980s. In the Central New York area alone, from 1944 until his last appearance at a high school dance in 1986, Woody made 12 visits.

Trumpeter/arranger Billy May summed up his feeling about Woody to Al Julian in the Woody Herman Society Newsletter (Fall, 2000). "Woody always had a good band, because, like Charlie Barnet, he let the individual band members contribute what they wanted. It was always relaxed and fun to go to work (not like Glenn Miller, I might add!)."

What brought the crowds to see the big bands? What excited the audiences and why was the sound so different than the jazz that Louie Armstrong had brought from New Orleans to the North just a few years earlier?

Swing bands produced a much broader, pleasing sound than Dixie groups, says a web site called "Between the Wars." The music was more harmophonic in construction. Thus, it sounded more organized, more melodic—less complex and certainly less harsh to the average listener.

Block chords became a harmonic style. Said another web site called "Swing," the new music gave leaders new roles, too. Older leaders like Paul "Pops" Whiteman and Paul Ash and others who merely led bands were replaced by players; men like clarinetists Goodman and Shaw, trombonists Miller and Tommy Dorsey, saxophonist Jimmy Dorsey and piano players Count Basie and Duke Ellington. It also offered sidemen who were usually only heard in an ensemble a chance to solo, too.

Featured players like trumpeter Cootie Williams, saxophonist Johnny Hodges, drummers like Krupa and Buddy Rich added more firepower to a band's showmanship. There were others, too. Dizzy Gillespie and Roy Eldridge on trumpet, xylophonist Red Norvo, bassists including Duke Ellington's Jimmy Blanton and Stan Kenton's nimble fingered Eddie Safranski. And, a talented but mercurial alto saxophone player, Charley Parker, who stopped conversation when he soloed but whose addictions made him an erratic musician most of his playing days unfortunately.

"Swing music became a corollary to every event from New York's swankiest night clubs to school proms, 'Juke joints' and even to Young Communist League parties. Every portion of society found some form of swing suitable for their dancing or listening. Country Club couples fox-trotted to 'Moonlight Serenade;' college students did 'The Big Apple' as a circle dance; and Harlem Ballrooms exploded to the aerial acrobatics of 'The Savoy Swingers' and the Audobon (Ballroom) Lindy Hoppers," says the Swing web site. Ballads became more sentimental—slower tempos—and fast music became faster. Bands playing gigs in ballrooms carefully varied so many slow to so many fast numbers during a set on an evening. Bandleader Kay Kyser said it best, the swing web site reported: GIs longed for home and the girls they left behind. Songs of the heart dominated touring band books.

At the same time, jazz historians explained, the swing era was already declining. Musicians like Dizzy Gillespie and Charlie Parker were unhappy with the commercial restrictions and started inserting phrasing that challenged a listener as well as other musicians. My obsession with the sound and different patterns used for rhythm didn't advance my career with conventional territorial bands. Some called it for lack of a definition "art music."

I'll always remember a four-day stop by the Gene Krupa band at the Lake Breeze Pier Ballroom, Buckeye Lake, OH when Don Fagerquist, a young, crew cut trumpeter, was with the group. I met him at the bar where I gave my best imitation of a 20 year-old that a 15 year old could give. He ordered me a Root Beer to "help me out." Not exactly talkative, he told me he liked the traveling, new places and playing. Krupa section mate Roy Eldridge and Dizzy Gillespie inspired him he told me. He said the band had put in several great bop charts that had "groovy phrases" and chances for solos. He told me to listen for them on the next set. Don went on to play with Shorty Rogers, Dave Pell, Les Brown, Woody Herman's third herd and a number of backup gigs with vocalists like former Krupa singer, Anita O'Day. Considered the leading soloist of the West Coast Jazz Movement in the 1950s, Don worked with Kenton arranger Pete Rugolo, guitarist Laurinda Almeida, Mel Torme and drummer Louie Bellson in his last decade. But he only cut one album as a leader in his short life in the business. He died young at 47 from kidney disease.

His one album? It was called "Music To Fill A Void," recorded on Sept. 14, 1957. In my very brief encounter with him, he made an impact on me I never forgot.

How much did we pay to see the big bands of the era? Ken Nihiser of Granville, OH found some of the advertising that promoted appearances of the touring stars at the Pier and Crystal Ballrooms and the Lake Breeze Hotel's Mayfair Room at Buckeye Lake. It cost 75 cents plus tax to see Benny Goodman but you had to pay a $1 plus tax to see either Jimmy or Tommy Dorsey and their bands that summer in the early 1950s. Ten years earlier, you could see popular big bands for no more than 60 cents admission. Guy Lombardo and the Royal Canadians charged 90 cents and tax but singer Vaughn Monroe, the Moon Maids and his band charged $2 and tax or $2.15 and tax at the door. It must have been the Moon Maids that raised the rate. At the same time, you could see Gene Krupa as I did that summer for 98 cents and tax. Since I was a Pier volunteer doing everything from helping musicians set up to taking tickets...I remember getting in free by showing up so early nobody noticed a blonde tousle headed kid inside the place with the bartenders and the delivery people.

It was more expensive elsewhere. Lou DiSario, manager of Hamid's Pier Ballroom in New Jersey, remembers that Harry James and Glenn Miller cost $4 to $5 with an "extra entrant fee" that could bump the price as high as $10. "Each band played 9 till 1 with a half hour intermission when we played records," he recalls.

House bands at the Pier and the Steel Pier would play "continuous music, he said, taking 15 to 20 minute breaks when the "house would play record music."

What was the appeal, the magnet of the bands of that decade?

National Public Radio Disk Jockey David Miller has his own theory. "Forget the 1950s...the vocalists had taken over by that time...I'd say the appeal in the 1940s was based on two attractions; dancing and listening. I always remember a photo of college kids at a Stan Kenton dance date. The guys were gathered around the bandstand watching and listening intently. Their dates are with them but look as though they'd rather be dancing. I think it was a definite guy-gal thing. Both liked to dance, but it was the guys who knew the musicians and could name every instrumental after the first two bars. It's the same today. Ninety percent of my trivia contestants are male, while women call in to request a romantic tune they danced to in high school."

How about those band uniforms that would turn heads off the stand?

Says Miller: "It was just taken for granted that the band would dress up for a gig, just as a college marching band does. The antics were few and far between and I don't think they did anything except add a bit of pizzazz to the band's presentation. Jimmy Lunceford was a past master at the visual effect of section men moving their instruments in intricate patterns and it had to add to the appeal of the band from a visual standpoint. Ditto Glenn Miller who borrowed the idea from Lunceford."

A 21st century DJ in Carmel, CA, David Kimball, who gives his listeners his view of the great days of traveling big bands, ballrooms and dancing to good music on www.letsdanceradio.com examined the bands and leaders and put together his top 40 list. "Admittedly, this is a biased list and my criteria," he says, but he used methodology at least. The criteria? General popularity during a tenure leading a big band, long-lasting popularity after the early years, years on the circuit at ballrooms, hotels and radio remotes and recording popularity, he explains. At the top of the roster are Glenn Miller, Benny Goodman, Tommy Dorsey, Artie Shaw and Harry James. At the bottom, Will Bradley, Ted Heath, Xavier Cugat and Vaughn Monroe. Unlike some swing and jazz purists, he includes bands such Lawrence Welk, Kay Kyser, Guy Lombardo, Jan Garber and Sammy Kaye. But he doesn't mention bands like Tommy and Jimmy Dorsey, Horace Heidt, Blue Barron and Ralph Flanagan among others.

The US, meanwhile, was still struggling with economic troubles. Unemployment hovered around 8 million with 14.6 percent of the workforce idle, France, Belgium, the Netherlands, Luxembourg, Denmark, Norway and Romania were being trampled by the German Wehrmacht and a popular song of the period somberly told us "The Last Time I Saw Paris" as the country worried over the news from abroad.

And the entertainment business was enduring the same kind of financial slump. Peter J. Levinson in his interesting book "Trumpet Blues: The Life of Harry James (Oxford, 1999) told how the band was "hot" with hits like "Ciribiribin" and "Flight of the Bumblebee" on the charts but Harry was trying to evade bill collectors. He had to avoid the Greyhound Company by taking the band bus on back roads because he owed the company thousands. Some nights, Levinson reported, he would engage a suite of rooms and share the bathroom with his musicians because he didn't have the money to pay for separate accommodations. Yet, Harry was known to splurge on new suits and shoes and drive a new Chrysler convertible because he believed bandleaders had to present a good image.

At the same time, Americans celebrated the beginning of the WPA's four lane, 160 mile long Pennsylvania Turnpike which opened Oct. 1, 1940. And we watched and heard our favorite animated characters when Walt Disney presented "Fantasia" on the screen.

Music was now charted on paper with notes, symbols and arrangements for sections of the band—brass instruments, reeds and rhythm—and musicians were forced to read or memorize a composition instead of so-called "head" stuff that came by feel, whim and impulse. Contemporary songs as well as old favorites were prepared by skilled musicians like Fletcher Henderson, Duke Ellington, Harold Arlen and a young southern gentleman from Georgia who also sang occasionally, Johnny Mercer. Henderson, a chemistry and mathematics major at Atlanta University, has been considered by some to be the man who really invented swing. Others contend it was Don Redman who gave us block passages. That's the place on the chart where one section plays the same lines as the others.

What was so unique about these musicians and their music?

Listen to former DownBeat editor Gene Lees in his book, "The Leader of the Band; The Story of Woody Herman" (Replica Books, 1995):

"For a brief, magical moment in history, a moment that lasted only about 15 years, good music was popular and popular music was good. There were some corny bands to be sure, but some of the men of that era, men such as Count Basie, Woody Herman, Duke Ellington, Claude Thornhill, managed to achieve great personal popularity and financial success with music that was genuinely superb."

Gene was right about their popularity but, sadly, few of the big band leaders or musicians of the 1930s and 1940s finished with the wealth rock musicians and professional athletes of the latter part of the 20th century acquired.

While the band business looked the best it had ever been by 1941, leaders found personnel shortages a nightmare as engagements multiplied. Selective Service boards began taking the cream of the musical crop by mid-1942 and bandleaders and their road managers began scouring college campuses and high schools for talent to fill section vacancies.

But America's world was turned upside down Dec. 7. And for Billy MacDonald and his band which had extended an engagement in Honolulu it was a personal and business disaster. They had finished a Saturday night gig and had hoped to sleep in like any group of musicians would do on a Sunday morning. Falling Japanese bombs jolted them into the streets where band members "pitched in to help clean up and care for the wounded." It took more than 60 days for the MacDonald band to get back to the mainland where a number of them found induction notices waiting.

It got progressively worse. In 1942, Will Bradley, who decided to keep his band together when co-leader and drummer Ray McKinley left, lost six men including a number of trumpet players to the draft. He gave up the band for the war.

Others continued the search for players. High schools and college music instructors didn't teach jazz or swing let alone allow students to use music rooms to play it. A large number of schools forbade any playing of jazz or swing on school grounds. The big band recruiters usually found young players by contacting territorial band leaders, record and music store owners and, of course, the local musicians' union halls. For young musicians who heard the records and listened to the big bands on the radio like I did, the allure for the exciting times, places and people were similar to earlier generations when the circus came to town. We memorized the music in the hard drives of our minds.

Don Cantwell, a former high school and college music instructor, bandleader and arranger in Central New York, has nostalgic memories of those days when the country heard the popular music on radio and went to the record stores to play the 78 records. "Each evening from 7 p.m. until midnight there was the radio 'Make Believe Ballroom.' Whether it was Sammy Kaye, Benny Goodman or Artie Shaw, we listened to that music. As a high school musician, I could buy the arrangement as it was recorded. Whether we performed it at the level of the recording or not, we memorized it. Then we would go down to the record store and play those great numbers over and over again to get them right."

A multi-talented musician, cartoonist and painter, Don remembers the excitement and career deciding performance he gave as a high school soloist with the Poughkeepsie, NY, Symphony when he won the clarinet competition and received the great Benny Goodman's autograph.

The dream? To go on the road with a big band.

Quincy Jones remembers he tried to join Lionel Hampton's band at 16 but Lionel's wife, Gladys, ordered him off the band bus and told him to go home and finish his schooling, he laughed during a radio interview. He had the last laugh, of course. He was back on the Hampton bus the next year and touring. Red Rodney had only been playing the trumpet for two years when he joined the Jerry Wald band at 15. Ray Anthony was 5 when he became a member of the family orchestra in Cleveland. Stan Getz, meanwhile, joined the Jack Teagarden band at 14. Artie Shaw heard a saxophone solo at a show he went to and, at 12, immediately rented one. By 18, he was one of the most sought after saxophone players in New York City...even though he refused to take lessons, Cantwell said. It wasn't uncommon in the 1940s for 16 to 18 year olds to be playing along side 40 to 50 year old professional musicians.

And such stories continue today. Chip Davis, award winning composer, leader and bassoonist turned drummer with the Mannheim Steamroller, composed his first piece, a four part chorale, when he was six and joined his father's chorus in Sylvania, OH at 10. Music, he says, filled his parents' house. His dad was a high school music teacher and his mother, Betty, was formerly a trombonist with Phil Spitalny's All Girl Orchestra. His first teacher? His grandmother, also a music teacher, who started him on the piano at four.

America during wartime was different than America during the Depression, too. Blackouts caused much more caution about night life and relaxation after work hours. In addition, there was rationing of food, the A, B and C gas cards and other basic products which limited those in the entertainment business as well as the public. On Feb. 8, 1942, President Franklin D. Roosevelt and Congress took the dramatic step to increase productivity by placing the country on year round daylight savings time for the duration of the war. The daylight savings time ended more than a month after the Japanese surrender, Sept. 30, 1945.

"Girl" singers, who had become popular addition to big bands in the late 1930s, blossomed in the 1940s. Anita O'Day spent several years singing in a club called "Off-Beat" before she stepped up to the mike with the Gene Krupa band and scored one of her biggest hits singing an upbeat duo with trumpeter Roy Eldridge called "Let Me Off Up Town." It became a $1 million record overnight. She was chosen Down Beat's new star of the year. A year later, she was selected one of the top band vocalists in the business (1942). In a matter of months she would join the Woody Herman band only to leave it and return to Krupa.

Connie Haines celebrated her 21st birthday at the Hollywood Palladium but her big band career took off at the end of the next decade (1939) when she became the "girl" singer with the popular Harry James band and shared the stage with a skinny kid from Hoboken, NJ named Frank Sinatra. Several years later, newspaper entertainment reviewer Robert W. Dana of the New York World Telegram (Craig's Big Band Reviews), assessed Connie's performance with the Tony Pastor band at the Terrace Room in New York City. "Miss Haines...programmed her numbers well, with contrasts to suit it. I would say she's at her best with zippy rhythm numbers, the finest of which was her concluding song titled "Sugar Coated Lies' where she enlists the aid of Tony Pastor, no mean song-phraser himself, in putting across the number." Her phrasing at times, he said, sounded "uncannily like that of Lena Horne."

The Great American Big Bands web site said that, while "boy" singers had been with swing bands from the beginning, women singers were the exception not the rule until the 1940s. They were called thrushes and canaries, endearing terms, but life for any woman singer with the big bands was lonely and tough.

"It was common practice then for a band to become known via some—usually remote—radio broadcasts. Once they had achieved a little fame, their agency would immediately book them on a tour of ballrooms, theaters, schools, hotels and such. Accordingly, the sole female in the group of—say 17 men—would be traveling, too. If some of the sidemen were sexual predators, the gal would have had to do a lot of defending. If the bandleader was predatory...that made life very difficult indeed. The leaders certainly deserve a word of praise for putting up with some of the 'shenanigans' that must have taken place on these band tours," the site continued.

It was no different in territorial bands either. Occasionally, it could be worse. A territorial band I worked with had a leader who wasn't good at firing people. One holiday period he decided the "girl" singer had to go. So he gave her only two songs in two nights in a brief tour in northern Ohio. She fumed and indignantly accused everyone of harming her career before she left...stomping off midway in a set the second night.

Other "thrushes" enjoyed themselves although some decided somewhere along the way it wasn't a career. Mrs. David "Doe" James has fond memories of her first engagement, most of her experiences and the people she met while "on the road in Pennsylvania and Maryland."

It started in the fall, 1946, on the campus of Bloomsburg State Teachers College, Bloomsburg, PA. Like many colleges and universities a year after World War II there were thousands of veterans returning to campus and education administrators had to find quick solutions to the lack of dormitory space.

"I was there because Penn State where I had enrolled had been inundated and sent a number of us temporarily to Bloomsburg. A band was being formed, many tried out and I came in second for the singing vacancy. I can't remember what we called ourselves but I sang with the band because the gal who did was either ill or away," she told me.

Her first night couldn't have been worse, she laughs.

"I was so sick with a cold, sore throat and a fever...but I did it because I didn't want to miss my chance. My speaking voice was not too good but my singing voice was okay. It came out kind of Keely Smith-ish. I remember riding in their small bus leaning my head against the window hoping I'd get through it okay so they'd ask me again. I think I made $10."

She sang six or seven times with the group in that first year, she remembers. "We played places like the Elks Club in that area...of course, there weren't too many places to play off campus in Bloomsburg."

By 1947, Doe was singing with several bands. "We played big fraternity dances and I picked up my first steady job with a good band that led to work in the surrounding towns. I also remembered that not too many listened but I didn't care. I was so happy to be doing it," she says.

Of course, there were obstacles to her singing life. "In those days we had housemothers and weekend curfews at 1 a.m. Fortunately, we usually were finished by midnight. So I would have about an hour with my steady (who would hang around about an hour or so) and then we'd go for a snack and head home so I could sign in.

"We also played places like a country club near Pittsburgh which was quite a drive with all the guys and instruments poking me in the back. I was plenty tired when we got back at about 3.m. I'll never forget when I stayed over one night and the band paid for my hotel room. I loved singing and those fellows were such fun, never flirted, and just took care of me. But after a few of those nights and engagements I began wondering if this is the way I wanted to spend much of the rest of my life."

Her life as a band singer continued, though, her last two years at Penn State. "I sang with the same group through my junior year, not every weekend, understand, but as often as they got jobs. We practiced at the bandleader's fraternity house (ATO, I think) Saturday afternoons. I was usually there in comfy clothes, hair up on rollers. They loved to tease me about that. And we practiced. I mean we really practiced! In fact, every band I sang with definitely had rehearsal time. My music was usually transposed into my key—B flat (listen to Diana Krall who is fabulous and that's my key not necessarily my voice). I sang whatever was selected for me...I wasn't a diva," she continues.

Fraternity dances were terrific, she remembers, because "I had lots of support because many of my sorority sisters from Kappa Kappa Gamma and other friends came and always clapped when I sang. It was great support." Other places demanded real fortitude, she recalls. "Much of the time? Crowds paid little attention to you. We sang in sets, usually four numbers a set and I had one song each set. I filled my time playing maracas and clicking other instruments to the beat. It gave me something to do. Sure took the boredom out of sitting there doing nothing. Only once in a while did I wear a gown. When a dance was formal I'd wear my own gowns. The rest of the time I'd wear a tailored knit dress or something like that. I found weighing 101 pounds I could wear almost anything and I could add special belts, scarves and costume jewelry and it looked good."

Central New York jazz historian Dick Robinson remembers how gigs could test your resolve to ever sing again. "When I was in high school, we formed a singing group that patterned ourselves after the popular Four Freshmen. We sang on a couple of radio stations but our first paid appearance was at a cattle auction outside of Governour, NY. We were paid $10 which we divided by four to give us $2.50 each. If you think singing in a loud night club or ballroom is bad try singing over the sounds of cattle mooing and auctioneers chanting!"

Doe believes she had a good big band education during her college years. "I probably sang about 14 songs a night. Even sang some that were requested which was difficult because of key, beat and the band arrangement and all. I still marvel at our guys. They were young and so accomplished that they could transpose immediately in my key. I had a pretty good range...but I was surely no soprano."

By her senior year at Penn State, academic life crowded her singing career and she focused on finishing with a good average. After graduation and at the beginning of her first teaching assignment, a chance meeting with another teacher put her back in front of a band on weekends. A different band, a different leader but new experiences, she says. "When I sang at the NCO clubs many of the guys were alone or with dates and they really did come to hear me, I think. In fact, if I changed a note, ending or bebopped a chorus they would come up to me at intermission and ask me not to change the original. I was flattered that they noticed but also offended because I liked to improvise. The leader was the only leader I had who requested that I sing certain songs. I remembered he insisted that I learn and sing 'These Foolish Things.' It evidently was he and his wife's favorite song. I didn't like the quick up and down vocal range it required and there were a lot of words and, frankly, I didn't like singing it. But he was the boss so I did it."

She married Navy officer David James not long after and flew off to Hawaii for his first duty assignment ending her big band life.

"Even though I had decided early on that I would not opt for that kind of exciting but lonely career...I'm now a bit wistful about not being a part of a group like that," she says with nostalgia.

But big band singers who went on tour with major organizations found leaders, arrangers and, occasionally, musicians weren't sympathetic to their needs. An exhaustive web site devoted to the vocalists of The Great American Big Bands (www.nfo.net) by Murray L. Pfeffer, shows that there were approximately 214 "girl" singers and 198 "boy" vocalists during the period. Leaders, I found, in my research could constantly be searching for singers because of temperament, range, ability to handle new arrangements, rigor of the tour and a variety of other important and less important qualifications. In his 52 years fronting a big band, Benny Goodman, known by most of his sidemen as a difficult taskmaster, had 12 girl singers including such talent as Peggy Lee, Martha Tilton, Helen Forrest and Mildred Bailey. He had five male singers including Dick Haymes.

In Harry James tenure as a bandleader, some 44 years, he had only six "girl" singers and five "boy" singers. Helen Forrest, Connie Haines, Kitty Kallen and Helen Ward, all veteran singers, were with the James band over the decades while Haymes, Buddy DeVito and Frank Sinatra were among the top male vocalists with the band.

On the other hand, in more than 50 years as a bandleader, Ray Anthony had only two female singers—JoAnn Greer and Dee Keating—and the two Mercers, Johnny and Tommy, on the other side of the stage. Like any business that requires positive personalities, touring with big bands for days, weeks, even months took flexibility, stamina, confidence, dedication and, at times, courage to stay focused.

On the West Coast, meanwhile, a number of East Coast musicians and singers were finding the kind of gigs that made southern California so attractive in the 1940s. It wasn't just the sunshine, saxophonist Bud Shank of the Kenton band said in a radio interview in the 1950s, "it was the gigs you could find."

John Coppola, a trumpet player from Geneva, NY, moved to California where it appeared his future was going to be as an apprentice shoemaker for his uncle. But that was before he got his first playing job at 13 with a territory band during the summer of 1945. The family had journeyed to Oakland in 1937 and there was steady work in the area because so many men had been drafted. John was working virtually every night as a senior in high school, he told V. Vale of Swing! The New Retro Renaissance. Monday night, he recalls, was what was known as "colored" night which drew all the hip white folk to Oakland. A big military service town, there were about 100,000 men constantly coming and going through the Oakland repro depot. He remembers you could take your pick of Harry James, Lionel Hampton, Duke Ellington all in town at the same time.

Stan Kenton trumpeter Ray Wetzel heard John when both were with Charley Barnet and when Wetzel decided to leave Kenton for more money on the Dorsey band, he recommended John. Kenton and some of the guys, including trumpet sensation of the time Maynard Ferguson, came to hear him at the Oasis. He got an offer. Barnet, John remembers, headed one of those straight-ahead, take no prisoners bands; Kenton, meanwhile, was experimental and constantly seeking changes. Later, John worked with Billy May, Ray Anthony and Woody Herman and organized his own group and backed Tennessee Ernie Ford. A versatile musician, he later did a tour with Henry Mancini.

John's wife, Frances Lynne, was a big band vocalist with a sweet sounding voice that made people think of Deanna Durbin. Actually, she told interviewers, she was influenced by Billie Holiday and Anita O'Day. She hasn't forgotten her first gig. It was in San Francisco in 1946, she told V. Vale of Swing! The New Retro Renaissance publication, while she was visiting a friend in the business. She hung out, she remembers, with Kenton vocalist June Christy and thought there could be a chance she could join the Artistry in Rhythm band. Instead, she went on tour with Charley Barnet and Gene Krupa. Refusing Charley's request to dye her hair red, she later left the band and joined Krupa who she called a real gentleman. Gene and band members, she recalled, kept themselves busy on the bus trips playing 20 questions and working crossword puzzles.

Some bandleaders could make your night in those days. A friend of mine, a decent trumpet player himself, John Imhoff, tells the story of his encounter with Harry James at Buckeye Lake. "People were going up to him and giving him a bill (a dollar I think) and whispering something to him. So I tried it. I handed him the dollar and whispered I'd like to hear "Ciribiribin."

"That's nice kid," Harry said, "but I was going to play it next anyhow."

While there was demand for the big bands, the competition was fierce. More important, bandleaders had to find distinctive ways to catch the public's "ear" with quality arrangements and individual sounds. The Miller band was on top of the Billboard college dance band poll three years in a row, 1940-1941-1942, for good reason. Glenn had a different sound, very danceable and memorable arrangements and a band that played the same way night after night. It was very successful, too. While Benny Goodman was named the best swing band in 1941, Miller was chosen the best sweet band, Downbeat Magazine said.

"The Miller band's sax section had a controlled shimmer to it and that is a challenge for saxophone players especially to get the whole thing balanced," says Monk Rowe, bandleader, music teacher and director of the Hamilton College Jazz Archive. "You have to listen to the lead player—a clarinet—but the writing Glenn did was very balanced. It was impeccable work. It was something to aspire to from a technical standpoint."

In one of his Archive interviews, Rowe says, saxophonist Jerry Jerome told him that one night after he had played a solo with the Miller band, Glenn came to him and said "why don't you play it the way you did the other nights and on the record? People will remember that." Memorability, it seems, was more valuable to Glenn than soloist creativity.

The Woody Herman sound a few years later, by contrast, was much different by design.

"The thing about the whole section (saxophones) with Herman was four tenors. The sound immediately comes down in pitch. Tenors are voiced lower. It had a real sexy kind of sound...very distinctive really. Tenor players, of course, loved it. There was good balance between the ensemble work and those great tenor soloists he had, too," Rowe continues.

But technique could also create a different sound, too. "Billy May's sound is a classic," Rowe suggests. "The definition of 'slurping' saxes which May employed...that came from sliding between notes and when you get a five man sax section bending the pitch like trombonists do is a really a challenge. For five guys to do that together, wow. You can't have four guys slurping...and one not."

The irony, some suggest, is that both Miller, a trombonist, and May, a trumpet player, relied on a softer woodwind lead to create their sounds, not brass instruments.

Arrangements and arrangers were certainly as important. During the war years, Glenn Miller had two charts among the most popular tunes. They were "Juke Box Saturday Night" and "Elmer's Tune."

The latter wasn't really Glenn's number. He acquired it from bandleader friend, Dick Jurgens. A young mortician named Elmer Albrecht was doodling with the tune when Jurgens heard him play it. Dick liked the clever ditty, got it from the funeral director, arranged it as an instrumental and named it appropriately, "Elmer's Tune." Miller caught the Jurgens band on the road, heard the number and decided it would fit the Modernaires and his band. He approached Jurgens who graciously offered it to his friend and even had lyricist Sammy Gallop put lyrics to it before he gave it to Miller. The rest is a part of Millermania.

I saw the Jurgens band in the late 1940s but I only heard the Miller group on records and radio. Their bands had different sounds and styles and the leaders different personalities. Miller was very disciplined, efficient in management and a tough taskmaster.

Jurgens, jazz critic George Simon said, was a handsome collegiate type out of California, who occasionally played fourth trumpet and tried to handle comedy. Yet, the band had a solid following and a number of redeeming values.

"His band was blessed with a wonderful trumpeter named Eddie Kuehler whose great tone and facile command of his horn enabled the band to achieve some especially attractive dynamics. Good arrangements, too, by Lou Quadling. It was a romantic-looking band. Jurgens was handsome, athletic...looking and his men deported themselves well."

And the Jurgens band had fun...something that didn't always take place in other bands.

Ann Freeman was the wife of longtime Jurgens trombonist Virgil Freeman. She remembered how she and other wives and their families toured with the band in a day when such travel would be like a group of transient gypsies. But Dick Jurgens, she said, did his best to make it possible for members of his band to have family companionship.

According to Annie, the band would do 48 or so one nighters a year during the 1940s.

"We didn't enjoy the packing every night," she said. Who would? Motel stays could have there own difficulties, too. At one stop, Annie continued, the band encountered a nosy landlady.

"When the men were taking turns driving to work at night she would stop them and ask why they all had the same suit on. She would inquire where they were going in the evening and why they all came back together...She had a key to all the rooms and since her room was over the front entrance, when she saw someone leave she would go check out their room. Imagine her surprise when she spotted me sitting in our room one night when she let herself in with her passkey. I yelled 'surprise' and she beat a hasty retreat."

Entertaining themselves on the road was mentally daunting, Mrs. Freeman explained. "For example, we'd have members of other bands over to our small hotel room and I'd serve them one of my knockout platters of food. We had to cool the beer and soft drinks in the bathtub by running cold water on it. Ice was very expensive back then and there were no hotel ice machines like now...Any band that happened to be appearing where we were usually brought us together. It became our social life. Sometimes during the day some musicians would just walk the streets to exercise and relax."

Dick Jurgens? "He was one of those great leaders who really cared about the men who played for him and the sound they created. He was a man who wanted perfection, clean cut dressers. That required two tailor made suits a year (no tuxes). That way the men could use them like business suits. He also insisted they have their shoes shined every night and their hair cut and trimmed. No question he had a good looking band and it was talented too," she recalls.

What kind of money could bands make during those days?

Sy Oliver remembers being happy to be working when he arranged for Jimmy Lunceford in the mid-1940s. He did some great scores for $2.50 an arrangement. Tommy Dorsey who hired Sy to arrange for his band paid him $5,000 more than Lunceford. In the mid-1930s, Paul Whiteman was carrying 34 players—one of the biggest traveling rosters—and paying musicians from $150 to $300 a week. Featured players could earn $350.

Lou DiSario, who managed ballrooms during the period and later, said that such arrangements were as secret as wartime security. In some instances, only the ballroom owners knew the final agreement. On average, he said, bands were usually paid between $2,500 and $3,000 with the leader getting double. Elliot Lawrence remembers when he was making $60 a week and his sidemen got $45 playing with the CBS orchestra in the 1940s. Woody Herman remembered his first gig as a bandleader at the old Roseland Ballroom in Brooklyn in 1936 when he was paid $75 a week and his sidemen got $50 each.

Imagine telling any musician of that era that U2, the Irish touring band, made $61.9 million from its records and publishing and gigs in the first year of the 21st century.

Hotels, it was noted, were steady gigs with decent hours and money during the 1930s to 1940s. Property and travel manager Ed Gabel, who authored the book Stan Kenton, said that musicians were usually paid union wages and big bands like the Dorseys, Barnet, Krupa, Miller and others used such dates to stimulate record sales. The earnings from records helped to meet payroll and travel expenses since there were no guarantees of steady work. In fact, many musical groups had to try to find creative ways to raise their asking price. Said Gabel in his book on Kenton, Carlos Gastel who managed Nat "King" Cole wouldn't try to book the trio until he could get $800 a week. It finally happened at the Orpheum Theater in Los Angeles.

Of course, many musicians of the period were very aware of what happened to top drawer musicians like King Oliver. King and his Circle Jazz Band were abruptly put out of business when clubs in Kansas City closed. He ended up operating a fruit and vegetable stand in Savannah, GA in the early 1930s. Later, he worked as a pool hall janitor. He died broke in 1938 at 43.

The Vincent Lopez band had, by far, the best hours of the big band era, some believe. The band had a long term contract—over 20 years—to play the dinner hours at the Hotel Taft in New York City which meant it was usually finished by 9 p.m. every night.

It was an era of turmoil, destruction, futility and survival...yet, it was also a decade of significance if you enjoyed the changing musical tastes.

"There was a certain kind of conformity at the time if you owned a ballroom and wanted music played a certain way...that was the way it was. On the other hand, I think there was a certain amount of experimentation that took place as well," says Richard "Dick" Robinson, a onetime high school administrator in Central New York who traded his desk for a turntable and teaches jazz, swing and serves as a disk jockey at the Mohawk Valley Institute for Learning in Retirement (MVILR) at the

State University of New York Utica/Rome IT campus. "Youth receptivity…young people tend to set the trends whether we like them or not. Older people become more nostalgic about what was, young people like to think about what will be. Young people reacted enthusiastically to Benny Goodman's music at the Palomar in 1935. They really had no experience base but they were so eager to experiment with new sounds. And they did in a big way."

It was, perhaps, a fitting way to end the first half of the 20th century.

J.R. Monterose plays the soprano at an impromptu Utica College (NY) performance.
Photo courtesy Utica College

Don Cantwell (second from left) and his Clef Dwellers, a Dixie band that traveled to Taiwan for an international festival in 1995. Photo by Bill Parker

Lou King, aka DiSario, East Coast entertainer, ballroom emcee, in the typical "zoot suit" of the 1940s.

...and now a short solo
by HARRY JAMES
The Nation's Number One Band Leader
"Sure it's fun, to play solo. But there's more to it than blowing your own horn. You've got to be in tune with the gang...know when to make a big noise, when to soft-pedal your own part and let others sound off.
"When everybody's in the groove, and nobody hogs the spotlight, that's solid sending...whether it's my band, your glee club, or our new 'world symphony,' the United Nations.
"Thanks to the Fleer people for letting me sing out on my pet subject. I like their democratic thinking . . . and I like their gum, too."
You'll join the chorus of cheers for Fleer's yourself, once you try this delicious gum with the extra peppermint flavor. Twelve snowy fleerlets, just 5¢. There's a trend to candy-coated gum . . . try Fleer's today!
Frank H. Fleer Corp.
Philadelphia, Pa.
Established 1885
FLEERS
Candy Coated
GUM
PEPPERMINT
Candy Coated—Chewing gum in its nicest form!

III. The Fifties: Bands Battle To Survive

Woody Herman told jazz critic and radio host Ralph J. Gleason on the "Jazz Casuals" broadcasts of the 1960s that his band didn't change arrangements when they played the usual dance gigs. They usually set aside about a half hour to 45 minutes of the four hour performance for concerts when they were on the road, he said.

Such "concerts" would have been unheard of for a touring band in the 1930s and even the '40s when danceland owners wanted soft dance music...nothing else. Major big bands on the road in the 1950s, by contrast, were already experimenting with a mixture of dance music and other entertainment. The reason?

Lots of them. It allowed the band to feature better paid soloists and vocal groups and resolve the ego problems some bandleaders and sidemen faced from night to night. Listen to Ralph Burns, pianist, composer and arranger for the Herman band as he reminisced in 1993 about the very popular instrumental "Early Autumn" he scored.

"When Stan Getz (tenor saxophonist) joined Herman there were no numbers written for him...and he played tunes written for others and became 'remorseful'...he kept after Woody to get him some numbers and so I when I had to write an end to the 'Summer Sequence" score—a larger piece to record—Woody said: 'Ralph, will you please, please give him something to play on this?' That's how Early Autumn came about. I wrote every change in the book on it and the first time Stan played it was just like magic...Here's to Stan and Woody up there."

Big band musician Bud Shank remembers how Stan Kenton helped him develop his own creative abilities. "Stan tried to bring out your best," he once told a radio interviewer. "I was hired to be lead alto saxophone player and I got paid to do that in the section. Art Pepper was the soloist but Stan knew that I wanted a chance to solo too and he found ways to give me chances even though it wasn't what I was hired to do. He did the same for guys in the trumpet and trombone sections too. He was like a father figure to many of us."

The '50s performances gave bands the chance to feature singles and albums in the record stores (later in the 1970s and 1980s, bands took their tapes, T-shirts and other memorabilia along to sell). Band personnel could show off their talent, too. Butch Stone, the baritone saxophonist with Les Brown, was a comic singer, for example. Trumpeter ClarkTerry developed scat singing or "mumbling" to a fine art and performed it everywhere from the "Tonight" show band to a Whitesboro High School, NY Jazz Festival. Leaders even got into the act; Dick Jurgens could always be counted on for a few laughs, Harry James loved to pick up the bongos on Latin numbers and Stan Kenton, who told radio interviewers of his early shyness and stage fright in front of a microphone, could burst into a monologue to fill time or amuse himself. One of his best occurred when he was changing personnel and musical direction. He called it "This is an Orchestra!" but studio producers at Capitol took this Bill Russo orchestration and called it "Prologue."

Sometimes, band warm ups before engagements were like board room brain sessions where new ideas emerged. Shorty Rogers, the talented trumpeter/composer and arranger, remembered how such "head" numbers emerged with the Herman organization. "One of the most frequently played jazz numbers was an old standard called 'Fine and Dandy' and the guys in Woody's band would get together back stage and just have fun doing it in jam sessions," Shorty told a Woody Herman Band Reunion crowd in Newport Beach, CA in 1993. "Woody came to me and asked if I would write a piece of music and use the chord changes of 'Fine and Dandy.' He said 'we'll call it 'Keen and Peachy.' I wrote the first chorus and I think Woody talked to Ralph Burns and he wrote part of it, too." While the crowd roared, Burns protested he didn't remember a thing Shorty was talking about.

Yet, some bands, in their attempt to create and change, ran into stubborn opposition.

Kenton led the list. Trying to explain his very progressive style of the late 1940s and early 1950s, Kenton told a Palladium audience that the band's "long works" of the "Innovations in Modern Music Group" which featured 40 strings and modernistic arrangements like Bob

Graettinger's 'City of Glass' concepts, might separate his loyal fans. "The fellow there has been so much heated controversy over in the music business is Bob Graettinger. Some people say it's not music...some people say it's great music...some people say I can't find a melody...and some people say there is no melody, listen for sound."

What a way to introduce a program to those who came out to dance! Kenton refused to change his innovative trend. He lost money on several big orchestral enterprises but he never gave up his dream. He recognized his need to please fans that came to dance but his heart was certainly going in another direction. A poor kid from Kansas by way of California, he made money and, said Ed Gabel, a road manager in the early days, he spent most of his wealth on his 12 bands.

While the big band business was experiencing a noticeable economic slump in 1951...My aspirations for becoming a road musician soared. Late the year before, I had started work with Dick Trimble's territorial band and, at the same time, acquired "wheels" (my mother's bright red Dodge convertible which became mine to use since my mother didn't drive) and I was making the awesome sum of $20 a gig. The band had a regular Friday night YMCA dance at the armory in Lancaster, OH and we would pick up another gig on Saturdays at special Elks Club events. Dick's impeccable reputation for good dance music gave us high school proms as well as plush country club outings each year during the six I played.

Like many others, I reluctantly left for college (Bowling Green State University) in the fall, 1951, but it would take me time to hatch a plan to get my drums to campus. Returning World War II veterans crammed every land grant college in the country and, consequently, living space in a dorm was down to three drawers in one chest in a temporary barracks hastily constructed under the concrete stadium bleachers. You had to vacate Saturday afternoons in the fall or live through what sounded like explosions on the roof especially when either team scored. My bunkmates and I had the added attraction of a drain pipe beside our beds so we knew when the quarters ended, too. By the end of the semester, however, I had met a few other musicians and gotten involved with fraternity life. When I came back for my second term I had a room off campus that permitted me to return with my big Slingerland set. But I had to put a covert operation in place to make it work. I transported the set piece by piece in unmarked bags and boxes past a wary landlord. The bass drum was stored at the fraternity house.

I played with so many "no name" groups, trios and big bands that, looking back, the only memories are of guys like Vinny, Blue Flame, Jim, Fran and others who have since faded with the years. Each group was an experience. There was the noon I was called at the fraternity by a friend in one of the big bands in Toledo who said I could play with their 16 piece group that night. The regular drummer, a schooled professional, had gone south for National Guard duty. Could I read? I said "yes" but I should have been honest and said "no."

When I got to the gig I discovered that one of the numbers for the upcoming holidays was a special arrangement of the "Nutcracker Suite" which called for kettles, not tom toms. I had never played kettles except to fool around on them while in high school. I gave myself a crash course and when we finished the quick rehearsal I sensed the leader was as troubled as I was. Too late to get someone else. Thanks to a good memory which stored the score in some part of my brain after I heard the number once...I brought it off. I was good enough, the leader said, to work for him again. The pay? We ended up with $7.50 each for four hours. Three dollars for gas and I think I made $4.50 an hour that night!

The Toledo leader's experience was typical of the national dilemma among big bands to find and keep good players in a rapidly declining segment of the music industry. Alto saxophonist Shank, a Dayton, OH native, told the Wayne State University radio station WDET in the late 1950s how he had arrived in Los Angeles in 1946 and connected with Charley Barnet before joining the Stan Kenton band in December, 1949. He said the Selective Service System had already contacted him and Kenton's staff had been able to put it off while the band was touring. In 1952, however, selective service tried to draft him again when he was 25 and "they found out I was 4-F and so they let me go.

What a bunch of nonsense!" he told the interviewer. His biggest thrill? "That first Kenton Concert...the Innovations Concert in January, 1950. It's what I joined the band to do and it was a thrill I'll never forget."

The United States was at war again; this time, Korea, 1950, and the draft was reaching deep into a depleted manpower pool. Meanwhile, colleges and universities were still very reluctant to recognize swing or jazz. There were no minor leagues for big bands to recruit from really. Jazz historian Monk Rowe's interviews with a number of players from the period left vivid impressions about the decline of such music.

"Lots of the fellows I interviewed got their start in their teens because more experienced musicians had been drafted," he told a Central New York radio audience. But other factors influenced changing tastes, too. "Youth is always looking for something new. It's the same today. Teenagers in the early to mid 1950s listening to what was their parents' music simply said let's find our own. Must be something in their genes. One of my interviewees told me with a half smile and scowl 'If I could' I'd ring Elvis Presley's neck!'"

Discordant notes that masked melody were replacing the danceable music with a familiar beat. Yet dance music was still popular among college age young people. Sandi and Bruce Haning of Lancaster, OH, were among the millions who couldn't wait to get on the dance floors whether the music was a dreamy slow one or a good swing number. The music took away the worries of a Cold War, a struggle to start housekeeping and to make a living.

I have this wonderful memory of a trip from Bowling Green to Finney Chapel, Oberlin College, outside Cleveland on a wintry night, March 2, 1953, to hear the new sounds of a West Coast ranch hand who became a polished new age piano player. Listen carefully to the album...you can hear me clapping strenuously from my 2nd row seat! Pianist Dave Brubeck and his quartet featuring Paul Desmond, Ron Crotty and Lloyd Davis were worth a year of fraternity parties and giving up beer money for a month to pay for the gas for the trip. Later, I read of the internal squabble on campus about bringing such innovative music to a conservatory best known for the classics and classical training. The two-hour program was a terrific success and resulted in the Oberlin College Jazz Club planning three more concerts the next year.

Brubeck's strength? His commitment to his own music was more important than commercial successful. For example, he had to battle record company execs to put Take Five, a number often considered a Brubeck signature piece and most creative, in his albums. They wanted to feature more conventional numbers with titles people knew. Later he went against those who argued he could make more money on tour, and wrote a Broadway musical about cultural exchange that was never commercially pursued. Brubeck told a PBS audience in December, 2001, that his dream was far different than that of musicians of the big band era who sought to get on the road with traveling groups. "What I really wanted to do? Play area spots at union scale and be close to home and family," he smiled. His Connecticut home satisfies his needs today. It has not one but seven pianos!

Was there a significant difference in players and playing as rock'n'roll bands became prevalent?

"Players I talked to of the early days placed great importance on the individual sound. Fellows like Sweets Edison (trumpet) believe that after a few notes you should really know who's playing. I think older guys don't hear that today. They believe today's players are more schooled, better readers and have a better variety of skills. I don't think that today's musicians are more talented. Guys like Lester Young, who supposedly didn't know chords at all, could play marvelously. His talent was innate. Those are really the differences generation to generation, I suppose," Rowe believes.

Few seem to remember the dawn of the 1950s. While American factories had downsized in 1946, they had to be mobilized again much like the beginning of the war to transform tanks built in the same plants into autos and weapons to washing machines. Furthermore while our social lives continued without blackouts and we returned to standard time zones, we kept Summer Daylight Savings Time. It was also the beginning of America's so-called "Silent Generation," teenagers who were expected to be seen...not heard.

An older, wiser generation that had fought the "war to end all wars" was in command. Youngsters could dream, of course. Many did. There was a preoccupation with Sloan Wilson's novel "Man With the Gray Flannel Suit." The story was about how the war had created a new kind of social economic fabric that veterans had to adjust to in post-war America. Author George Orwell, whose book "1984" predicted a future ruled by telescreens and automation and was required reading in my college literature classes, was dead at 46, days after the book was published. We never had the chance to discover the true meaning until years later.

Kirk Douglas, Lauren Bacall, Doris Day and composer and sometime singer Hoagy Carmichael gave us the other side of the big band business from what we saw on the screen a few years earlier in such happy tales as "Orchestra Wives" and "Sun Valley Serenade." The 1950 film was called "The Young Man With A Horn," the turbulent story of Midwestern born Bix Beiderbecke, the self-taught cornet player who was considered one of the real sensations of the era but whose excesses with booze, women and vanity, not to mention ambition brought an early death at 28. His appeal at the turn of a half a century was his lifestyle and his talent.

What movie goers took away was the story of a business that seemed to have cost him his life. Yet the film offered great contemporary music to accompany Dorothy Baker's novel. Doris Day numbers abound in this film thanks to songwriter Carmichael. Harry James did the trumpet score. The songs, numbers like, "The Very Thought of You," "Too Marvelous For Words," "I May Be Wrong" and "With A Song In My Heart," were popular for years. You came away humming...even if you didn't find a happy ending.

Entertainment was no longer indoors either. Americans, all 150 million plus according to the US Census that year, flocked to drive-in theaters—more than 2,000 of them—and began spending more time at home with 16 inch Capeharts, Dumonts or GE black is blacker and white is whiter television sets. Breadwinners marveled at Boston Red Sox slugger Ted Williams and his record breaking $150,000 salary.

Yet, we worried about our future when President Harry Truman ordered a hydrogen bomb, 100 to 1,000 times more powerful than the atomic bombs used against Japan, built to ensure the United States "is able to defend itself against any possible aggressor." We saw the Cold War clouds rumbling toward us and seriously considered the government's call to build bomb shelters complete with days of supplies. We practiced "duck and cover" drills in schools and our parents examined whether they wanted the vault shelter away from the house that featured the concrete walls eight blocks high in the back yard or an extension of our basement to function as a place to survive. My dad ruled that out when we remembered that our basement walls had shed waterproofing twice in one year and still had leaks. Once it came off in large slabs with a loud crash. It was no joking matter although we tried to make light of it.

Big bandleaders, meanwhile, were talking about dropping the 15 to 16 men they carried and surviving with smaller groups in the sunny sections of the country they loved to visit. Henry "Hot Lips" Busse was an example. A trumpet playing leader, Henry enlarged his band to 19 during World War II days and then dropped five men in the post-war era. By the 1950s, his band had 10 sidemen and vocalists. Tragically, according to Leo Walker in his book, the Big Band Almanac, Henry was playing a convention of undertakers in April, 1955, when he was stricken and died of a heart attack in his room at the Peabody in Memphis, TN.

The fifties created new visitas for musicians, though. Cities, for example, weren't megaplexes like today. Said Gaye LeBaron of the Press Democrat, CA: "The newspapers still announced the birth of every baby and ran photographs of everyone in the military. Young people, now on wheels, discovered drive-in restaurants and drive-in movies. Alcohol was definitely the drug of choice. There were nearly 30 bars, lounges, saloons and taverns in Santa Rosa's downtown."

As a teen playing country clubs for the wealthy and locally famous I never ceased to be amazed at after hours conduct. One night, I was playing a New Year's Eve dance which started at 9 and was to end at 1. By 11, few people were dancing, a great number of couples were close to or totally smashed and a guy asks if he could sit in. The leader knew him and verified that he played drums. I gave him the sticks and he told me to go sit with his wife. I spent most of the next two hours dancing with his wife, eating his dinner and enjoying myself while being paid for playing four hours. It gave me new enthusiasm for the life of a musician!

Small was in along with background sound. The traveling big bands of the '40s found far fewer audiences and touring costs much higher so the lure of the road, which had already diminished, caused musicians who wanted to make the band business a career to stay near major cities like New York, Los Angeles and Chicago where clubs were plentiful and studio work was much more likely. Listen to bassist Ray Brown who started working with Oscar Peterson in 1951 and stayed another 15 years before going out on his own.

He believes playing with the "best in the business" influenced him to continue. "(Oscar) would write something for the band and we would play it, and then when everybody got comfortable with it, he would make it go twice as fast. So you'd be scuffling all over again. But, when I reflect back on that, that has helped me maintain myself."

Oscar's high school friend from Montreal and a child prodigy at CBC, Maynard Ferguson, a trumpet player with one of the best upper ranges heard in that era, made his debut at 21 in the states with the Stan Kenton Orchestra. He spent three years as the sensational member of Kenton's screeching brass section and then worked another three as a first call musician at Paramount Studios where, in 1955, he was the strong trumpet sound on the motion picture, "The 10 Commandments."

He started at 4 on the piano and violin, discovered the trumpet at 9 and by 13 had soloed on CBC. At 16, he recalled for me, "I led the warm-up band in Canada for all the great orchestras when they passed through Montreal, including Basie, Ellington, Woody Herman, Kenton, Dizzy and both Dorsey brothers."

A musician I'll always remember from my years at Buckeye Lake was Leonard Stoppelaire—aka Lenny Dee—a one-man band who made the Hammond Model A, the first commercially available electronic organ, his trio and quartet in the 1950s. Lenny was that nightclub comic who made music create his place in an entertainment world that included popular groups like the Page Cavanaugh Trio, the Dave Brubeck Quartet, Nat King Cole Trio, the Four Freshmen and loads of others who found opportunities in the thousands of supper clubs, grills, nightclubs, hotel bars and catered parties. Lenny took lessons on the accordion and was working professionally before he enlisted in the US Navy in 1943 and served on an aircraft carrier in the Far East. When he returned from military duty, he used the GI Bill to study the organ at the Chicago Conservatory. A series of bookings in prominent southern hotels helped but it was country and western star Red Foley who engineered a gig on a weekly radio network while Lenny played the exclusive Nashville Plantation Club that brought a recording contract from Decca and prominence. I wrote a piece about Lenny from memory while I was in the service in the late 1950s. What I said then certainly is the nostalgia I had for the little man on the big Hammond years later when I thought about his performances at a place called the Mayfair Room, Lake Breeze Hotel, a few steps from Buckeye Lake.

"What wouldya like to hear?" he'd asked, coaxing the audience. The answers gave him the evening's performance. "That's what makes it a great job whether the bar is full or empty," he told me. You could hear Lenny do a multi-faceted organ imitation of Eddie Haywood's Canadian Sunset and later close your eyes and see and hear Henry Mancini's Baby Elephant Walk or Pink Panther.

His style gave him the chance to use his appearances throughout the country—just as television was emerging—to acquire a special kind of popularity. His albums (more than 12 over his performing career) kept you in touch from the summer engagements to the long winter layover when he was playing the balmy South or big city hotels and club gigs. Decca shrewdly seized on his draw and took his specialty to the studio. Each of his albums was a focus that touched someone somewhere. Lenny Dee Down South could sell a northern Dee follower as well. The titles and his mastery of the console were potent. South, Georgia on My Mind, Carolina in the Morning, Alabamy Bound...the songs said it all. Few bandleaders at that time had figured out how you cluster what people recognized and wanted to hear to make it a signature. Lenny Dee was definitely a head of his time.

Admirers traveled anywhere to hear him. Some went south for vacations when they knew Lenny had a two week or a month at a resort, especially on Florida's West Coast where he later bought a club in the late 1960s called Lenny Dee's Den in St. Petersburg and would play from time to time. The late Johnny Jones of the Columbus, OH Dispatch, a popular entertainment columnist in his day, used to make sure he saw Lenny on his trips to nearby Buckeye Lake. "Using Duke Ellington's Caravan, Lenny Dee will start an imitation of Harry James, then bring in Harpo Marx and his harp, Bobby Haggart on the bass fiddle, Gene Krupa on his drums and even Tommy Dorsey. A great evening's entertainment," he wrote. Without a doubt, Lenny was the 1950s compact, one-man big band whose sound could fill a room.

Milt Bernhart can't forget when he was a 23-year-old trombonist playing with the great Benny Goodman on the road. He remembered a January, 1949, closing night at the new Flamingo in Las Vegas he said on the web site, www.jazzprofessional.com. Benny wanted to put bebop into the band so he got Gerry Mulligan, Fats Navarro, Lee Konitz and a few others to join him. Konitz, a boyhood friend from Chicago, had put in the good word for Milt to join Benny. Two weeks of grueling rehearsals and the only guys left were Wardell Gray, Milt and a few others. Benny, Milt said, was a taskmaster; the band wasn't paid for rehearsal time.

The young Chicagoan remembers getting up that January day, packing his suitcase to leave for Los Angeles and checking out. Then he had to find something to do until the first show at 8 p.m. that night. There was no place to practice...so all he could was walk around Vegas in the hot sun. Milt also remembered how angry Benny became that last night. Wardell was Black and, typical of the times, he had to use the back entrance, not the front, to enter the Vegas hotel. He also had to stay in the backroom between shows. The intolerance was impossible even for a gentle person like Wardell. He shrugged it off until the last night when he ended up drinking too much and teetering onto the stage when the band began. Benny wasn't in a good mood, either, Milt said. Wardell had a solo on "Memories Of You," and he got up late and missed his opening notes.

Benny stopped the band, Milt continued, enraged. A capacity audience sat in those uncomfortable, embarrassing seconds that seem like an eternity. He told Wardell to "get off this stand, pops!" Then he followed him to the wings and took away Wardell's clarinet which Benny had given him some time earlier. You never really knew what to expect at times.

Many musicians and leaders, looking back, believe that racism that permeated the period certainly didn't help the growth of music either. Ken Burns, creator of the blockbuster PBS television series "Jazz," offered us the same description.

Longtime musician, bandleader and friend of major players of the 1930s to 1950s, Don Cantwell, told a New York radio audience that Artie Shaw used to battle racism with the proprietors of dance establishments. "He resented the fact that some owners had the ability to dictate how or who he should play. When Roy Eldridge (trumpet player) played in the band, a ballroom owner wanted Roy to sit 16 steps to the right of the band. Artie said he's in the band and that can't happen. The owner said he had to sit away from the band, that's it. Artie said 'forget it,' and the band didn't play."

Musicians always had to have a sense of humor as well as a sense of indignation. Bassist Milt Hinton told the story of jazz pianist Perry Bradford that always drew a smile from other musicians. Perry became ill when he was 77, Milt said, and he had to be hospitalized. As the doctors and nurses collected personal information about him, he mentioned that he had written more than a 1,000 songs and sold a book about jazz. "It just must have seemed too unbelievable to those doctors," Milt said Perry recalled. They sent him to a psychiatric center because they thought he was hallucinating!

Dick Robinson tells his jazz classes in Central New York how black and white were conditions as well as racial terms during the era. Ballroom and dance hall owners were proprietors period, exclamation point. "There was a certain kind of conformity at the time if I owned the ballroom and I wanted you to play a certain way that's the way it was. I think there was a certain kind of experimentation that took place as well. I call it 'youth receptivity'—young people tend to set the trends whether we like them or not—older people became more nostalgic about what was, young people like to think what will be. Young people reacted very positively to Benny Goodman's music. They had no experience base to start with so they were eager to experiment with new sounds...and Goodman did it in one night."

Racism and segregation, said the web site "swing," were dominant in the era. A good number of states restricted seating in theaters and clubs and the few mixed bands traveling at the time met police officers ready to enforce local law. Southern states would be difficult through the 1950s and even into the civil rights battles of the 1960s. Yet, it wasn't merely a Dixie problem. Stan Kenton, Ed Gabel said in his book of the Kenton early years, found tolerant and liberal California could also resist mixed bands. In a Downbeat article, October, 1939, musicians talked about integration of swing bands and, while no conclusions were reached, the story did demonstrate that southern sidemen were nearly unanimous in opposing it as a bad idea.

One anonymous bandleader offered a view that probably is still reflected today:

"When a Negro enters a White band, he loses his identity as a Negro musician. I think the musical progress of all Negro groups such as Duke Ellington and Count Basie has been tremendous and has contributed originality and a freshness to American music we would never have had if there were mixed bands. But after all, it is really up to nobody else but John Q. Public. If the public wants Negros in its white bands, it'll get Negros in them. If it doesn't want them, well, the box office will always tell us what the answer will be."

Entrepreneur Norman Granz of Jazz at the Philharmonic and record labels such as Clef, Verve and Pablo fame, is credited with leading the battle to integrate jazz and the business community. He demanded equal pay and dining and better living accommodations for musicians wherever he took his tours. He saw himself, said the New York Times in his obituary, Nov. 21, 2001, as a businessman who dabbled in the economics of music but he wanted people to hear jazz the way others listened to Bach. It was an uphill battle, observers said, but he brought many to see a light at the end of the long tunnel.

The irony, says jazz historian Robinson, "The Afro-American contributions to big band era and jazz in this country were absolutely outstanding...Henderson's arrangements in the early 1930s, interestingly enough, were played mostly by Afro-American musicians and white musicians weren't able to play those complex arrangements or at the speed of them. Goodman was smart enough to use Fletcher and a number of his arrangements. Other people used Fletcher and so did others too as time went on. That whole scene evolved from the Savoy where Chick Webb, another outstanding Black musician, played. They had band battles. Goodman and Webb. And Webb's band would blow them away. The neat thing about this was that when they finished their gigs at 2 or 3 in the morning, the Afro-American musicians would get together with white musicians and the Afro-Americans would learn the style and finis and white musicians would learn improvisational techniques. There was a mixing and a growth of music that came from it."

Of course, not all bands had the big image of a Shaw, Kenton, Goodman, James, Herman, Lombardo and others. Yet, they acquired a loyal following and were certainly bands that could draw crowds. That's a good description of the Dick Jurgens band. George T. Simon, a harsh critic of most "sweet" bands, called Jurgens a handsome, athletic looking leader with a "collegiate and romantic looking" organization. Ironically, Billboard college polls from 1938 to 1942 claimed Kay Kyser, Jan Savitt, Orrin Tucker, Sammy Kaye, Will Bradley and Wayne King were the popular sweet bands. But Leo Walker in his book "The Big Band Almanac" said that Jurgens led a first class, very popular dance band that drew large crowds especially in Chicago, Denver and Catalina Island.

Anne Freeman, wife of Jurgens' trombonist Virgil Freeman, said the secret (if there was one) to the success of a band was the personal style and the approach of the leader. "Virgil chose Dick (he had other opportunities)...those were the happy days. They had the appearance of a very clean cut band on the road. No scandal, no drugs, no heavy drinking. Where any drinking was done at all it was made clear that it had to be after working hours or you were fired. A few tried it and were replaced. It was Dick's policy to hold the band together with the same men as long as possible. He didn't believe in changes. He encouraged the men to bring their wives and children along when on long locations such as the Hotel Claremont where we would spend three months every year and always at Christmas."

It was no picnic yet band wives found a way to make it work for their spouses and kids.

"Our excitement through the band travel days was a newspaper and once in a while a movie and anything that was free from museums and zoos to parks on our days off from Hollywood to New York. We saved our money for a business we wanted to open after we retired in later years. Exercising was something else we tried to do We tried golf and tennis, too."

And, Anne said in the Dick Jurgens' web site,www.dickjurgens.com, which is devoted to the family life of the band, wives and musician husbands did their best to bring quality to their lives on the road.

Musicians and their wives "would entertain themselves the best they could. For example, we'd have members of other bands over to our small hotel room and I'd serve them one of my knockout platters of food. We had friends on the Eddy Howard band. In fact, any band that happened to be appearing where we were usually brought some of us together. It became our social life. Sometimes during the day some musicians would just walk the streets to exercise and relax," she wrote. "Virg and I didn't keep musicians' hours. We would go to sleep after he had a snack when he got home and then get up early. Most musicians would stay up late and sleep late. In 51 ½ years of marriage Virgil never broke the habit of getting up early."

But her father, she remembers, was convinced the marriage wouldn't last. It was a familiar story and one I could relate to because my wife and our families had the same uneasy feeling about what was ahead for us if I chose a musical life. Anne and Virg were determined to prove her father wrong...and they did for more than a half century of marriage. Yet things didn't start smoothly. "The band was playing their usual three weeks at the Aragon Ballroom in Chicago, Virgil and I scheduled our wedding for the day off, being a Monday. He flew to Pittsburgh late Sunday night after the job. We made it, the wedding went off as scheduled...after the traditional dance, its time to go to the airport at midnight. Virgil had to work the next night. No honeymoon...no sleep for Virgil for two nights because of flying and none the next night either. We got back in time for him to go to work," Anne recalls.

"We did have a lot of fun on this band. I remember we played a ballroom at Walled Lake, MI and after the job we all had a huge roast with a nice fire outside the ballroom. That was such a fine evening, the pictures we took are still in my scrapbook."

Jurgens, a number of musicians remembered, realized the necessity of marketing, too. Walker wrote that when the band was playing Claremont on Catalina Island, CA, it launched a promotion called "I like Dick Jurgens because..." The campaign drew the largest amount of mail the island ever received.

The band business, said Chuz Alfred in his limited issue book "Gigography" (1994), was always a struggle filled with plenty of hassles. Before a major gig he had put together in the 1950s, he received a telegram from American Federation of Musicians headquarters regarding one of his players: "Because Charlie Crosby, who had been with Phineous Newborn Jr. and BB King, a member of the Dayton Local 683, plays with your band, the telegram said, you are classified as a traveling band...(therefore) you must increase the contract price by 10 percent for traveling surtax. The rest of us belonged to the Local 103 in Columbus, OH. The club owner refused and the gig was off. No wonder it's tough to make it in the music business."

But he loved it. He paid his dues as Roots' author Alex Haley, who wrote the fascinating Playboy story about trumpeter Miles Davis, said whenever he heard a story about the love of one's work. Talk about love of work...Haley couldn't get Davis to meet with him for an interview until he discovered that Miles was an amateur boxer who loved to work out in the ring. Haley met him at the gym and took his lumps in the ring to get the musician to finally sit down to talk.

Chuz, meanwhile, had stumped much of Ohio drawing good crowds and comments before the president of Savoy Records happen to hear of him while passing through the Buckeye state. The record exec decided the Alfred group should be heard and set the date. The album "Jazz-Young Blood" was their first. "The three youngsters blow well on all the compositions and show promise For the future. They have been favorites in and around Ohio ever since they began working as a group and after hearing them here the rest of the country will be sure to recognize their capabilities," the liner jacket said. But what happened years later demonstrated the value of those 1950s cuts. When Nippon Columbia bought Savoy, it selected a group of old hi-fi masters to be reproduced in the then new Denin Digital Remastering of 1993. Recording executives examined who to feature and selected such greats as Marian McPartland, 1940s big band leader Ray McKinley, George Shearing, Sun ra and...Chuz Alfred. The album, incidentally, featured Chuz's work as a composer, too. His numbers "Manta Wray," and "Love Comes to Mehitabel Brown" were on the Young Blood CD.

As one who was there in the beginning backing Chuz, his dad George, the piano player, and others at cottage jam sessions on Buckeye Lake on lazy summer holidays...I felt good about his success, too.

Woody Herman, of course, came as close as anyone to defining the success or failure in leading a band for a living. He told Willis Conover in MusicUSA: "There are only two kinds of bandleader. One is a businessman who plays what the public wants to hear and is interchangeable with the accountant. The other is an artist who plays (or coaxes his sidemen to play) what he wants to hear and hopes he can find a manager to market the results. To the businessman, a night on the bandstand is a day at the office. To the artist, the money is important but secondary, he is never really happy except when his band is playing." I didn't find a musician or bandleader from any era who disagreed with Woody's assessment.

The informality and casualness of getting gigs was the reason trust in the 1950s became an issue. While with Trimble I had always been paid. Perhaps not what I thought I was worth...but I was paid. Later during my years playing with collegians who thought others would be honest and a handshake was a contract, I worked with one group that played two clubs and neither proprietor paid us. The owners took advantage of the fact that we didn't have a "doing business as" (dba) and we didn't have an identifiable business address. I'm still waiting for the checks!

Of course, contracts during wartime didn't have the guarantee of peacetime either. Ronnie Kemper found that out. Ronnie had been with Horace Heidt's "Pot 'o' Gold" radio show during the early 1940s. He decided the time was right and his reputation was strong enough to launch his own band. He got financial support but when sought a release from his contract, the bandleader refused. Heidt had seen war coming and his attorney added a clause canceling the contract if "an act of war caused the US to be attacked." Said Leo Walker in his book The Big Band Almanac: "Fate intervened on Kemper's behalf in late summer 1942 when a Japanese submarine fired a few nondestructive rounds at a mountainside near Brookings, OR. Kemper's attorney was successful in convincing Heidt's attorney that this constituted an attack (on mainland US) and Kemper became a bandleader. His band leading career was cut short after little more than a year when he was called in to the service...He did not resume as a bandleader at war's end."

Gabel in his book on Kenton recalled that Frank Dailey, once a bandleader himself, would pay as little as possible to groups playing the Meadowbrook but offered plenty of national radio exposure to bands he thought had potential. Kenton, he said, got plenty of time.

The sounds of the late 1940s spilled over onto the '50s for musicians...but they didn't excite an apathetic public unfortunately. Improvisation was rampant; trios, quartets and even sextets which didn't require tightly written arrangements were popular. I played a series of gigs with a pickup trio that used 30 basic melodies from standard sheet music. Who ever acted as the leader would call out the numbers, step off a beat and everyone would drop in where they felt they fit. One of our biggest problems? Figuring ways to end the tunes so they sounded rehearsed.

Yet, there were big bands playing a limited number of larger audience engagements trying to put new musical sounds into orchestral arrangements. The results, most music critics said, were Uneven at best and usually short-lived commercially. The touring bands of Woody Herman, Stan Kenton, Boyd Raeburn, Charley Barnet, Harry James, Gene Krupa and a few others tried to bridge the swing and bop music prevalent among musicians but, outside of providing a quick change of pace to give dancers a break, the fusion wasn't successful.

Claude Thornhill probably provided the newest big band sound with scores by Gil Evans that incorporated French horns, piccolos, bass clarinet and even a tuba. Thornhill introduced some bop-tinted numbers like Robbins Nest, Lover Man and Anthropology to whet audiences' appetites. Said one critic: "Thornhill's orchestra acquired a totally fresh and subtle sound, one considerably softer and more opaque than the bright, loud, brash sonorities of the late swing era bands."

But the timing, not the musicianship, was wrong. People appeared far from interested in trying to understand such music. We were trying to understand the "Beat Generation" writers of the time. Coffee houses were vogue on the coasts and so were writers like Jack Kerouac and a brash but sedate man named Hugh Hefner who launched an upscale girlie magazine called Playboy.

Teddy Powell, who had hired top talent like Goodman, Tommy Dorsey and Bunny Berigan when he started in 1939, later took on Pete Condoli, Boots Mussulli, Charley Ventura, Ray Wetzel, Milt Bernhart and Lee Konitz and hired Ray Conniff to arrange for this all-star crew of jazz stars. He was determined to have one of the best of the swinging big bands. By 1950, Teddy had given up. He reorganized, added strings and became a society band that attracted bookings.

The struggle for a smaller and more isolated audience put older musicians against younger, more individualistic players. We had already been given a taste of new interpretations in the early 1940s. Composer/arrangers like Buster Harding, Neal Hefti, Gerry Valentine and Budd Johnson along with Ralph Burns and a Mills College student named Pete Rugolo who studied with Darius Milhaud on the West Coast were exploring new ways to develop melody. Some caught and became a whistler's fancy…most did nothing for anyone and were forgotten like some of the wartime ditties.

But ultimately the experiments and forward thrusts of bebop—many of them instilled in such places as Minton's Playhouse in Harlem, in small lounges and obscure nightclubs, on tours, and in even more private situations such as homes and hotel rooms—had to break through to an expanding public via record companies and the larger, more popular club venues," one midwestern critic surmised. The new players? People like Charley Parker, Dizzy Gillespie, Bud Powell, Kenny Clarke, Max Roach, Oscar Pettiford, Ray Brown, Milt Jackson, JJ Johnson and Miles Davis…for starters.

Parker, for example, created dazzling speed executing 4/4 into 8/8. Meanwhile, drummers became much more involved in driving or creating poly rhythm while trying to keep the sound behind the soloist. Wire brush drumming artistry was powerful with smaller groups at the time.

But unlike the days of the 1930s and early 1940s, instrumental music didn't create the enthusiasm to dance or to be remembered in the 1950s as bop altered the jazz scene. "Bebop was made for listening, not dancing," said one wag in an Ohio newspaper, "it was not intended to be played to the accompaniment of clinking glasses and nightclub merrymaking…"

Bop, of course, was spontaneous, creative thought that took form like jazz had decades earlier. But its flatted fifths and discordant notes always made it more a freefall than melodic music.

Diehards, especially musicians, loved it. The average patron, though, had little feeling for it. In an earlier day, big band arrangers were careful to repeat clever chords and keep the beat simple. Even then, the sound didn't always bring million record sales. Big band numbers had melody, shout choruses and a solid beat, thanks primarily to the arrangements.

"The arranger was really the unsung hero of the era. Jazz moved a small group thing going back to its beginning in New Orleans but when you started adding on more people you couldn't have everybody improvising obviously. Someone has to be behind the scenes writing the charts and creating what the band sounds like. Often the leaders could be fine musicians but not writers. They could be just good businessmen, too," jazz historian Monk Rowe told a radio audience.

While Paul Whiteman, Frankie Carle, Carmen Cavallaro and Freddy Martin had introduced some classical sounds to dance bands, Rowe didn't find such efforts that popular during the swing era.

A number of jazz musicians, though, were studying Bach and Bela Bartok to expand their horizons and find more compatible ideas. Gunther Schiller called it "third stream" with ideas flowing in both directions. Some in the music world call third stream cross over or fusion music.

"I think most experiments mixing classical and jazz music at that time didn't end up highlighting either form of music, frankly," Rowe argues. "You seem to have diminished what's good about each one in order to combine these music forms. I'm not so sure the public, for example, was ready for Stan Kenton. I'm not sure even the musicians were that happy either. I remember a story about his larger organization when Kenton was complaining about how the band had to do something dramatic to increase its strength and trumpeter Al Porcino yelled out "Why don't we try swinging?" Kenton reportedly didn't respond. But he did answer manager Carlos Gastel when the band played a gig in Providence, RI. Carlos told Stan the booking agency had taken complaints the band was too loud. "Tone it down," Stan was told. He refused.

But Kenton did create a distinctive style, beginning and ending productions to virtually each number if you listened closely as I did and a showmanship that was unique at the time. Listen to the cymbal crescendo that opens Artistry in Rhythm, which was called "Production on a Theme" for lack of a title when it was recorded in 1943, and you appreciate the excitement the band brought to an engagement. Take a quick journey back to a dance date at March Field Air Force Base, 1959, and listen to the Kenton band handle such standards as "Where or When," "Street of Dreams," "Early Autumn" and you can appreciate the originality of the band number to number.

That transcribed evening didn't start smoothly. It appears that while the contract called for a quality piano...the Air Force must have forgotten it. Stan's piano is missing throughout the performance, said Michael Sharpe in his liner notes. But the show must go on...and the band did. It played in Peterboro, Canada, when conditions for everybody were far more miserable. It was an ice skating rink with a portable wood floor down for dancing. The temperature, unfortunately, was 48o BELOW freezing when the program began. According to Ed Gabel in his book on Kenton, gas heaters couldn't warm the pavilion. To make matters worse, the brass section couldn't play its instruments for fear the trumpets and trombones would freeze and the moisture on the lips could cause injury to the player.

I met the popular Kenton band in the summer of '47 when it visited Buckeye Lake, OH after finishing a date outside Cincinnati. It was a one nighter before heading for Lake Erie for a stay at Cedar Point. I helped unload the band bus and met and interviewed the tall Californian visitor for a story that was never published until three decades later. Capital Records had signed the band a few years earlier and I had already put sidemen in my memory bank. Guys like Boots Mussulli, Al Anthony, Red Dorris, Chico Alvarez, Bob Cooper, Bob Gioga, Ken Hanna, Bart Varsalona. Harry Forbes, Eddie Safranski, Buddy Childers, Kai Winding and others made my afternoon memorable.

There was something about a Kenton performance that made you think it was special regardless where it was played. Some bands just started with the first number whether it was the theme or not. A few, like Kenton, made the beginning notes and chords a production in itself. His first performance in November, 1941 at the Hollywood Palladium is still remembered by oldtimers in the business.

Kenton waited nervously across the dance floor until all the musicians were seated and then he gave a loud shout and ran across the floor through a bewildered crowd and hopped up on the bandstand. When his feet touched the stage he gave the downbeat for Artistry in Rhythm. The crowd loved it.

Frank Galime, a former first chair and solo trumpet player for the Utica, NY Symphony, jazz musician and music teacher, remembers his first time seeing and hearing the Artistry in Rhythm Band. "It was a most progressive band...big and brassy compared to others I had seen and with new ideas. I remember when I saw him how he showcased Maynard Ferguson and as a trumpeter I thought that was really great. I would have loved to have played in that day," Frank said as he mused about his 1950s evening at Ithaca College.

Unlike leaders who once they found their "sound" stopped growing, Kenton would make changes without hesitation. In the 1970s, he told a radio audience that he had changed Artistry in Rhythm from a march to a rumba to a Afro-Cuban beat to a waltz just to give it a different twist. Years earlier, the tall Kansan thought Glenn Miller's clarinet lead might be an interesting harmonic blend to his reed section so he tried five clarinets and had composer/arranger Gene Roland score some numbers. The saxophone section had to rent clarinets, said Ed Gabel in the Kenton book, to make it work. The experiment lasted three days. When Stan heard the new "Eager Beaver" he decided it wasn't going to work.

South Korea wasn't the place I expected to hear the Les Brown band. Envision a lakeside ballroom, a nice evening breeze and the soft "Sentimental Journey" sound with Jo Ann Greer singing. Switch the setting to a portable bandstand with the distinct odor of Kimchi and the stench of rice paddies wafting across what could have passed for a farmer's market and you've got the overseas location. It was 1957 or 1958 and the Bob Hope Thanksgiving-Christmas Special was island hopping from Japan to South Korea to Okinawa. I became friendly with Pacific Stars & Stripes entertainment columnist and man about Tokyo, Al Ricketts. He had introduced me to a great all-night Russian restaurant-bar called, naturally, "Volga" where I listened to an Oscar Peterson/Dave Brubeck Japanese piano stylist do American standards. Close your eyes and you thought you were stateside. Al wasn't about to leave his comfortable digs in Tokyo and Ginza nightclubs to wade in rice paddies, eat military food and billet in drafty Quonset huts somewhere south of the DMZ.

I volunteered and since I was permanently stationed in Korea there was no argument. I covered the USO show from Tachikawa Air Force Base, Japan, to Kimpo Air Field, South Korea, and spent some moments chatting with Les Brown's trombone-playing brother Stumpy, arranger Frank Comstock, bassist Rolly Bundock, my favorite drummer, Jack Sperling and Miss Oklahoma who was along with Jerry Colonna, Hope and the rest of the gang.

It was essentially the same band that made a sensational appearance at the Hollywood Palladium, Labor Day weekend, 1953. Thanks to the efforts of Bob Thiele, the "Band of Renown" broke from its typical routine on that memorable date and demonstrated what a swinging group it really could be. Thiele took time constraints off the soloists and, as Leonard Feather would later write, "the Les Brown band comes into focus not only as a great dance band but as a superlative jazz orchestra with several top-grade soloists."

Unfortunately, the band merely did warm up numbers on stage when I saw them but I did get a chance to hear several Skip Martin arrangements like "Back In Your Own Backyard," "You're the Cream in My Coffee" and the beautiful "Midnight Sun." I also discovered up close and very personal why my future wouldn't be as a working drummer. Watching Jack Sperling, one of the best technicians I'd seen with wire brushes, sticks and general versatility that became such a seamless style on the drums, I realized how much I had to improve to get a chance to audition let alone play with a major band. My real destiny, I rationalized, was with pen, pad and a typewriter. I wrote my wife about the experience. "Some of these sidemen are my age and they have deferments or wives with kids. Strange how fate intervenes and gives you a different stage to play on," my letter home mused.

The 1950s brought movement of laborers and professionals and certainly musicians who sought better places to work as well as others whose stylings and musical interests were similar. Gone were the days when to join a band was the goal. Typically, there were comparisons of musical tastes that focused on the two coasts. Others left our shores for extended tours through Europe and Japan where the demand for American jazz and artists was much greater. That, said JR Monterose, was why he journeyed to France.

Entertainment writers talked about a West Coast sound that was new and fresh. A number pointed out how a few former East Coast musicians had become residents of California and weren't returning to their roots. Jazz curator and bandleader Monk Rowe, a native New Yorker, has his own theory:

"A few of the musicians I talked in gathering archival material insisted the differences were a critics' thing. The critics, they said, jumped on the East vs. West thing because it gave them something to write about. Yet, if you listen to many albums of that time you'd find there is a different kind of energy from the West Coast. It tends to sound more relaxed. Maybe it did have to do with the sunshine after all. If you were in New York City there seemed to be a higher energy...a little more frenetic. I think when those fellows moved out there they were affected by the laid back scene and atmosphere. They also started using instrumentations that hadn't been used before. The sounds—Bud Shank on flute, for example, Chico Hamilton with the cello and Shorty Rogers with the flugelhorn—were different and they were much mellower and that gave the West Coast music a signature. Gerry Mulligan with his piano-less quartet that had to have a different feel. I think the writing they were doing for film and TV may have influenced the writing for jazz, too."

There was no question, music historians and contemporary writers said in encyclopedia descriptions of the period, jazz had been damaged by the Depression. "It retired to backrooms, to speakeasies and to rehearsal halls. Not until the phenomenal success of the Benny Goodman band in 1936 did it come into the open again. Goodman's triumphal march across the United States brought with it an almost insatiable demand for jazz. It made new careers possible for many who had been living in semi retirement and re-established many other bands," said Collier's in a 1960s review.

The celebrated return carried midway into the next decade and began to fade as technology, musical tastes, industry turmoil and the public turned to other forms of entertainment.

Television was certainly an influence, so was the growing popularity of singers who had come the big bands and now were now more popular as singles than the groups they started with. Production of records and the manufacture of jukeboxes became erratic because of a musicians' union battle with industry executives over what royalties performers should earn. The year long strike in the middle of the war had repercussions for the rest of the decade, some insist.

Popular bandleader of the 1920s, Paul "Pops" Whiteman, who resurfaced to appear in a nightclub revue called "New Faces of 1928" in the late 1950s, probably offered the best assessment of the failure of the big bands from the 1940s and 1950s. One of the first bandleaders to feature singers like Mildred Bailey and Morton Downey, Whiteman told Daily Mirror Entertainment Editor Dick Williams in June, 1958, bandleaders caused their own demise.

"...You're digging your own graves when singers are featured and crowds gather around the stand to listen instead of dancing. They (leaders) began to quit playing dance numbers. But I made them (the singers) sing in dance tempo. I didn't want to do anything to stop the dancing."

Unfortunately, his comments came far too late to have an impact. The era was for all practical purposes...over.

Howie Schneider, the trumpet playing leader of the Jan Garber Band that tours the US these days.

Ed Shaughnessy, formerly of the Tonight Show Band, demonstrates his drumming style on a double bass set at a Whitesboro High School, NY, Jazz Festival in the 1970s. Photo courtesy of Don Cantwell

Chip Davis

M A N N H E I M S T E A M R O L L E R

AMERICAN GRAMAPHONE

One of the new genre of band leaders playing a combination of classical, jazz and religious music, Chip Davis, of the Mannheim Steamroller. Photo courtesy of American Gramaphone

RALPH MARTERIE
And His Marlboro Orchestra

MERCURY RECORDS

Chuz Alfred (third from left) on a solo at a Mercury Records Recording session in Chicago, IL, in October, 1958. Left is Stan Edson, Larry Ragon and Chuz. On the right is bandleader Ralph Marterie. Photo courtesy of Chuz Alfred

IV. Beyond Rock and Rap...A Return to Swing Music?

It's hard to imagine a group of fans of Harry James, Benny Goodman or Glenn Miller in the 1930s to 1950s going berserk when a song was played and destroying the bandstand, tables, cars and even committing assault.

But that's what happened in the summer of '99 in Rome, NY when a rock headliner named Limp Bizket is alleged to have set a crowd of thousands attending Woodstock '99 loose with a song called "Break Stuff."

Yes, crowds went wild listening to Goodman and James and were known to have danced and swooned in the aisles of the old Paramount Theatre when Sinatra sang with the James and Dorsey bands. Entertainers even had to have uniformed escorts to leave buildings and police had to control mobs trying to buy tickets to attend big band nights. But the behavior was sedate compared to the chaos seen at Woodstock.

The "bad boy" image which contemporary touring groups seem to welcome was exactly the opposite of the persona musicians, leaders and singers during the middle of the last century wanted. Some think musicians of that period carried a stigma; I believe they were intimidated by the public's perception of their lifestyle. In small towns they were "big city people" who were treated like transients and in the cities they were accused of causing disturbances and performing in places that attracted low life, some insisted.

What made musicians a target?

A tougher law enforcement "no nonsense" response to after hour establishments and those associated with them and the attitudes of the time that equated musicians to traveling gypsies.

It wasn't helped by celebrated arrests of the famous like drummer/bandleader Gene Krupa for alleged marijuana use. Then there were the alcohol and drug antics of musicians like Charlie Parker, Chet Baker and Gerry Mulligan as well as other entertainers. Whether you were guilty or not, being identified as a musician seemed to add more guilt.

A fellow musician and I were traveling through Detroit in the early hours of a Saturday after playing a 1950s gig in Windsor, Ontario. We were wearing typical colorful blazers and zoot suit pants with pegged bottoms. We weren't speeding and, thankfully, we hadn't been drinking. But we must have fit a profile on a police station bulletin board. Two officers pulled us over with guns drawn and demanded we get out of the car. We were spread eagled on the hood of the car and grilled about our whereabouts and why we were in Detroit. Our car was searched. My friend, who was driving, was actually handcuffed. The ordeal lasted about 30 minutes when the officers abruptly took the cuffs off my friend and literally jumped in their cruiser and sped away without an explanation or apology. It gave us one more reason to remain in the closet during a period when to be different courted harsh treatment, ridicule and loss of work.

But it's a different day and age and, although the media only acknowledge it when a big band icon passes, the swing sound still continues on a summer village green, at a holiday country club or Elks Club Saturday night party, a cruise ship or a community festival that features a myriad of musical appetites. The music has courted young people thanks to energetic music educators who connected with friends in the big bands and leaders like Stan Kenton, Chuck and Gap Mangione, Maynard Ferguson and others and incorporated them in high school and college programs.A sound that once was banned in music rooms is now more welcomed (*see Jazz Education*).

Sometimes the performance surprises young audiences who possibly come out of curiosity. Jazz pianist Georges Cables took his blend of classic jazz and his own music to a summer concert outside Sheldon Memorial Art Gallery at the University of Nebraska-Lincoln and literally blew the crowd on lawn chairs and blankets away. Founder and director of the Berman Music Foundation, Butch Berman, told the assemblage it would beautiful and unpredictable. Reviewer Bart Schaneman told a Daily Nebraskan audience it was that...plus. "Whether or not people came because they knew it would be great, they should have all left knowing it was," he concluded.

As I looked at entertainment sections and reviews from more than 60 newspapers throughout the country, his comments about such free concerts on the green are found elsewhere enticing others who possibly didn't know much about the "old" music until they heard it translated through young, new musicians.

Former tenor saxophonist in Midwest territorial and military dance bands, Jim Booker, now spends his days listening and assessing an era he believes can never be replaced. But, he continues, the death of the big band sound is quite unlikely. "Jazz and big band music are still very much alive. For me, of course, they never left."

Yet to those who play or played professionally for years, it is a powerful rollercoaster ride that you want to savor as something you had to do because you loved it...but knew you had to leave it or you might have to sacrifice much more than simply money and fun.

Said former Ralph Marterie saxophonist Chuz Alfred in his recollections of the road on March, 1959:

"The fact was...even though I was featured a lot...I still wasn't able to just stand up and blow all night. Plus, it's hard to relax with someone else's tune selection and tempos...especially when you're used to calling the shots night after night, year after year...Maybe, years ago, being featured on a big band could have paved the way to 'who knows where?' But now...and especially since Elvis...the big bands were on their last swing. And, in my opinion, small group jazz didn't have much going either. I started to think a lot...about a lot of things!

"I'd said to my buddies back in high school that I wouldn't get married until I was about thirty. Until then, I was just going to go with the flow...wherever that led me. Now, I'm 26 years old and think I'm getting a pretty good handle on what's happenin'...If I want to finish school (college)...maybe hope to meet a nice gal and settle down and raise a family...I'd better start flowing in another direction. I sure didn't want to wind up where many of the guys...guys I had met along the way, had already wound up or were, in many instances, heading. Quite a few of them had been with all the big bands at one time or another when they were hot! Now's the time to prepare for something else...other things to learn...Many more things to do."

Chuz left the business, finished college, got married to a lovely lady, Maggie, entered real estate but still found time to organize groups to play in and around Columbus and cut some appetizing sounds of the past and present on special CDs. Even after he had decided to quit the business for good, the emotional tug to return was powerful, he told me.

"Upon graduation from OSU in June, 1961, I took Maggie (her music was the Everly Brothers, Elvis, etc) out to Buckeye Lake to hear Ralph's big band at the Crystal Ballroom. Before the night was over, Ralph had talked me into coming back on the band until Labor Day. This time, he needed an alto sax, not tenor. So I figured it would be worth delaying my first 'day job' search. At this point, I thought, what's another couple of months? Anyway, we wound up at Freedomland in New York backing Paul Anka. After one week of that fiasco, I was more convinced than ever that I wanted off the road and on a day gig. There were probably 5,000 kids at the shows, all trying to get onto the bandstand and grab some part of Paul. Cops had a rope line in front of the bandstand and were standing there to keep order...Anka's manager would survey the screaming urchins clutching at Paul, pick out the most delirious, lift her onto the bandstand and bend her head onto Anka's shoulder as Paul sung those soothing words, whereupon she immediately collapsed and was hauled off stage on a stretcher by a couple of paramedics who just happened to be standing in the wings...and all this while Paul's singing away and the band's still playing and 4,999 other kids are screaming louder. Whew! Twice a night for seven nights was more than I could handle. I knew the earlier decision was the right one."

A Rochester musician offers a bleaker picture for the younger professional who wants to play in the 21st century. "As a player, I regularly bemoan the graying of the audience for big band music. Those old folks love to come and dance but their kids, the ones with the money who could be spending over the bar, are generally home watching TV. This doesn't bode well for the future of the genre. And club owners are helping to kill it as well. There are real pros—some with PhDs—playing in NYC for $75 to $100 a gig. It's a sin…From where I sit, there isn't much hope."

Steve Early, Duke Ellington's drummer with the 1966-67 band, vividly recalls his time on the road. He continues to play in New York City. You can hear his work on an Ellington chart called "His Mother Called Him Bill" which won the big band Grammy award in '67. He remembers backing celebrated players such as Johnny Hodges, Harry Carney, Lawrence Brown, Cat Anderson and Cootie Williams and playing the many Ellington compositions while touring.

Said David Hajdu, president of the Duke Ellington Society, of Ellington's style and musical writing habits: "I can think of only one thing that Ellington even appeared to hate: endings. He didn't like to finish his songs and frequently left the finale blank on a piece of sheet music…

To his final days, he dreaded facing his own mortality—like most of us, surely, though with a lot more cool, since he was Duke Ellington, after all."

"I came in at the end of the big band era really," Early told me. "Strange as it seems I got to play with some of the best big bands because a lot of these leaders had less work and they had the best of their former sidemen available at the same time. I was there from 1958 to 1968, I guess. I played with Lionel Hampton and recorded with his Newport band as well as his all-star alumni band. Played with Charlie Barnet in his Live at Basin Street East recording and others. Worked with Tex Beneke, Claude Thornhill and Les Elgart, too.

"Duke's band was different from any other one in the business. The scope was vast, every one in the band had their own sound, and you couldn't take people in and out as in most bands without completely changing the sound. The Ellington sound was, in my mind, unique. These so called recreations of his music are ridiculous because the guys in the band including Duke were the music period. They created the true sound and that will live on."

Steve recalls the difficulty of playing drums in big bands as the era changed from traditional bands of the 1940s to the rock music of the late 1950s. "I remember Shelly Manne making the statement about playing drums and chopping wood in the 1950s when I was in high school. This was a long time before Rock'n'Roll and amplified instruments. I played the Ed Sullivan Show with Duke and there was a group called Vanilla Fudge. In terms of audience reaction I can only say that they wiped us out. Once and for all, I decided that I had better learn to play this stuff. I can only say that any drummer at the time hit their instrument harder than Shelly ever dreamed of while playing for Stan Kenton. Rock took up the level of sound of music. Even classical music! Do you know that percussionists in symphony orchestras now use bigger drums and cymbals to play the same music they played in the 1940s and 1950s? It's true.

"Duke had no drum charts. You just sat there and played by ear. That could be very daunting because a lot of the music was long compositions. I ask him once when we were on the road what records of the band I should listen to so that I could learn the music. He said that he didn't want me to listen to any of them. He said: 'I don't want you to sound like Sonny Greer. Do your own thing.' That is almost unheard of in the business, everyone has preconceived ideas.

How could Duke keep guys like Johnny Hodges and Lawrence Brown? I am afraid that my answer to that might shatter a few idols. The fact is that a lot of the older big band and jazz musicians of that era were very unschooled in any other kind of music and really had very few work opportunities, especially later in the era. A lot of them did try to leave and eventually came back."

Dick Jurgens' son Dick Jr has a similar view based upon his experiences in the 1970s.

"I played with the band (his dad's band) in the 1970s and met with Woody Herman, I remember. I even got an offer to play with Ray Anthony, met with Count Basie and Duke Ellington but the '70s bands weren't always the real road weathered all for one, one for all groups that had been so popular in the heyday of the big bands. Don't get me wrong…some of the bands were good but not seasoned like years of living together will do for a group."

But then there are bands like the Jan Garber Orchestra which celebrated its 75th anniversary in 2000 and continues to attract audiences, especially dancers, and applause for a style that changed only once. Listen how Howie Schneider, trumpeter, pianist, singer and arranger who signed with the Garber family in 1995 to continue the orchestra, describes the transition:

"Jan never had particularly big hits such as 'In the Mood.' However, Freddie Large, the lead alto saxophone player and former leader of the group, had a very nice tone that was well accepted by the general public. It was this 'sweet style' from Canada that Jan joined in allegiance with the likes of Guy Lombardo, his main competition, to build on. Jan did change his format to swing music from 1942-44. People didn't accept it and Jan lost about $50,000. He went back to the sweet sound that continued to make his band popular."

Called the 'Idol of the Airlanes,' Jan retired from the bandstand in 1971 and his daughter Janis, who accepted the stage name Kitty Thomas and sang with the band, took it on the road in the early 1970s. A diminutive violinist fans from the 1920s and '30s recall, Jan was a fixture in the South and Southwest playing horse shows and later at the Lady Luck Lounge of the Desert Inn in Las Vegas during the 1960s as the nation's gambling city emerged as an international show place.

In recent years, Howie and Garber Orchestra were featured in a special big band series offered by the Sheraton Hotels. In the spring of 1997, The Sheraton showcased the Garber Orchestra, the Russ Morgan band with Jack Morgan, Buddy Morrow leading the Tommy Dorsey Orchestra, the Dick Jurgens Orchestra with Don Ring and finished the series with Al Pierson and Guy Lombardo's Royal Canadians.

Have the big bands of the past disappeared?

"Actually, big bands never went anywhere; they have, to some extent, succumbed to economics; more importantly, to the many modes and styles of music which constitute simplicity and lie under the umbrella of what is considered today as, pop music," Richard V. Duffy wrote in a critique entitled "Big Band...What's Big?" at www.jazzreview.com

The reality, say booking agencies, is that big bands actually return from time to time to play different formats and arenas with younger talent and traditional books that fans love. The economy, the availability of featured sidemen and leaders and the desire to go back on the road are the keys to who's performing and who isn't, I'm told. Pick up your daily newspaper or turn on your favorite radio jazz station and you'll quickly realize the name bands you danced to are still touring and playing perhaps in your hometown. But there's a caveat. The band's name is the same but you sometimes realize there are fewer gray heads among the musicians than you thought. Like Chuz Alfred, a large number of the veteran touring sidemen are gone or they've stopped traveling.

There are far more freshly minted Eastman, North Texas State, Cincinnati Conservatory and graduates of other music schools among the sidemen. Bandleaders who put such touring groups together do their best to recreate the sound people remember, introduce contemporary music and somehow make your musical evening as memorable as it was four or five decades ago.

"Fortunately, we live close to one another and we still get together from time to time. Very few of the older guys want to go beyond a day's travel for any gig but if there are solid dates, decent money and a good feeling about playing for a group of people who we think will enjoy us...the odds are we'll have a band with good sections. Some bands that go on the road coast to coast have to sacrifice those things to get much younger players willing to travel, play a book they don't know that well even after rehearsals and simply do a job. All of us have had that disappointment when we've gone to see a name band that couldn't play the original theme song that well, haven't we?" said a Florida veteran of the big band days.

Legendary big band names continue to traverse all sections of the United States and Canada today. The very popular Glenn Miller band with the energetic Larry O'Brien probably leads the list in total engagements in any given year but certainly close by are the Tommy Dorsey band with Buddy Morrow, the Woody Herman Herd with Frank Tiberi and Maynard Ferguson, perhaps the only one of the originals still fronting his own band, the Big Bop Noveau. Travel to England and you can hear the great English recreation of the Glenn Miller sound with the UK Orchestra, Bert

Kaempfert's Orchestra with Tony Fisher, Syd Lawrence's big band and a number of Ted Heath influenced orchestras.

Take the QE2 Big Band Cruise yearly and you'll likely get a chance to hear "Music in the Morgan Manner" with the Russ Morgan band led by his son, Jack; the Larry Elgart Band, the Charlie Spivak band with Nick Russo or the sound of one of America's great arranger/composers, Nelson Riddle. His band is led by his son, Chris.

Creative bandleaders have found ingenious ways to attract listeners, dancers and music lovers to the sounds of the day. Bob January of Mohegan Lake, NY certainly leads my list. Formerly a big bandleader at the Village Gate, Studio 54, the Roseland and the Rainbow Room in New York City, he has organized not one but six different and complete musical groups, each with its own music library. His organizations include; the All-American Concert Band, the Original Swing Era Big Band, Metro-Swing Big Band, Dance Orchestra New York or the Satin Swing Orchestra and the intriguing Strauss Festival Orchestra which plays Strauss waltzes, polkas and quadrilles. He's able to play for virtually every kind of event and professionally satisfy himself, his musicians and his audiences.

Most important to any big band event, though, is the music and the expectation of hearing nostalgic sounds that are easily recognized. Certainly prominent singers feel the pressure to handle the old songs the way people wanted to hear them and, at the same time, add contemporary pieces to please younger audiences.

Bobby Darin didn't need "Mack the Knife" to show the public he had tremendous talent. He sang with the enthusiasm and verve that had created older singers like Sinatra, Crosby and King Cole and others. But there were significant differences. Darin didn't start with the big bands as most male vocalists of the period did. Says Bobby's archivist Jimmy Scalia:

"Remember, Darin was much younger than other vocalists singing this type of music. He knew to work with the best in the business whether a household name like Billy May or someone like Bobby Scott, Shorty Rogers and Torrie Zito. Torrie, by the way, was very good and his affiliation with Bobby helped give Darin credibility and great music to vocalize to. It's in the grooves…and the wax don't lie, man." Darin admired Torrie's genius that brought all parts together to "get that 'solid sock' in the brass that gives such excitement…(and) he has a very attractive way with strings, too, to showcase a love ballad with delicate tenderness."

Zito is a member of a talented musical family from Utica, NY. His brother Fred was a trombonist with the early Artistry in Rhythm sound of Stan Kenton, Artie Shaw and Charlie Barnet. His other brother Ronnie, a drummer, backed Peggy Lee and was a member of Woody Herman's Herds. Torrie not only wrote for Bobby Darin, you can find his name among the credits with such stars as James Moody, Herbie Mann, Quincy Jones, Billy Eckstine, Sarah Vaughn, Barbra Streisand and Tony Bennett. He has written for the Tony Awards and the Kennedy Center honors programs. It's the kind of talent that inspires others.

Jazz composer, player and archivist Monk Rowe certainly agrees. In the late 1990s he gathered an all-star cast of musicians and produced his first CD dedicated to the lives of nine outstanding artists of earlier years. He gave it a simple but declarative title: "Jazz Life." He wanted to honor them and, at the same time, give the audience a taste of his musical salute to each.

"If people can hum it…that's what I'm after," he told me. "When a tune is done, whether mine or anybody's, I like to know people will be able to remember it. In the industry they call it a hook. It sticks in your ear. Sometimes, of course, you get tunes that stick you wish would go away. But I've always tried to be remembered by writing melodies that are easily recalled. Mine are usually in the jazz genre, of course. I think that jazz can be innovative but still can be memorable too. Just listen to Glenn Miller."

Monk wrote a piece called "Jazz Class," for one of his interviewees, Milt Hinton, a bassist who played with about everybody during a career that spanned over a half century. He started with a violin given him by his mother for his 13th birthday, switched to bass and studied music theory at 18 and he was one of the most sought after bassists as he turned 80. An accomplished photographer, his photos were published by Downbeat, Popular Photography magazines and a book he later published called "The Jazz Photographs of Milt Hinton."

"He's such a classy guy as is his wife Mona. I was getting a class in jazz and social history talking to him. Then there was Nat Adderley, Cannonball's brother, who always drew people to his music. He was a composer and cornetist. I wrote a tune for Nat that I felt captured his sound and his writing," Monk said. He tried to do the same for Lionel Hampton. "I wrote a tune and I called it 'The Gates of Swing' which had a melody I could hear playing on the vibes and then there's a part in the middle that's chaotic which, I read, was typical of his band because it could get pretty wild."

The term "gates," Monk noted, was what Hamp called everybody during their interview. "It certainly was a great idea because you didn't have to remember names."

The jazz historian loved the personal anecdotes vocalist and jazz composer Jon Hendricks told of growing up in Newark, OH. "The way he earned his money was to go to public men's rooms with pay toilets and wait for customers. He'd take your nickel and go under the door at the bottom and open it. Saved you several minutes," Monk laughed.

Jon would also hang out at the jukebox "and memorize all the parts of the records and when someone went to the jukebox, he'd stop them and coax them to pay him to vocalize the number…and he'd do a dance along with it."

While museums and repositories are great places to visit to become acquainted with the past, a number of band leaders and musicians I talked to feel that music, like professional sports, keeps evolving, living and breathing new sounds. "People go to Cooperstown and Canton to see legends of a bygone era but they also continue going to baseball and football games today. I believe big band entertainment is no different," I was told.

Popular bandleader/singer Harry Connick Jr. opened at Syracuse, NY's Landmark Theatre in 2001 and continued his quest to bring big band sounds to various parts of the country the way his musical predecessors like Benny Goodman, Tommy and Jimmy Dorsey and Vaughn Monroe used to.

"I want to please the audience and the listeners," he told the upstate audience. "But I want to do what I like to do, too. I'm lucky to do what I love. Of course, I want the audience to love it also. But I guess what I'm trying to say is; my motivation is to sing great songs." Bandleaders like Monroe, Sammy Kaye, and Johnny Long would have echoed his views I believe.

And while entertainment observers point to statistics that clearly show that jazz/big band music continues to lose audience share, nostalgia and events continue to attract people for fund-raisers and to recreate the fun of earlier days.

A good crowd, for example, turned out at Muncie, IN's Horizon Center for a dance party to celebrate the ageless USO in the summer of 2001 and hear a band billed as "America's Hometown Dance Band." Ball State University dance instructors showed people basic dance steps to get the audience dancing again. Said a Muncie resident after hearing Pennsylvania 6-500 and April in Paris, "I love the big band sound and it's great to hear the Ball State student talent playing."

At the North Texas State campus, meanwhile, the university's talented and heralded "One O'Clock Lab" band plays for capacity crowds in such places as Japan, Hong Kong, Australia and Europe as well as at the university. This is a band of college players that has brought four Grammy nominations to the school's music program.

In Detroit, meanwhile, Gary Greenfelder believes a band of semi-professionals and hobbyists called "onebeatback" keep swing music alive in the Motor City area. The band started as a rehearsal group more than 10 years ago. "We started an Annual Dinner Dance for an opportunity for the band to play. Within a short period of time, we developed a following and a reputation and we started working on a regular basis," he told me. Onebeatback works events from Summer in the Parks programs to weddings and corporate parties. "Our premise really is that we are doing this for the love of swing music and gigs are the icing on the cake. We pride ourselves on what we've done and the standards we're worked to attain."

The musicians, he says, come from all parts of the community. "I have a gentleman trombonist in the band that is 82 and is the historian for our group. He grew up listening and playing this music and he knows many of the greats that have been in the business. At the same time, our lead alto saxophone player graduated not long ago from Central Michigan with a music degree."

The band book includes music from the 1930s but Gary says diversity is the key. "We do some modern music but it's limited and it probably comes more from requests. We do the Beatles song 'I Saw Her Standing There' as well as an arrangement of Mustang Sally...but most of what we do is standard swing arrangements and some jazz. My goal though some day is to have at least one song from every major big band from the Big Band Era."

NPR disk jockey, David Miller, offers a partial explanation to paradox of economic bad times for bands and a resurging popularity.

"In the 1980s, my audience was composed almost exclusively of people who were at least teenagers during WWII. They were listening to 'the music of their lives,' and they found it a welcome contrast to what was saturating the airwaves during that period. In recent years, I've noticed a subtle shift. The older people still love my program because it brings back pleasant memories of 'real music.' Young people, too, are coming to appreciate the big band sound. At first, I thought it was because of the retro-swing movement, but I'm not so sure anymore.

"The teenagers who contacted me don't make reference to Big Bad Voodoo Daddy or Cherry Poppin' Daddies or whoever—instead they talk as if they have just discovered music of 60 years ago and like what they hear. Honestly, I think they find it quaint. They often describe it as 'cool' but that's an all-encompassing word for the under-25 set these days."

Robert J. Robbins of the Big Band International organization and newsletter describes how his passion for the music, the musicians and their values has preoccupied him.

"When I was about 10, my aunt gave me a batch of 78 RPM records which contained titles by Tommy and Jimmy Dorsey, Benny Goodman, Harry James et al and I was immediately attracted to the sounds of the big bands which was anything but current at the time. About four years later, I became enamored with the music of Glenn Miller at a time when psychedelia was flowing from every pop chart. I did follow Blood, Sweat and Tears and Chicago during my high school and early college career but when I was 19 I attended two concerts which permanently altered my musical outlook and directed it unmistakably toward big band jazz. The first of these concerts featured Maynard Ferguson with his all-star British band, which showed me that the music of the big bands was not merely nostalgia but could be decidedly contemporary.

"Two months later, I heard the Stan Kenton Orchestra for the first time and the Kenton band with its five trumpets, five trombones, five reeds, piano, bass and drums and Latin percussion. It roared over me like a tidal wave and I have been a committed Kenton fan ever since."

But the economics of the business from its very beginning have continually made it vulnerable to domestic and world events. The entertainment field was already struggling to survive before 9/11/2001...and it got much worse after the attack on the World Trade Center on that sunny September morning in New York City, still considered the jazz mecca by the devoted. There were very few live jazz clubs in the WTC but those in the vicinity were closed either because of the loss of public utilities, tourists, the pungent odor of toxic fumes and the shock and rage felt by a city and a nation.

The Blue Note in the West Village reopened three days after the attack to smaller audiences and so did the Village Vanguard. But the Iridium at Broadway and 5lst offered more hope that music could help soothe and start the road to recovery. Saxophonist Michael Brecker helped the club reopen Sept. 14 with a capacity crowd. In return, he donated his fee of about $15,000 for three nights to causes supporting the victims.

Musicians, like entertainers everywhere, could always be counted on regardless of the pain, suffering and personal inconvenience or risk. During wartime and uneasy armistices, the show must go on.

Woody Herman and his band heard of JFK's death in Dallas as they returned from lunch after taping one three-hour session in New York City. There were two more sessions to go. Woody went into the studio to talk to his musical family and they agreed that they couldn't meet their commitments if they didn't continue the recording. Said Jack Tracy in a piece called "A Day To Remember" in the Woody Herman Society Newsletter, fall, 2001, "When it was over, everyone quietly packed up their instruments and headed off. Professionalism shown. It was a fine album by the way."

That could be why former Ellington and Dizzy Gillespie sideman Marvin "Doc" Holladay, who created the jazz studies program at Oakland University, MI, told North Texas State students (North Texas Daily, Feb. 7, 2001) about what was missing from Ken Burns' famed documentary on PBS called "Jazz."

"From my perspective as an ethno musicologist, I can tell you that there were many exclusions…If you want to understand a culture, get acquainted with their music. The world equates American culture with jazz; that's how the world sees us. It isn't European, it ain't African—it's American. It embraces both European and African characteristics but it created a culture of its own," he explained.

Furthermore, said Monk Rowe on a radio program about jazz, the music originates from a typical American trait; inspiration. "It's a funny thing…sometimes it comes from hearing something, sometimes it comes from meeting people. I would get these little 'gooses' of inspiration and come up with tunes and they would be really closely identified with persons I was affected by. Some cases the tunes were an attempt to capture pieces of their musical personality."

The best examples of such musical inspiration, says the Guinness Book, are the tunes "Star Dust" and Beatles' John Lennon and Paul McCartney's "Yesterday." The Guinness Book of World Records says that there are 1,500 recorded versions of Star Dust and 2,500 of Yesterday.

Remembering and honoring our past is vital, Monk adds, but it demonstrates the importance of schooling. The fact that there are so many variations of one song on sheet music or recorded and the numbers of copyright litigations over plagiarism certainly cause any intelligent musician to master the mechanics of this field as with any other.

"The last 15 to 20 years have created major changes. You can now go to school to become a jazz musician (*see Jazz Education)* or a jazz teacher. Golly, there are classes on rock'n'roll and all kinds of things really today. The schools that most smart kids pick if they're interested in such music are places like North Texas, Berkeley, Eastman and other campuses where traveling bands look to when filling chairs. Some of the people I've interviewed for the Hamilton College Jazz Archive said they went to music school but in the practice rooms were signs saying no jazz playing. Now jazz music has been institutionalized. I guess the days of the traveling bands and jam sessions and all the venues to play have been greatly diminished. Jazz is looked upon as a legitimate art form so that it is justifiable to study it. In fact, there are places now that offer doctorates in jazz and you can dissect the music and pass it on. But it's a two-edge sword, too. I think of jazz as an art form but I hope it doesn't become music only heard in a concert setting or that's put above the listening audience because it's a music that was free form created in typically low settings. It doesn't have to stay there but we don't want to lose the vitality of such music either."

The complaint one hears from a number of professional players, Monk continues, is the lack of feeling but technical soundness of younger players. "Veterans in this business think that younger musicians all sound the same and there is an element that says when you learn logistics and techniques of a classroom such elements don't seem to allow them to play with the feeling that offer individuality that produced people like Lester Young or Paul Desmond. After a few notes, you know who it is because style shines out. Most young musicians say they aren't out to copy what the masters did. They do their own thing they insist. I don't think Lester Young was trying emulate anybody…he was trying to do his own thing, too. The story goes that Lester was canned from a big band because he didn't sound like Coleman Hawkins. I guess it never ends."

Others, like Monk, are concerned about loss of vitality or sameness that can evolve from institutional programs. So many of the popular professionals on the road and recording today tell of real commitment to the discipline of the work even though they're not playing an instrument they started with. Rob McConnell, whose Boss Brass and lusty big band sound came roaring out of London, Ontario, in the late 1960s, remembers how he had to accept reality regardless of his horn preference. "My older brother was a trumpet player and I knew every jazz trumpet player at the time and I heard all that music. And when I was 15 years old, I wanted to play trumpet but by the time they got to me in the school band they didn't have any. They said all that's left is the slide trombone." Two Grammys, 12 Grammy nominations and four Junos (Canada's equivalent awards) show us that the jazz world's good fortune is that his school didn't find a trumpet.

His roots were musically expressed a few years ago when he cut his own nostalgia…a Big Band Christmas album of favorites like Away In the Manger, which, he said on the album cover, has three melodies like the one he sang as a child in the church choir. "There have not been many Christmas recordings by big bands but as we are usually in the vanguard of these trends, I'm sure that every Tom, Dick and Harry with a band will be on this case soon," Rob quips. Not with the big band treatment he offers.

McConnell's music, the sounds of the Airmen of Note, Spyro Gyro and others certainly tell us that quality music is not only available, it's probably next door considering the growing number of Jazz Festivals and Concerts being held in the United States and throughout the world (*see Jazz Festivals*). Some worry that fusion music and a fickle public have already damaged the image.

Said the web site "The Great American Big Bands/Melodies" (www.melodyb.html):

"A great many musicians, and others, have called the 1960s and beyond the era of NOISE.

Electric string boards (erroneously called guitars), are teamed up with 'gazillion' watt amplifiers. 'Ears' are turning from gold to tin to lead. And, finally, deaf. The amplifiers and the earphones do take their toll. This is a generalization, of course. There is good music being produced. The TV, record companies, concert promoters are all catering to the lowest common denominator of musical intelligence. But, a large number of people still listen to and immensely enjoy the big bands and their acoustic instruments, playing in a sophisticated style. And, wherever these bands appear, they are winning converts."

Again, the festivals, concerts at your town's park and the dedication of men like Monk Rowe, Don Cantwell and Dick Robinson and thousands like them throughout America offer the hope that there is a vibrant future.

If you've got doubts, check the littlebigband of Virginia (www.littlebigband.com). Here's a music program designed to introduce children of various ages to music experiences like singing, listening and dancing. Classes have been offered in Norfolk, Tidewater and Virginia Beach schools, community centers and religious houses. "It's so much more than simple tunes for tots," says Cathy Francis, the contact person. "Little Big Band is designed to promote socialization skills and build self esteem and confidence. That way, Little Big Band members will grow both educationally and personally. And along the way, they'll have lots of fun. We perform at birthday parties, special community events and festivals on both the south side and the peninsula. We offer weekly sing-a-longs at several area pre-schools." If musical experiences start early enough there will never be any doubts about the big band future, I believe.

Where, though, is big band music headed?

"I wish I knew," says the Big Band Newsletter at the turn of the century. "I think it's improved in the last five or six years even in the contemporary field. As far as jazz is concerned, I don't know if I can take it any more. If I hear any more be-bop and a guy playing the same chord for about three minutes. I can't take that. It doesn't swing much; they just play a lot of notes. Every time I see one of those current jazz guys I ask 'Do you get paid by the note?' They rarely answer."

More importantly, say past and present touring musicians, is the interest shown by city fathers, community leaders and civic groups. A jazz history, written by Joe Mosbrook, (www.clevelandjazz.org/history.htm) describes how orchestras have sprouted in communities small and large similar to the John Philip Sousa military bands that offered concerts in village squares at the turn of the century.

"Cleveland has been far ahead of the rest of the country in this development," he wrote with pride. "Cleveland has had its own repertory big band since 1984, pre-dating almost all of the big bands that are now getting national headlines."

Equally significant are the popular musical celebrations, which offer a diversity of music tastes that have dotted the countryside coast to coast in recent years. They've merged major corporate donors with civic groups and brought community governments to recognize the fun, the popularity, attention and the money for causes that such events can bring.

M&T, a regional bank in Central New York, spearheaded an annual celebration in Syracuse, NY in the 1990s and the week-long affair attracts grade and high school as well as college musical talent along with some of the great names in swing and jazz. Syracuse, which has been the butt of late night talk show humor as the city that gets little sunshine, found its niche by adding musically talented youngsters to its jazzfest. Said reviewer Mark Bialczak, high schoolers "lighted up the Scholastic tent…the music was so bright it made you forget the clouds had yet to melt away." The players, 6th graders and up, were just building steam and heading downhill on Herbie Hancock's "Watermelon Man" and then showed their stuff on Bill Basie's classic "April In Paris" in one session. Old Bill would have smiled and said, "One More Time."

In fact, Basie would have loved it all. It was music with an inescapable beat and sections and soloists playing relaxed and mindful of one another. Artie Shaw in the late 1990s at a rare public appearance captured the essence of the Count.

"Basie was right down the middle of the road. He did what he did in a very straight-forward way. He understood the blues, he understood the beat. He had a beat like nobody in the world…I used to watch Basie rehearse. I knew Bill a long, long time. When he rehearsed he was not vocal. He didn't say much. He didn't have a lot of vocabulary…spoken vocabulary. But when he nodded the band knew exactly what he wanted, and when he frowned they'd say 'What's going on, what's going on?' And then they'd finally hit the right thing, and when they got it, Basie would nod again. Basie would never fool around with anything complicated. 'One O'Clock Jump' was the prototype of what he could do. And it was simple. But it had a beat that wouldn't quit."

The renaissance of big bands has even found an audience in churches. Riverside, CA has featured a group called "The Praise Big Band" that plays the big band sound in neighboring chapels, bible colleges and denominational schools with a brass section that includes a French horn player and a flutist as well as its own arranger.

Of course, there are those who believe that swing, this uniquely American musical style, has returned to the coasts and is slowly working its way toward the midlands. They further believe it has brought a rivalry between the East and West.

East coast swing, such observers insist, is purer and faster while the West Coast offers a subtler and noticeably more deliberate beat. Free style dancing was out by the passage of the 20th century. The new form "brings couples together, touching in fact instead of keeping partners at length with the volume so loud that no conversation can be held." Sounds very much like the 1930s and 1940s but dance bands today have such odd-sounding names. Big Bad VooDoo Daddy, The Flying New Trends, Squirrel Nut Zippers and Flipped Fedoras don't conjure a big band image but neither do the California Collegians, Champagne Music Makers and the Kay Kyser Kollege of Musical Knowledge to those born after 1965, I suppose.

Murray Pfeffer, whose massive web site (www.nfo.net) is a must for any devotee, says dancers today are returning to favor an old fashioned elegance in touch dancing. They show up in gabardine suits, shirt and tie while females are wearing lace and crepe dresses.

Age, said jazz reviewer John Fordham, didn't matter to listeners, dancers or musicians of the era. You either felt the music or you didn't. "When the great drummer Art Blakey in his 70s and in his last years on the road, found listeners young enough to be his grandchildren improvising new dance steps to music he had been playing for 40 years, it bore out a dictim he had repeated most of his life. 'From the creator to the artist, direct to the audience, split-second timing, ain't no other music like that." And the same elements apply today.

Bruce Boyd Raeburn, curator of the Hogan Jazz Archive, Tulane University, and the son of the innovative and respected bandleader, Boyd Raeburn, and the popular singer Ginnie Powell who sang with Raeburn, Gene Krupa, Charlie Barnet and Harry James among others, offers a different perspective on the music of the past era and the future.

"I have mixed feelings...I have come to appreciate what a huge logistical undertaking the organization and maintenance of a big band actually was...and is. My father made many sacrifices to keep his bands together, especially from the period 1942 to 1958 and yet when you hear the music that was made possible as a result of these efforts I have to agree it was all worth it. What the big bands accomplished from the late 1920s through the late 1950s (and, in some cases, beyond) is one of the greatest accomplishments in the history of American music in the 20th Century. Yet, today it is difficult, if not impossible, to keep a big band together. Most of what I see now are repertory efforts which are only partially successful because band chemistry is something that does not occur with a few rehearsals (usually too few given budgetary restraints). The great virtuosi of the big band era, musicians who had technique, plus something more, were too numerous to name...but Lester Young, Roy Eldridge, Red Allen, Coleman Hawkins are great examples."

For those who remember such players and the environments in which they played, it's difficult to relate to the present. "Those voices can't be replaced. So even when the section work is happening, solos are too often a disappointment today," Bruce adds. "Thank goodness the bands of the past recorded prolifically, making it possible for young people to learn about a musical age that has, in fact, become a part of history. For those raised on rock and roll, this can be a hard sell, but given time, younger generations will find something of value in the big band legacy. Who knows what surprises are ahead of us? For anyone interested in learning why it is that the world loves American music, however, investigating the music of the big bands is inevitable. That music defined an era, and its preservation is an American cultural imperative. In essence, that's what the Hogan Jazz Archive is really about, I believe."

What are the mystical ingredients that made the music of the past so successful? Musicians and bandleaders differ on specific reasons but longtime observers, like former ballroom manager Lou DiSario, believe it comes down to melodies and tempos.

Says jazz historian Dick Robinson:

"Take 'In the Mood,' the internationally famous Glenn Miller number. It's recognized everywhere more than half a century later. The chart was a classic opportunity to improvise and people like Tex Beneke did. Swing was basic enough to attract the average person with a beat, a tempo sound that would attract people to dance and, at the same time, cause them to enjoy listening as well. It was an era comprised of music for the common individual and yet a jazz musician could jump on it and enjoy it as well through improvisation."

Some music can have a different kind of impact, too. While swing was thought to induce moods that some psychologists of the 1920s thought would turn us into primitive savages because of the hypnotic rhythm of the "jungle," today we're faced with music that contains raw, explicit language and an electronic loudness that emits deafening sounds.

A young pipe bomb suspect who terrorized the Midwest played guitar in a punk rock band and claimed he was influenced by the music of grunge band Nirvana's late leader, Kurt Cobain. A

Federal Trade Commission study on marketing in late 2001 said that three-quarters of the offensive music sold to children was classified as "rap," the second best selling records after rock, the number one seller. What worries investigators are the haunting words played over and over again. Here's a portion from Eminem, a popular rapper: "(female dog) I'm going to kill you. You don't want to f...with me...These motherf...are thinking I'm playing, think I'm saying the s...just cause I'm thinking it."

Is there a precedent from an earlier time? Certainly. Lyrics on Duke Ellington's "The Mooche" were so provocative while he was appearing at the Cotton Club in 1928 that protests were organized. Outraged citizens said the song had increased rapes in the United States and women feared for their safety. Ellington was placed on a list of performers banned from the NBC network and he suffered from the stigma for years. At one time, there were 147 songs banned because of sexual or emotional overtones and among the performers and composers affected were Cole Porter, Billie Holiday and Bessie Smith.

By contrast, President George W. Bush's Attorney General John Ashcroft claims singing and playing the piano have been a great pastime and an inspiration, too. He takes an electronic keyboard to his office and accompanies himself while singing pop classics, gospel, blues and jazz.

In 1995, he was a member of the Congress's "Singing Senators." Good music, Ashcroft says, relaxes him and helps him handle the stresses of his long days and nights.

Robinson believes that "listener ability" can create a sound in the ear that offers pleasure. "Hearing the number over and over and still enjoying it has always been important. When I hear Artie Shaw's 'Stardust' I enjoy it every time I hear it. It never loses value for me. Look back at the times before television. You had to go hear the bands because you loved the sound or particular numbers and it wasn't that expensive. Radio was big. You could create images from what you heard. The creativity that resulted from radio was certainly valuable to a lot of us."

The difficulty for many today in seeking nostalgic music from the big band era involves expectations. They have the old records, digitalized sounds of the masters on CDs and the notes and numbers are imbedded in their minds. The disappointment occurs, sometimes, when the same fans go to hear a band from the past. It may not be what they expect. "When you haven't had a steak dinner in a while and you go to a restaurant famous for it you can be noticeably upset when your dinner isn't cooked to your liking or worse, the steak tastes like leather. Big band fans have similar kinds of taste buds," big band enthusiast John Imhoff told me. When possible, he travels to big band fests.

A growing number of name bands from the 1930s to '50s have returned since the 21st century began. Among the orchestras that tour with veteran former musicians leading a variety of young and older sidemen are; Sammy Kaye, Russ Morgan, Jan Garber, Guy Lombardo, Dick Jurgens, Ray Anthony, Glenn Miller, Tex Beneke, Artie Shaw, Woody Herman, Tommy and Jimmy Dorsey, Larry Elgart and others.

An example of such organizations and their success are Buddy Morrow and the Tommy Dorsey Orchestra. Morrow joined the Dorsey band more than 20 years ago and the group—17 musicians usually—do about 275 shows a year. The band plays a book that features Dorsey favorites, progressive, rhythm and blues, swing, Dixie and traditional big band numbers.

Says musician, bandleader and jazzfest coordinator Don Cantwell: "As long as the quality of the band is tops then I think it's good and can even make the band more desirable for those who never had a chance to hear its sounds before. If the band, however, is sub par then people who have been enticed to attend are somewhat turned off and they won't return. That's a reasonable assumption. A really disciplined and rehearsed band can recreate good music. Those on the road just for the money can ruin it. The quality of musicianship has got to rise to the occasion. One of the ironies is that the level of music that is exposed to young people has diminished in quality and that's because there are groups that aren't up to professional standards."

Jazz historian Dick Robinson adds that because people are living longer, there are far more who remember the era as "their day and their music. Re-issuing famous old cuts has become very popular. There is a renaissance of big band music now on CD, for example. Our college courses on the era are packed because there is a demand to go back to music from a different time. I think that if school jazz programs are to be good they have to realize that students are more alert to the difference between mediocrity and excellence. I think we'll see quality emerge."

It's already happening. Ball State University Jazz Ensemble, directed by Larry McWilliams, was invited to tour Europe in 2001. The band had stops and concerts in Switzerland, Germany, France and Holland. There was a time when only traveling professionals could play such gigs.

"You don't just elect to do this, we've been accepted by taped auditions and it's an international event which we have successfully competed and gotten into," he said proudly.

Listen to Wayne Goins, director of jazz ensembles at Kansas State talk about his young musicians who may be music majors or studying engineering: "There are guys on campus I'd take with me to a gig. They know their music and they are great performers."

Three creative musicians in Rochester, NY, have added another dimension to the big band experience; a jazz fantasy camp. Bob DeRosa, a bassist when he's not involved in his day gig as a marketing and public relations specialist; Jim Doser, a full-time music teacher in a Rochester suburb and a former faculty member at the Eastman School and director of the award-winning New Jazz Ensemble and Fred Sturm, a composer and arranger, author, Eastman faculty member and director of jazz studies at Lawrence University, Appleton, WI, decided several years ago that jazz enthusiasts like sports fans needed a place to go to taste the experience of jazz playing. "You've heard of baseball fantasy camps where amateurs train with major league teams, sometimes sharing a tin of chewing tobacco with their favorite pro players," Bob says. "Tritone Jazz Fantasy Camps work the same way...without the tobacco. They offer a week-long opportunity for adult jazz musicians—regardless of your skill level (21 and older)—to learn a lot, play a lot and rub shoulders with professional jazz musicians whom they've only heard on CDs or admired from the balcony." The goal? "To create an atmosphere of fun, instruction and enjoyment of jazz and its practitioners."

For musicians like me from a day when clubs and ballrooms had intimacy and fans hung on every note and players pulled sounds that came from their being, not simply their instruments...it can never be the same, though.

Oscar Peterson, a piano-playing jazz player extraordinaire, best expressed it when he talked about performing with the great Lionel Hampton: "When I know I'm going to play with Lionel, I know it's going to turn into a stomping session somewhere along the line."

It's spiritually and physically exhausting...and refreshing. Bassist Ray Brown was playing gigs until his final weeks. Although he was recovering from a replacement of his right knee at 75, he didn't sit on a stool while at an engagement a few months later. He told Pittsburgh Tribune-Review music writer Bob Karlovits he'd stood his whole career and he would continue playing standing up. Physically difficult? Yes. Very professional? Absolutely.

And, said bandleader Les Baxter from his California home in 1993, the music is still the memories of great times, relationships and a far different era in the country.

"Sometimes I cannot get over the fact that my records still make money. When the band got together for those recordings we hoped it would bring some immediate response and pleasure. We had no idea those songs would be requested in high school gym dances some 50 years or more later."

Quality still has value.

A popular bandleader and saxophone player, Sam Donahue.
Photo courtesy Louis DiSario

Monk Rowe, bandleader, composer/arranger and director of the Hamilton College Jazz Archive. Photo by Steve Charzuk of Hamilton College.

My Big Band Time Line

(Selected events, highlights, groups and people who played roles in continuing the popularity of the big bands during the 1930s and beyond.)

1901—Buckeye Lake Park near Columbus, OH opened with two of America's 800 ballrooms or dance halls. The Park boasted the Lake Breeze Pier and the Crystal Danceria. Its most popular summer seasons were 1945 to 1950, according to Buckeye Lake historians.

1924—At 15, composer/lyricist, vocalist and big band enthusiast Johnny Mercer wrote his first song "Sister Susie Strut Your Stuff." Mercer composed more than 1,500 songs, had 750 published and scored hits with nearly 100. He won four Academy Awards.

1925—Duke Ellington's lst band is formed called "The Washingtonians." Lawrence Welk Orchestra first broadcast on WNAX, South Dakota. 16-year-old Benny Goodman went on the road with the Ben Pollack Band in Chicago.

1926—NBC began coast-to-coast broadcasts of bands from hotels, ballrooms and radio stations.

1930s—Dick Trimble, a saxophonist/clarinetist from Lancaster, OH, who played with The Strollers and Dick Fidler's band in Central Ohio, started a successful territory band which remained a popular dance group for nearly 30 years. Singer Ella Fitzgerald took over Chick Webb's popular band when he died at 30.

1932—Charlie Barnet, at 19, became one of the youngest bandleaders in New York City. Two years later, he recorded with vibraphonist Red Norvo.

1935—The Village Vanguard was opened by Max Gordon at 178 Seventh Ave, New York City. Lucky Strike Cigarettes Hit Parade Radio Show begins with the theme "Happy Days Are Here Again." Lenny Hayton's band 1st featured. Carl Hoff's band joins the show in 1936. Singers were Gogo Delys, Kay Thompson, Charles Carlisle, Loretta Lee.

Aug. 21, 1935—Benny Goodman's opening night at Los Angeles' Palomar Ballroom and a young audience goes wild. Considered the beginning of the swing era by many observers.

Nov. 2,1936—The Band That Plays the Blues led by Woody Herman opens at the Roseland Ballroom, Brooklyn. Woody got $75, his sidemen $50 each.

1937—Drummer Buddy Rich started his big band career with Joe Marsala at New York City's Hickory House at 20. He joined the popular Tommy Dorsey band two years later as a featured player. Twenty-year-old Nat "King" Cole started his trio as a piano playing leader.

January 16, 1938—Benny Goodman's hot band with trumpeter Harry James and drummer Gene Krupa became the 1st swing band to play at Carnegie Hall.

March 7, 1938—A group of Iowa ballroom operators formed an association which, three years later, became the Midwest Ballroom Operators Association. In the 1970s as the ballroom business changed, the group became what it is today; the National Ballroom and Entertainment Association.

April 5, 1938—First Gene Krupa Band opens at the Marine Ballroom, Atlantic City, NJ. He continued for 14 years and was featured in 15 films and produced 37 hit records.

1938—Les Brown, fresh from success with his collegiate band the Duke Blue Devils, opened his professional career with his first band in New York City. Trumpeter Sonny Burke began his first gig in New York City the same year. Glenn Miller puts failure behind him and launches a new and popular band with a clarinet lead.

March, 1940—Big band leader, saxophonist Sal Alberico, played his first gig at age 11 at Utica, NY's Palm Grill.

1940—Russ Carlyle, Lee Castaldo (later changed to Lee Castle), Sonny Dunham, Lionel Hampton, Teddy Powell, vocalist Vaughn Monroe, Claude Thornhill, Charlie Spivak and Georgie Auld all started big bands.

1941—Tommy Dorsey Band finished 1st among major bands in the popular Martin Block's Make Believe Ballroom contest. Minton's at 108th St, NYC, opened and swing musicians gathered after other gigs in the city. The Armed Forces Radio and Television Service (AFRTS) began as a GI Network in Alaska and Panama Canal Zone. In 1943-44, it broadcast the Bob Hope Show with Stan Kenton and his Orchestra.

1941—One of the top modern big band arrangers, Nelson Riddle, a trombonist, joined the Charlie Spivak Orchestra. Composer/arranger Bobby Sherwood launched a big band on the West Coast. While on May 30, out on the waterfront at a place called Rendezvous Ballroom, Balboa Beach, Stan Kenton gave the public an introduction to progressive jazz. On the East Coast, the Jerry Wald big band began along with Hal McIntyre's band. Collegians voted Glenn Miller the top band on campus, according to Billboard Magazine. Tommy Dorsey was second and Kay Kyser was third.

Aug. 1, 1942—American Federation of Musicians President James C. Petrillo ordered all musicians to stop recording because musicians weren't paid when recordings were used on radio and in jukeboxes. The order remained in effect until the following Fall.

Sept. 27, 1942—Glenn Miller's final civilian performance was given at Central Theatre, Paissiac, NJ, before he entered military service as a captain in the Army Air Force.

1942-1945—Pianist Dave Brubeck leads Gen. George Patton's 5th Army band. Stateside, singer Eddie Howard and drummer Ray McKinley, who had just taken over the Will Bradley band, started careers in front of the bandstand.

1942—Pianist Oscar Peterson joined the Johnny Holmes Orchestra in Montreal, Quebec. He was the first Black musician in the band. Playing trumpet when he joined the Holmes group was Montreal native, 14-year-old Maynard Ferguson. The first V-Disks are produced of bands and vocalists for armed forces' audiences.

1942—Song writer, singer and producer Johnny Mercer and colleagues founded the legendary Capitol Records Company. Mercer was the lst president. Singer Helen Forrest was chosen the top female vocalist by Downbeat and Metronome magazines and Frank Sinatra the top male singer. Forrest, who worked with Goodman and James bands, championed civil rights. She refused to appear while with the Artie Shaw band unless a theater owner permitted black singer Billy Holiday to perform.

Oct. 20, 1943—Popular bandleader Ben Bernie is dead at 48. He started as a violinist and vocalist. Armed Forces Radio and Television Service (AFRTS) begins coverage of everything from big bands to sports events in all military theaters. Fourteen years later, I participated with AFRTS as a radio announcer in Seoul, Korea.

Nov. 11, 1943—Stan Kenton recorded his first 78 for Capitol Records, "Do Nothin' Til You Hear From Me" at the MacGregor Recording Studios, Hollywood, CA. He was signed to record for Capitol by Johnny Mercer and Glenn Wallich in September after recording for Decca.

Oct., 1944—Maj. Glenn Miller's American Band of the Allied Expeditionary Force begins broadcasts over the American Broadcasting Station in Europe (ABSIE) to help the allied propaganda effort for the war.

Dec. 15, 1944—Glenn Miller left the Twinwoods Airfield, Bedfordshire, England, on a foggy morning flight for France. He never arrived. The aerodrome has become a popular tourist attraction/museum in the 21st century.

1944—Singers scored big hits while bandleaders struggled to keep orchestras touring. Jo Stafford and Perry Como recorded Long Ago and Far Away, Bing Crosby sang I'll Be Seeing You and the Ink Spots created the hit I'll Get By.

1944—Norman Granz launched the Jazz at the Philharmonic show in Los Angeles with Nat King Cole. It toured US and abroad with dozens of top jazz stars until 1957.

1944-46—The Merry Macs (Ted, Joe and Todd McMichael) a jazz, pop trio, performed on radio's Lucky Strike Hit Parade and recorded popular wartime numbers such as Mairzy Doats, Pop Goes the Weasel, The Hut Sut Song, Praise the Lord and Pass the Ammunition, Jingle, Jangle Jingle and others.

1945—Bop trumpeter Dizzy Gillespie began his band and in Los Angeles, former Glenn Miller arranger Jerry Gray started one, too.

1946—Dave Brubeck and his Mills College friends began playing as the Dave Brubeck Octet. In Chicago, Johnny Bothwell was playing a different kind of music with his big band in his first engagement at Tin Pan Alley. Overseas, composer/arranger and trombonist Sy Oliver was leading his first group in Paris. And in New York City, dazzling young drummer Buddy Rich became a band leader. President James C. Petrillo calls a strike of the American Musicians Union...again.

1947—Oscar Peterson fronts his 1st trio at Montreal's Alberta Lounge with Ozzie Roberts on bass and Clarence Jones on drums. Jazz at the Philharmonic producer Norman Granz, enroute to the airport, heard a live radio remote from the Alberta Lounge with Oscar. Realizing it was a live broadcast, he had the cabbie turn around and go to the bar where he met Oscar. Granz made plans for Peterson to join the Jazz At The Philharmonic to play in the group's Carnegie Hall performance. The rest is history. In Cincinnati, OH, bandleader Barney Rapp heard two sisters, 17 and 15 years old, on the clear channel NBC network affiliate WLW, and recommended them to fellow bandleader Tony Pastor. It was the big break for Rosemary and Betty Clooney.

1947—The first jazz studies program is begun at North Texas State University.

1948—Eight top bandleaders announce their retirement from the business; Woody Herman, Benny Goodman, Harry James, Les Brown, Jack Teagarden, Benny Carter, Ina Ray Hutton and Tommy Dorsey. Some critics said it was really the end of the Big Band Era.

Sept. 20, 1948—The Four Freshmen played their 1st gig at the 113 Club in Fort Wayne, IN. The group was formed at Butler University in Indianapolis, IN, during that summer. The group included: Bob Flanigan, Don Barbour, Ross Barbour and Hal Kratzsch. Later, Ken Errair replaced Kratzsch.

December, 1949—The original Birdland opened on Broadway, a few blocks west of 52nd Street in New York City, headlining Charlie Parker. Woody Herman bassist Chubby Jackson, one of the most enthusiastic rhythm men of the era, started his own band in the city. Meanwhile, a popular band led by Ralph Flanagan, started blocks away catering to the people who missed Glenn Miller.

1950—J. R. Monterose of Utica,NY, a tenor saxophonist, was invited to tour nationally with the Henry "Hot Lips" Busse Orchestra. Stan Kenton puts 43 musicians on tour with his Innovations in Modern Music orchestra and loses thousands in two years. Your Hit Parade, a popular radio show, becomes a weekly network TV program. The show, which is sponsored by the American Tobacco Co., features Dorothy Collins, Snooky Lanson, Eileen Wilson and Raymond Scott's studio orchestra along with the Hit Paraders (chorus and dancers). The Ray Anthony band is voted number one dance band in the country in all trade music polls for fifth consecutive year. The Airmen of Note, created to continue Glenn Miller's Army Air Corps dance band, begin. The group continues the tradition today traveling the country and abroad with 18 musicians.

1951—Dave Brubeck and alto saxophonist Paul Desmond organize the 1st Dave Brubeck Quartet. The Benny Goodman Trio, reunited after 13 years, played for Goodman's top arranger Fletcher Henderson's Fund on the Martin Block Make Believe Ballroom. The Bob Noval Orchestra, a popular West Coast band, co-led by brothers Ray and Pat and featuring some top sidemen, return to Catalina Island, CA. Iowa State Teachers College starts one the country's first student jazz groups.

1952—Composer, arranger and part-time trumpet player Billy May started his own band in Los Angeles. Arrangers Eddie Sauter and Bill Finegan put together the Sauter/Finegan Orchestra also on the West Coast.

1953—George Wein produced the world's first Jazz Festival at Newport, RI. In New York, trumpeter Jack Palmer of Rome, NY, started his band.

Aug. 2, 1954—Chuz Alfred Quartet opens in Lancaster, OH and begins a tour that includes supper clubs, evening spots and college campuses from Ohio to Florida.

1954—Movie star Jimmy Stewart played Glenn Miller in The Glenn Miller Story. Stewart's life had similarities to Miller. Stewart played the accordion most of his life and he also enlisted in the military (the Army Air Force) in 1942. Unlike Miller, a trombonist who joined the service as a captain and became a major, Stewart joined AAF as a private and retired a number years later as a brigadier general. Stewart died July 2, 1997. Jazz Pianist Dave Brubeck is named "Man of the Year" by Time Magazine.

Sept. 27, 1955—The Chuz Alfred Quintet is" discovered" in Ohio by president of Savoy Records of New Jersey. The group cuts first album "Jazz-Young Blood" featuring Chuz's compositions "A Message From Home," "Manta Wray," and "Love Comes to Mehitabel Brown" among others.

1955-56—Tommy and Jimmy Dorsey host their first television program, Stage Show on CBS.

1957—The 1st "Live at the Village Vanguard" recording was made with Sonny Rollins. Stratopheric trumpeter Maynard Ferguson, after several years with Kenton, launched his first band. Organist Jimmy Smith takes the former novelty organ, Hammond, and makes it a featured instrument in jazz at the Newport Jazz Festival. The Hammond was favored by soul players because it had rotating tone which gave a reverberating bass, piercing treble and wail sounds.

Sept. 14, 1957—Trumpeter Don Fagerquist, a leading voice of the West Coast Jazz Movement, cut the only album of his career, "Music To Fill A Void." He spent his musical life with leaders like Gene Krupa, Shorty Rogers, Les Brown, Dave Pell and a number of singers.

1958—Two Rochester, NY brothers who mingled with jazz greats from their earliest days thanks to their father "Papa", started a group called the "Jazz Brothers." It was the beginning for Chuck Mangione and his brother Gap.

1958—The Monterey Jazz Festival, CA was founded by Jimmy Lyons, and became the longest running jazz gathering in the world.

1960s—Symphony Sid Torin, a legendary broadcaster and disc jockey, started his "Live From Birdland" shows to radio listeners all along the Eastern seaboard.

March, 1961—The Love Swings sessions in Los Angeles for Bobby Darin feature arrangements by Torrie Zito of Utica, NY

1962—One of the last big bands to start (27 years after the beginning of the swing era), Frank Bettencourt's band, plays its first engagement in Dallas, TX

1965—As rock and roll gained popularity, the original Birdland in New York City closed.

1966—Dick Trimble, a regional band leader whose band played throughout Ohio and launched careers and part-time occupations for a number of musicians, died at 61.

1967—George T. Simon's comprehensive book about the musicians, leaders and singers, "The Big Bands," is released by MacMillan.

1968—Canadian Rob McConnell founded the popular Boss Brass and recorded his first album, Rob McConnell & The Boss Brass. McConnell's group has won two Grammys, 12 Grammy nominations and four Junos (Canada's equivalent to a Grammy).

1969—The Concord Summer Festival launched the beginning of car dealer Carl Jefferson's Concord Records. The annual Concord Jazz Festival continues annually at the Concord Pavilion, an 8,500 seat theater.

1970—Phil Collins, a former child actor/singer in the 1964 production of Oliver!, was chosen as replacement drummer in the British art-rock band, Genesis. He later led his own big band and cut the solid big band album, A Hot Night in Paris. In Rochester, NY, Chuck Mangione, while director of the Jazz Ensemble at the Eastman School and associated with the Rochester Philharmonic, performs and records his Friends in Love score which features the popular Hill Where the Lord Hides. He earns his 1st Grammy nomination.

August, 1975—Cannonball Adderly, alto and soprano saxophonist, brother of Nat, died.

1974—Chip Davis started the very successful American Gramaphone Records with a bread commercial for an advertising agency. Old Home Bread commercials were about delivery truck driver, C. W. McCall. The commercials were so popular Chip did a song called "Convoy" which became a movie starring Kris Kristofferson and Ali McGraw among others. Using the latest in state of the art technology, Chip put together the creative "Fresh Aire" series, original music with a classical soundbed.

1976—After an earlier Grammy nomination, Chuck Mangione's Bellavia, is selected winner of the Best Instrumental Composition Grammy.

1977—The Big Band and Jazz Hall of Fame is organized in Carlsbad, CA. It has inducted more than 200 persons who have impacted and educated the world through music. The repository contains biographies of over 2,000 musicians.

1979—The American Jazz Philharmonic is founded to commission, record and perform symphonic jazz through the Henry Mancini Institute, Los Angeles.

1980-81—Spyro Gyra evolved from a no-name band playing gigs at Buffalo's Jack Daniel's club. The club owner wanted a name for the band and leader Jay Beckenstein remembered spirogira as a name for pond scum from a SUNY at Buffalo botany class he took and jokingly told the owner it was the band's name. When he saw the club sign incorrectly called the group "Spyro Gyra"...the joke stuck...and so did the name. By early 21st century, the group had recorded 23 albums on three labels and toured extensively.

1984—Holiday arranger, composer and conductor Chip Davis produced the lst Manheim Steamroller Christmas album and earned accolades for fusing symphonic, jazz, folk and new age sounds of the holidays. The successful holiday sampler would be repeated in 1988, 1995 and 2001.

April 26, 1984—Count Basie, a simple one finger rhythm pianist who started out learning to play on a pipe organ, dies, ending a Kansas City era of big swing bands. He played the drums before drummer Sonny Greer told him he should look for another instrument...and he became a piano player.

1986—Rex Foundation created the Ralph J. Gleason Award for outstanding contributions to culture. Gleason was a jazz critic and pop music journalist for the San Francisco Chronicle and DownBeat. Birdland reopens at 2745 Broadway on the corner of 105th Street.

October 29, 1987—One of the great swing era band leaders of all time, Woody Herman, died at 74 in Los Angeles. He had toured on his 50th anniversary of the band business in 1986.

March, 1989—Leo Walker's chronological review of bands, musicians and the music business, "The Big Band Almanac," is published by Da Capo Press.

June 21, 1990—One of the "cool" singers from the 1940s and 1950s with the Stan Kenton Band, June Christy, died at 64 in Los Angeles. She won the Downbeat top female vocalist award four times from 1946 to 1950. Her recordings of Tampico, It's Been a Long, Long Time and Shoo-Fly Pie and Apple Pan Dowdy were hit records.

April 8, 1991—Ken Curtis, vocalist and actor, died. He's best remembered as Festus in the Gunsmoke TV series but those in the band business remember him as the singer who replaced Frank Sinatra on the Tommy Dorsey band and lasted four days. Previously, he sang with the Shep Fields band and the Sons of the Pioneers.

July 14, 1991—On his birthday, Don Cantwell launches his Central New York band, the Clef Dwellers.

April, 1993—An International Jazz Festival at Whitesboro High School, Whitesboro, NY featured Central New York's own featured players. Retired Whitesboro band director, musician and band leader,Don Cantwell, brought together saxophonist Chris Vadala, trombonist Mark Kellogg, Dr. David Blask, a trumpeter and pianist Rick Montalbano to play arrangements by popular jazz composers Jeff Tyzik and Rob McConnell.

Aug. 5, 1993—Former Kenton tenor sax great, Bob Cooper, is dead of a heart attack at 67. Cooper spent 6 years with the Artistry in Rhythm band and later headed his own jazz group called Juggernaut. He married Kenton vocalist and leading jazz singer, June Christy.

July 29, 1994—Longtime big band trombonist Fred Zito of Utica, NY, who played with Stan Kenton in the mid-1940s, died in Las Vegas.

Feb. 7-14, 1995—Don Cantwell and his Clef Dwellers perform at the 7th annual Folk Festival in Hsinchu, Republic of Taiwan.

April 23, 1996—Guinness Book of World Records names Les Brown and his Band of Renown the longest organized band in the history of popular music.

June 5, 1999—Mel Torme, a one-time drummer but a singer and composer for all time, is dead at 73. He was chosen male jazz Grammy winner. He entertained millions as a singer, drummer, actor, author and composer and will be remember annually for his yuletide composition, The Christmas Song.

1999—The Maynard Ferguson Reunion Band met at the New York Brass Conference. Players who had been with Maynard throughout his more than 40 years joined in the reunion including Dennis Noday, Buddy Childers, Mike Vax, Buddy Childers and others.

Fall, 1999-Hamilton College, NY, opened the Jazz Archive, the first jazz/swing repository with videotaped interviews of prominent players of the big band era. Monk Rowe is the director. Oct. 9, 1999, Milton "Bags" Jackson who formed the internationally renowned Modern Jazz Quartet, dies at 76. Partially deaf, he played piano, guitar, violin and drums before becoming an accomplished vibraphonist.

Jan. 2, 2000—Nat Adderley, trumpeter, composer, died in Tampa, FL. Nat joined Woody Herman in 1959 and recorded with the Woody Herman Sextet.

Jan 7, 2000—Big band trumpet player Jack J. Palmer died in Rome, NY. Jack roomed with Frank Sinatra while playing with the Harry James band. He later toured with Tommy Dorsey and Benny Goodman among other bands of the period.

September 26, 2000—Big band drummer Nick Fatool, who played with Benny Goodman, Artie Shaw, Claude Thornhill and others, died in Los Angeles. He was 85.

Oct. 30, 2000—Steve Allen, comedian, TV host, songwriter, died at 78. He composed more than 5,000 songs including his theme, "This Could Be the Start of Something Big."

Nov. 4, 2000—A longtime small group drummer, Vernel Fournier, who spent years with Amad Jamel, died at 72.

Dec. 19,2000—Milton Hinton, nicknamed "The Judge," who spent 70 years in the band business and was considered the most recorded jazz musician of his time, died.

He developed what was called the "slap bass."

January, 2001—PBS telecasts the 10-part documentary Jazz produced by Ken Burns and Lynn Novick.

Jan. 4, 2001—Les Brown, veteran bandleader of the 1940s who spent 18 years on Christmas USO tours with Bob Hope, died in Los Angeles at 88.

Jan. 23, 2001—Pianist Lou Levy who began a professional life in his teens with Georgie Auld and Sarah Vaughn and, later, with the Woody Herman band, died at 72.

Feb. 4, 2001—Trombonist, composer and bandleader J.J. Johnson died in Indianapolis, IN. He was 77.

March 7, 2001—Frankie Carle, considered the dean of the big band leaders, and remembered for co-writing his theme song, Sunrise Serenade, died at 97 in Mesa, AR

March 29, 2001—The originator of the Modern Jazz Quartet, John Lewis, died in New York City at 80.

April 18, 2001—Billy Mitchell, a celebrated tenor sax player with Count Basie, Dizzy Gillespie, is dead at 74. He spent some 34 years as a resident tenor man at a Seaford, NY club called "Sonny's Place."

June 1,2001—Tex Beneke, tenor saxophonist and vocalist with the Glenn Miller Orchestra, and leader of Miller bands as well as his own, died in Costa Mesa, CA. Started with Miller in 1938 for $52.50 a week. Born Gordon Beneke, it was Glenn who named the Fort Worth native "Tex."

July 3, 2001—Joe Henderson, saxophonist and composer, died in San Francisco, CA

Summer, 2001—Writer/musician George T. Simon, author of the Big Bands and supervisor of the Military V-Disc Program while in the US Army in 1944, died at 88. He is credited with calling Woody Herman's bands "The Herd."

June 22, 2001—Jazz clarinetist, saxophonist Norris Turney, a member of the last Duke Ellington band, died at 79 in Wilmington, OH. Born in Wilmington, he worked with Ray Charles in 1967 and joined Ellington in 1969. He stayed with Ellington until 1973. He was a member of the Lincoln Center Jazz orchestra from its inception.

July 20, 2001—Milton Gabler, dies, America's first independent jazz record label producer and the first to re-issue out of print jazz records. He operated the most comprehensive jazz record store in America, the Commodore Music Shop in NYC.

He produced Billie Holiday records when major labels wouldn't. He wrote lyrics for a Duke Ellington number called "In a Mellow Tone."

Aug. 17, 2001—Flip Phillips dies in Fort Lauderdale, FL at 86. A powerful tenor saxophonist with Woody Herman, Jazz At The Philharmonic and, during the 1950s with Gene Krupa, he was still recording at age 85.

Aug. 18, 2001—Former big band singer Connie Haines receives a Lifetime Achievement Award in Atlantic City, NJ

Nov. 23, 2001—Norman Granz, founder of Verve Records but more familiar to many of us as the man who brought jazz greats to the countryside and our hometowns as Jazz At The Philharmonic, died at 83.

Nov. 28, 2001—One of the creative big band arrangers who also won awards for his work on Broadway and in Hollywood, Ralph Burns, died in Los Angeles at 79. Burns was an Academy Award winner for his work on "Cabaret," "All That Jazz" and the 1999 Broadway musical "Fosse." It was Burns' arrangements for the Woody Herman band of the 1940s that demonstrated his talent. He wrote Apple Honey, Bijou, Summer Sequence and the popular Stan Getz, Four Brothers number Early Autumn which featured lyrics by Johnny Mercer.

Dec. 14, 2001—Conte Condoli, trumpet and flugelhorn player and younger brother of Pete, died in Palm Desert, CA. He started with Woody Herman at 16 during high school vacations in 1943 and later spent more than a decade with Doc Severinson and the Tonight Show band. He was 74.

2001—Popular bandleader Ray Anthony, who started his orchestra in 1946, released his 127th album. The compact disc is called "Dream Dancing IV: In a Miller Mood." Anthony was lst trumpet in Miller's organization at 18.

Jan. 16, 2002—Former band singer and West Coast entrepreneur Merv Griffin opens the first major supper club in decades at the luxurious Beverly Hilton in Los Angeles to entertain dancers and those who enjoyed the big band sounds of the past while they dined.

January, 2002—Lionel Hampton's Vibraphone, a classic custom model, enters the Jazz Archives at the Smithsonian National Museum of American History. His Musser Hampton Signature Vibraphone was a truly a limited edition.

Feb. 8, 2002—Nick Brignola, a big band baritone saxophonist, died in Albany, NY.

Nick was named Best Baritone Saxophonist in Down Beat polls over the years.

Feb. 22, 2002—One of the great British big band drummers, Ronnie Verrell, dies at 76. Was best known for his London Palladium 1955 "Concerto For Verrell" which demonstrated his creativity and his similarity to his idol, Don Lamond of the Woody Herman band.

June 29, 2002—Rosemary Clooney, who began a career as a big band singer with her sister Betty with Tony Pastor, dies at 74. They opened with Pastor at the Steel Pier in Atlantic City in 1947. Her 1951 "Come On A My House" recording made her a national hit.

July 2, 2002—Bassist Ray Brown, an original in the Dizzy Gillespie/Charlie Parker Quintet, is dead at 75. He was musical director and later husband of Ella Fitzgerald and served as manager of Quincy Jones. He spent 16 years with the Oscar Peterson Trio and was a regular on Norman Granz's Jazz at the Philharmonic tours. Ray played bass on more than 2,000 recordings which makes him one of the most recorded artists in the business.

Big Bands in the Movies, 1940 to 1960

Second Chorus (1940) This movie features Artie Shaw and his band with Nick Fatool on drums. A comedy starring Fred Astaire and Burgess Meredith. Artie has a role in this show which is about musicians trying to join the Shaw Band and he plays Concerto for Clarinet.

Ball of Fire (1941) Barbara Stanwyck is the star and actually sings...with the Gene Krupa Orchestra in this comedy from the war years. This was one of those screwball type shows you see every so often on late night TV where you wonder who could have written such a script filled with slang. Actually, it was Billy Wilder who had emigrated from Germany just a few years earlier. There's a good opportunity to see and hear Krupa playing his famous chart Drum Boogie.

The Birth of the Blues (1941) This musical featured Mary Martin, Bing Crosby and Jack Teagarden who sang The Waiter and the Porter and the Upstairs Maid. Meanwhile, Crosby and Martin sang the old favorite Wait Till the Sun Shines, Nellie. Johnny Mercer created the compositions and lyrics on this wartime film

Hellzapoppin' (1941) A wacky musical with some silly comedy routines. Featured are Slim and Slam and Whitney's Lindy Hoppers.

Sun Valley Serenade (1941) The first full-length feature movie to highlight Glenn Miller, Tex Beneke and the Modernaires in a cute musical romance story. Skater Sonia Henie stars in the film. For big band fans, one of the great parts of the movie is that it features members of the civilian Miller band. On the bandstand were: Beneke, Jimmy Priddy, Chummy Macgregor, Ernie Caceres, Hal McIntyre, Willie Schwarz, Al Klink, Ray Anthony, Johnny Best, Billy May, Maurice Purtill, Trigger Alpert, Paul Tanner, Frank D'Anolfo, Ralph Brewster, Mickey McMickle and Jack Lathrop. It was nominated for three musical Oscars thanks to songs like Chattanooga Choo Choo, In the Mood, Moonlight Serenade, I Know and It Happened in Sun Valley. Most reviewers liked this movie because it offered a variety of talent as well as smooth Miller music. Paula Kelly, Ray Eberle and the Modernaires played themselves, Milton Berle had a cameo and a young Dorothy Dandridge sings and dances. Even Sonia Henie tries to sing a few bars.

Birth of the Blues (1941) Here's a movie few people can remember. It featured Bing Crosby and Jack Teagarden, the trombonist.

Blues In the Night (1941) A famous band number through the 1940s written by Harold Arlen and Johnny Mercer. Film features Jimmy Lunceford Orchestra backing Mabel Todd on the legendary number and you also get to hear the Will Osborne Orchestra on a number that probably didn't make it past the next day called "Says Who? Says You, Says I" with Priscilla Lane.

Las Vegas Nights (1941) Frank Sinatra, Phil Regan and Burt Wheeler star in this musical film with the popular Tommy Dorsey Band. The songs make the movie. The show highlights TD playing Delores, Song of India, I'll Never Smile Again, Cocktails for Two and Mary, Mary Quite Contrary. Director Ralph Murphy made this hour and 30 minute comedy virtually fit the Vegas in the desert everyone knows.

What's Cookin' (1942) A Universal film that gives a brief look at Woody Herman and his band and offers an energetic Woody dancing and singing. Played the popular number "Amen." The movie features the popular Andrews Sisters.

Cabin In the Sky (1942) The story is based on a Broadway play and it featured musical numbers by Louis Armstrong and his group, Duke Ellington and his band, Buck Washington, Ethel Waters and Lena Horne. It was Vincent Minelli's first film.

Holiday Inn (1942) It is the annual movie to see at holiday time because of the music, the dancing and the carefree setting it offers while America faced a grim period during World War II. Perhaps that's what made Linda Mason (Marjorie Reynolds) and Jim Hardy's (Bing Crosby) story so acceptable in a world of divorce, cynicism and greed. Fred Astaire's dancing (remember the routine with firecrackers?) is clever and certainly Irving Berlin's introduction of White Christmas makes this a great film. Viewers thought so, too. It received a user's rating of 7.4 out of 10. Why is it a movie that involves big bands? You'll find Bing's brother Bob Crosby's band backing the musical numbers throughout the movie.

Orchestra Wives (1942) The second of the two wartime movies starring Glenn Miller and Tex Beneke. Says the film critic Satu: "I'm crazy about this movie...Splendid dance and song sequences by the Nicholas Brothers of 'I've Got a Gal From Kalamazoo.'" A number of critics rated it the best black and white of the movies featuring big bands.

Seven Days' Leave (1942) Lucille Ball and Victor Mature star in this comedy which has musical skits and highlights from the Band of Renown of Les Brown.

Syncopation (1942) A documentary of sorts which shows how jazz started in 1906 and evolved through 1942. It demonstrates the racism of the period, too. No Black musicians are included in this development of the genre jazz. It features Benny Goodman, Charlie Barnet, Joe Venuti, Gene Krupa, Harry James and others.

Springtime in the Rockies (1942) Betty Grable and John Payne are featured in this 91 minute film along with Carmen Miranda and a young Jackie Gleason. Miranda sings an offbeat arrangement of Chattanooga Choo Choo. Supporting the musical side of this movie is Harry James and his Orchestra.

Iceland (1942) The Marines landed at the top of polar cap during World War II. They needed to, of course, because skater Sonja Henie is featured along with John Payne. Somehow, someway Sammy Kaye and his Orchestra are on the ice cap with them.

Ship Ahoy (1942) Tommy Dorsey and his orchestra featuring a young, animated drummer named Buddy Rich playing numbers like On Moonlight Bay give this movie its music and backdrop for comedians Bert Lahr and Red Skelton and dancer/singer Eleanor Powell to perform.

Best Foot Forward ((1943) A military school setting with Lucille Ball, June Allyson and Nancy Walker who jitterbugs with band leader Harry James in a sensational set. The James band performs Two O'Clock Jump among others.

Girl Crazy (1943) Another musical that audiences enjoyed based upon the ratings. It generated a 6.6 on a scale to 10. June Allyson, Mickey Rooney and Judy Garland were the featured stars but Tommy Dorsey played himself and contributed to this comedy along with his orchestra. Imagine Mickey Rooney doing a piano solo with Dorsey & company. One commentator even suggests that the arrangements of pieces like Biding My Time, Treat Me Rough and Could You Use Me were experiments that would springboard the Hi-Los and the Four Freshmen more than a decade later. The Dorsey band plays numbers that became standards later like Embraceable You, But Not For Me and Fascinating Rhythm.

Crazy House/Funzapoppin' (1943) It only took Hollywood a year or two to figure out that one "zapoppin' could actually clone a second. This one introduced Count Basie along with Jimmy Rushing, the Glenn Miller Singers not the band and the Delta Rhythm Boys.

Here Comes Elmer (1943) Possibly the first appearance of Nat "King" Cole on screen with his trio in this black and white comedy without much of a script. You get a chance to hear one of Nat's famous numbers "Straighten Up and Fly Right."

I Dood It (1943) And we ridicule kids for kidspeak and rap! The title should give you a tip about what's ahead with this movie. The music includes Lena Horne, Hazel Scott, Lee Young and Jimmy Dorsey and his band.

Hit Parade of 1943 A music review of the year with Count Basie and his band.

Stage Door Canteen (1943) This was the beginning of a wartime Hollywood attempting to outdo itself in assembling literally a cast of thousands for patriotic purposes. This was a blockbuster for the time. Approximately 94 hollywood stars of various categories did cameos or feature roles in this Normandy-like production directed by Frank Borzage. Plenty of bandleaders and musicians, too. From guitarist Dave Barbour to his former wife Peggy Lee, Count Basie and his band, Xavier Cugat and his orchestra, Benny Goodman and his band, Kay Kyser and is College of Musical Knowledge Orchestra, Guy Lombardo and the Canadiens and Freddie Martin and his orchestra. Benny plays his solid swing numbers Why Don't You Do Right and Bugle Call Rag. Squeezed in all kinds of roles were people like violinist Yehudi Menuhin, Harpo Marx and Gypsy Rose Lee. It must have been a writer's nightmare trying to find interesting conversational dialogue. But the synergy this movie produced paid dividends for a country at war. Said a movie goer about movie some 50 years later: "It was a morale booster, and nothing more than a delightful musical with a lot of big bands and performers…I own it and I intend to see it again and again."

The Gang's All Here (1943) Here's a musical with Benny Goodman and his band. Another movie with a cute title that meanders for 103 minutes. Carmen Miranda, called the Brazilian Bombshell lives up to her name when she sings "The Lady in the Tutti Frutti Hat." She even plays a xylophone made of bananas which goes to prove how far prop personnel have to go to create the visual in these shows. And we can't forget bandleader Phil Harris's wife, Alice Faye, who does a number, too. The Goodman band shows its talent on the number "Paduca."

Stormy Weather (1943) Didn't meet expectations of some critics but the public gave it a 6.5 out of 10. Musicians abound in this all-Black film and with music by Nat "King" Cole and Fats Waller it was a toe-tapper. Singer Lena Horne, dancer Bill Robinson, Cab Calloway and Waller were in it along with tenor saxman Coleman Hawkins and trumpeter Zutty Singleton. And we got to hear Cole's That Ain't Right and Waller's Ain't Misbehavin' too.

Wintertime (1943) Picture Sonja Henie as a Norwegian skating champion and you can follow this musical story. Cesar Romero, Jack Oakie, Carol Landis and Cornell Wilde are co-stars along Woody Herman and his band.

Top Man (1943) Count Basie and his Orchestra join Donald O'Connor in this musical comedy.

Hold That Ghost (1943) Ted Lewis and his band along with Lou Costello and Bud Abbott.

Pin-Up Girl (1943) One of those wartime fun movies that focused on a starlet; this time Betty Grable. The band in the movie wasn't hubby Harry James…it was Charley Spivak and his trumpet and orchestra.

Hit The Ice (1943) A comedy with the popular and zany Bud Abbott and Lou Costello which also featured Johnny Long band and singer Ginny Sims

Bathing Beauty (1944) Originally entitled Mr. Co-ed, this MGM film starred swimmer Esther Williams, Red Skelton, Basil Rathbone and Harry James and his orchestra and singer Helen Forrest. You can hear I Cried for You and Tico-Tico.

Follow the Boys (1944) The tribute story to the wartime USO with Ted Lewis and his band and Louis Jordan and his popular Tympany Five.

Jammin the Blues (1944) The controversial film that featured the Benny Goodman and his integrated band and other Black musicians. To make the film photographer Gjon Mili had to get special permission from the studio to include white guitarist Barney Kessel. First, the studio wanted the photographer to stain Kessel's arms, hands and face with "berry juice" so he would look darker. Finally, the studio bosses accepted Mili's suggestion that he film Kessel in the shadows. In the film, Kessel turned out looking darker than Black tenor sax star Lester Young.

Atlantic City Honeymoon (1944) Here's another of the many musicals starring popular bands and leaders of the period. This one included Paul "Pops" Whiteman and his Orchestra.

Broadway Rhythm (1944) Tommy Dorsey and his Orchestra along with Hazel Scott and singer Lena Horne.

Hollywood Canteen (1944) Continuing the "canteen" series by the same writer who wrote the first; Delmer Daves. This movie featured about 90 stars in cameo and other roles and spotlighted the bands of Jimmy Dorsey, Carmen Cavallaro, the voices of the Andrew Sisters and the Golden

Gate Quartet among others. The voters on Amazon.com gave both Stage Door and Hollywood Canteens a rating of 6.7 out of 10.

Bathing Beauty (1944) Another Harold Arlen, Johnny Mercer extravaganza with an all-star cast. Red Skelton, Janis Paige, Carlos Ramirez, Bing Crosby, Betty Hutton join forces with two great bands of the period, Harry James and Xavier Cugat

Sweet and Low-Down (1944) The title makes it another genre film from the 1940s but this comedy probably needs a paid audience. The highlight for those who enjoy big bands is seeing and hearing Benny Goodman.

Two Girls and a Sailor (1944) One of the Hollywood extravangza movies that featured stars from comedy to drama to music. June Allyson, Gloria DeHaven and Van Johnson had principal roles but the walk ons included people like Jimmy Durante, Gracie Allen, Lena Horne, Harry James and his band, Helen Forrest and Xavier Cugat and his orchestra. Says one online viewer who enjoyed the black and white film, "I was enthralled by the movie. Lots of humor and sisterly love draw you into the plot. The mystery of who will end up with whom keeps you riveted." Time Magazine called it "a joy and a delight."

Atlantic City Honeymoon (1944)A musical comedy with similar plot to the others of the war years with one exception; it featured Paul "Pops" Whiteman and his orchestra. Whiteman, who called himself the "King of Jazz," was a popular fixture in the 1930s but wasn't as visual in movies during the war years as Harry James, Benny Goodman and others.

Dixie Jamboree (1944) Cab Calloway hi-de-hos his way in this comedy on a musical showboat.

Four Jills and a Jeep (1944) Another of the wartime sets featuring USO entertainers overseas and featuring Kay Francis, Carole Landis, Mitzi Mayfair and comedian Martha Raye—the jills of this movie—dealing with the elements, staging shows in Europe and North Africa. Also featured

Swing Big Bands At the Movie are Dick Haymes, Phil Silvers and Betty Grable. Jimmy Dorsey and his orchestra supply the music.

Wilson (1944) This was a 20th Century Fox production which had considerable star power but never really caught public attention. Stars were Charles Coburn, Dana Andrews, Thomas Mitchell, Red Buttons and Jean Crain and included the Stan Kenton band.

Weekend At the Waldorf (1945) The Waldorf Astoria in New York City is the site for this comedy-drama which features Ginger Rogers, Lana Turner, Walter Pidgeon, Van Johnson and who else but Xavier Cugat and his orchestra.

George White's Scandals (1945) Another musical with slapstick comedy that included Gene Krupa and his band. It featured Jack Haley and Joan Davis. You can enjoy another Krupa big band favorite, Leave Us Leap.

Sensations of 1945 (1945) A musical featuring Eleanor Powell and Dennis O'Keefe with Cab Calloway and his band, Woody Herman and his aggregation and Sophie Tucker. Watch Eleanor show you how to dance inside a pinball machine. Warning: Don't try it.

Earl Carroll's Vanities (1945) Earl's club was a natural for another musical since it was in Hollywood. The resident music director was Archie Bleyer who went on to fame on the Arthur Godfrey radio show. This film, however, features the red hot Woody Herman and sidemen like Billy Bauer, Flip Phillips, Chubby Jackson, Davey Tough, Bill Harris, Pete Condoli and one of the first women musicians in a popular road band, Marjorie Hyams on vibes.

Make Mine Music (1946) This is a 75-minute movie which was never released in its original form. Parts of the film, which features Benny Goodman, were released as part of Walt Disney's Mini Classics. But the music is solid: listen to Benny on numbers like Casey at Bat, The Whale Who Wanted to Sing at the Met, Two silhouettes, Without You, All the Cats Join In, After You've Gone, Blue Bayou, Peter and the Wolf and others and you'll see why this a terrific video for the early swing listener. Believe it or not, Disney thought the war between Hatfields and McCoys was too violent in animation and cut the segment later. It originally censored the movie.

Beat the Band (1947) Another Krupa film which he probably wishes he hadn't made. Krupa has speaking parts and he and the band are featured in two production numbers.

The Fabulous Dorseys (1947) Tommy and Jimmy play themselves in this plotless 88 minute black and white that traces the Dorsey brothers' careers. Some critics were especially critical of the lip-synching and fake piano playing. Some cameo roles for other musicians in this film, too.

You'll see Charlie Barnet, Bob Eberly, Henry Busse, Helen O'Connell and hear some good Dorsey sounds like Marie and Green Eyes…if the story doesn't bore you. Don't be surprised to see Paul "Pops" Whiteman, too.

Hit Parade of 1947 Another review of music of the period with Woody Herman and his Band.

This Time For Keeps (1947) A Mackinac Island setting for this musical comedy with Esther Williams and Jimmy Durante and his famous Ink Dinky Do routine. Xavier Cugat and his orchestra offer big band Latin sounds.

New Orleans (1947) Woody Herman and his band again this time teaming up with musicians like boogie-woogie king Meade Lux Lewis, Billie Holiday, Barney Bigard, Kid Ory and Zutty Singleton. The fictional plot focuses on the birth of jazz music.

A Song Is Born (1948) A gangster's musical that rated fairly high among movie goers. Danny Kaye and Virginia Mayo star in this and an array of big band talent that includes a sprinkling of academic titles. Benny Goodman, the King of Swing, is Professor Magenbruch which is a stretch.

But the gang's all here: appearing as themselves are Tommy Dorsey, Louis Armstrong, Lionel Hampton, Charlie Barnet, Page Cavanaugh and his Trio and the Golden Gate Quartet. Among the crew on this film was trumpeter Sonny Burke.

Luxury Liner (1948) A musical starring Jane Powell and George Brent and Xavier Cugat and his orchestra. It features the popular Latin number Yes, We Have No Bananas.

Melody Time (1948) Another animation, family musical which emulates Fantasia but offers much more music. And the music is a potpourri of contemporary post-World War II bandleaders and singers. Fred Waring and Freddy Martin are here along with singers Dennis Day, the Andrew Sisters, Ethel Smith, Frances Langford and Buddy Clark

Make Believe Ballroom (1949) Anyone who listened to New York radio and the big bands remembers Martin Block and his great radio show of the same name. This movie conjures the scene and includes cameos by Jimmy Dorsey, PeeWee Hunt, Charlie Barnet, Gene Krupa and Nat King Cole.

Neptune's Daughter (1949) Esther Williams and Ricardo Montalban join with Red Skelton in this MGM film about bathing suits and designers. Xavier Cugat and his orchestra played the background music and gave us Baby It's Cold Outside and My Heart Beats Faster.

The Glenn Miller Story (1954) Hollywood had virtually shutdown big band spectaculars in the 1950s but this special movie was created because of the post-war interest in the man who swept popular music polls before and during the war. Glenn Miller's life was considered to be a role model for American musicians and many others. A patriot, a journeyman trombonist, composer and arranger and the leader of America's legendary dance band, the show featured two of the country's top performers; June Allyson and Jimmy Stewart. And the public responded. It rates a 7 on the rating service. There was a mixture of musicians playing themselves and actors taking the parts of musicians in this film. MASH star Harry Morgan played Glenn's piano player and confidante Chummy MacGregor but Frances Langford, Louis Armstrong, Ben Pollack, Gene Krupa, Barney Bigard, Marty Napoleon, Arvell Shaw, Cozy Cole and Babe Russin played themselves.

Obviously Glenn is credited with the music but if you look carefully among other credits you'll find the name of a young music adapter who went on to make music and film in another era, Henry Mancini.

The Wild One (1954) Marlon Brando and Lee Marvin terrorize the West Coast in this original biker movie. What does it have to do with swing and big bands? Check out the sound track of Leith Stevens' compositions arranged by Shorty Rogers. It's West Coast jazz of the 1950s at its best.

Daddy Long Legs (1955) Fred Astaire and Leslie Caron star and dance in this 20th Century Fox production which features Ray Anthony's band in a college dance scene.

The Benny Goodman Story (1955) Noticed the similarity in titles? Hollywood figured, it seems, that the leader's name was attractive enough to elicit public response and made three of these movies virtually back to back. Benny told a critic a short time after the movie was playing around the country that "the music was good." Steve Allen, of course, played Benny and Donna Reed starred as Goodman's wife. Like other bandleader movies there's a cast of plenty of sidemen. Gene Krupa, Lionel Hampton, Harry James, Ziggy Elman, Teddy Wilson and Martha

Tilton are walkons in this glimpse of a bandleader's bandleader who may have been more quietly explosive than the movie portrayed.

The Eddie Duchin Story (1956) Considered a society pianist, this story includes the personal drama the other stories lack. Duchin, a popular high society musician, started his own band and at the height of his career was diagnosed with leukemia. Carmen Cavallaro does the piano dubbing on the show which featured Tyrone Power as Duchin, Kim Novak and James Whitmore. A longer than normal film of more than 2 hours, it was nominated for four Academy Awards including Best Motion Picture story award. If you are a careful viewer and a boating enthusiast you'll see some vintage Century boats in the waterfront scenes.

The Girl Can't Help It (1956) In a year, Ray Anthony and his band were back on a 20th Century Fox lot and this time Ray has some lines to say. Jayne Mansfield, Tom Ewell and Edmund O'Brian starred in this movie and you see and hear the Anthony band in a recording studio and a dance scene.

Mister Rock and Roll (1957) Lionel Hampton and his band and Allen Freed in a movie about the music fad of the time. Unfortunately, the type of music was partly responsible for the end of the big band era.

This Could Be The Night (1957) MGM produced this up tempo plot which featured Jean Simmons, Paul Douglas and Tony Franciosa. The Ray Anthony band is seen throughout the movie in a nightclub setting.

Five Fingers (1957-59) Ray Anthony in an acting role that wasn't too difficult as the leader of a small band in a 20th Century Fox movie that starred David Hedison and Oscar Homolka.

Jamboree (1957) A boy singer meets girl canary as female singers were called in this movie which features Fats Domino, Count Basie and his band and Kay Medford whose voice is dubbed on singing numbers by Connie Francis.

The Big Beat (1957) Once more, you won't find a plot of much interest but there are big band sounds emanating from this movie. Popular leaders like Charlie Barnet, Harry James, Fats Domino and their bands are featured along with the legendary Mills Brothers.

St. Louis Blues (1958) Some wish producers would have rethought the script of this salute to WC Handy's life but, once again, the music makes it appealing to big band aficionados. You'll find Nat King Cole, Pearl Bailey, Cab Calloway, Ella Fitzgerald and Curtis Counce in this film.

Senior Prom (1958) A very low budget musical with Louie Prima and Bob Crosby and their bands.

The Gene Krupa Story (1959) Hollywood finally got the message about bandleader movies just as this film was in production. It was the last of the genre. Unfortunately, it wasn't a historically accurate account though. Yet Sal Mineo as Krupa was superb. Most drummers gave him good marks for duplicating Krupa's style on screen. While the music was good it did appear to be music of the 1950s instead of the swing and jazz period of the period when Krupa was at his peak in popularity. Some interesting cameos of the big band musicians. Shelly Manne, a great drummer of his own day, played Davey Tough, Red Nichols played himself as did Krupa vocalist Anita O'Day. It was interesting to see Bobby Troup as Tommy Dorsey in this film.

This film was dubbed Drum Crazy for release in the United Kingdom.

Hey Boy! Hey Girl (1959) I guess the title matched the antics of the stars Louie Prima and Keely Smith in this typical Vegas musical with typical Prima antics, showmanship and music.

The Five Pennies (1959) A highly fictionalized Hollywood view of Red Nichols' life. Nichols was a cornet player who appeared on more than 4,000 records during the 1920s. Danny Kaye played Nichols in the film.

Cinderfella (1960) Sometimes it gets tough to find a title without infringing on the copyright of another film, and, of course, this film is a Cinderella story with a guy not a girl in the lead. And it has lots of stars with no real plot to follow. There are two zany guys—Jerry Lewis and Ed Wynn—a young Anna Maria Alberghetti as Princess Charming. And somewhere in here you find the swinging Count Basie and his band along with band vocalist Joe Williams. But said a film buff in 1999: "This was the cutest movie I've ever seen. Jerry Lewis is absolutely hilarious."

Alphabetized Big Band Theme Songs

Most popular songs used by bands and approximate date band began

A

And the Angels Sing…………… Ziggy Elman Band, late 1940s

Apurksody, Star Burst…………… Gene Krupa Band, 1938

Auld Lang Syne……………… Guy Lombardo Band, early 1920s

Alexander's Swinging…………… Van Alexander Band, 1938

A Kiss From Me To You…………… Ray Pearl Band, 1937

Anita…………………… Skitch Henderson Band, 1947

Ain't Misbehavin'……………… Fats Waller Band, 1932

Angry…………………… Tiny Hill Band, 1933

Artistry in Rhythm……………. Stan Kenton Band, 1941

After Hours…………………. Ted G. Buckner Band, 1946

Arsenic and Old Lace……………. Jerry Jerome Band, 1942

Amazing Grace, Just a Closer Wall With Thee, When the Saints Come Marching In Medley …………………….. Don Cantwell, The Clef Dwellers, 1991

B

Blue Lights…………………. Bob Astor Band, 1940

Blue Flame…………………. Woody Herman Band, 1936

Blue Mood………………….. Teddy Powell Band, 1939

Busybody…………………… Hal Pruden Band, 1946

Blue Rey, Nighty-Night…………… Alvino Rey Band, 1939

Blue Nocturne………………… Dick Stabile Band, 1936

Bubbles in the Wine…………….. Lawrence Welk Band, 1925

Billy……………………… Billy Bishop Band, 1931

Boston Tea Party……………….	**Mal Hallett Band, 1920s**
Breezing Along With the Breeze……….	**Lou Breeze Band, mid 1930s**
Body and Soul…………………	**Coleman Hawkins Band, 1938**
Business on the O……………..	**Archie Bleyer Band, late 1930s**
Blue Sonata………………….	**Sonny Burke Band, 1938**
Bye Bye Blues…………………	**Bert Lown Band, 1928**

C

Cherokee, Redskin Rhumba…………	**Charlie Barnet Band, 1933**
Contrasts……………………	**Jimmy Dorsey Band, 1935**
Coral Reef…………………..	**Neil Hefti Band, 1951**
Careless…………………….	**Eddie Howard Band, 1942**
Ciribiribin……………………	**Harry James Band, 1939**
City Lights (Nights)……………………	**Jack Jenny Band, 1939**
Cocktail for Two…………………	**Spike Jones Band, early 1940s**
Call of the Wild…………………	**Jerry Wald Band, 1941**
Carla………………………	**Ralph Marterie Band, 1946**
Christopher Columbus……………	**Fletcher Henderson Band, 1946**
Cherry Pink and Apple Blossom White……..	**Prez Prado Band, 1948**
Can't We Be Friends?……………..	**Johnny Messner Band, 1930s**
Chant of the Weed………………..	**Don Redman Band, early 1930s**
Commanderism…………………	**Irving Aaronson Band, 1925**

D

Dance of the Blue Devils, Shangri-la, Leap Frog……………………	**Les Brown Band, 1938**
Danny Boy……………………	**Bobby Byrne Band, 1939**
Dipsy Doodle, My Reverie……………	**Larry Clinton Band, 1938**
Desert Serenade…………………	**Jerry Gray Band, 1945**

Doodle Town Fifers..................	**Sauter-Finegan Band, 1952**
Daydreams Come True at Night...........	**Dick Jurgens Band, 1939**
Drifting and Dreaming, I Love You..........	**Orrin Tucker Band, early 1930s**
Does Your Heart Beat for Me?...........	**Russ Morgan Band, 1935**
Deep Forest, Cavernism...............	**Earl "Father" Hines Band, 1928**
Doodle-Doo-Doo....................	**Art Kassell Band, 1924**
Dreams of You.....................	**Frank Bettencourt Band, 1962**
Daybreak Serenade..................	**Jess Stacy Band, 1939**

E

East St. Louis Toodle-oo, Take the A Train, Solitude......................	**Duke Ellington Band, 1920s**
Elks Parade.......................	**Bobby Sherwood Band, 1941**
Eight Bars in a Search of Melody...........	**Will Hudson Band, 1938**
Embraceable You....................	**Bobby Hackett Band, 1938**

F

Flying Home.......................	**Lionel Hampton Band, 1940**

G

Gotta Have Your Love.................	**Ina Ray Hutton, 1934**
Good Evening.....................	**Del Courtney Band, 1933**

H

Hot Lips...........................	**Henry "Hot Lips" Busse Band, 1931**
Heart to Heart.....................	**Elliot Lawrence Band, 1944-45**
Howdy Friends.....................	**Ray McKinley Band, 1946**
Holiday Forever....................	**Randy Brooks Band, 1945**
Heart of My Heart, Sophisticated Swing,......	**Les Elgart Band, 1945**
How I Miss You When Summer Is Gone.....	**Hal Kemp Band, 1925**

I

I've Got A Right to Know................ **Georgie Auld Band, 1940**

I Wish You Love..................... **Jack Palmer Band, 1950s**

I Can't Get Started With You............... **Bunny Berigan Band, 1937**

I'm Getting Sentimental Over You........... **Tommy Dorsey Band, 1935**

I've Got A Date With An Angel............. **Skinnay Ennis Band, 1938**

It's That Time Again.................... **Buddy Moreno Band, 1947**

It's A Lonesome Old Town................ **Jimmy Palmer Band, 1945**

I've Got A Right to Sing the Blues............ **Jack Teagarden Band, 1938**

I Want To Be Happy..................... **Dick Wickman Band, 1941**

I Love You, Oh, How I Love You............ **Tommy Tucker Band, 1928**

I'll Love You In My Dreams............... **Horace Heidt Band, 1923**

It's A Lonesome Old Town................ **Ben Bernie Band, 1921**

If Stars Could Talk................... **Nat Brandwynne Band, mid1930s**

I'm Looking Over a Four-Leaf Clover......... **Art Mooney Band, 1940s**

J

Jazznocracy, Uptown Blues............... **Jimmy Lunceford Band, 1927**

K

Kaye's Melody........................ **Sammy Kaye Band, early 1930s**

L

Let's Dance......................... **Benny Goodman Band, 1934**

Listen to My Music............. **Ted Heath Band, London, England, 1944**

Lean Baby......................... **Billy May Band, 1952**

Love Thy Neighbor................... **Paul Neighbors Band, 1948**

Last Night......................... **Joe Venuti Band, 1932**

M

Melancholy Mood..................... **Teddy Phillips Band, 1944**

My Sweetheart..................... **Paul Pendarvis Band, early 1930s**

Mr. and Mrs. Swing.................	**Red Norvo Band, 1936**
My Day Begins and Ends With You.........	**Henry King Band, early 1930s**
My Time Is Your Time................	**Rudy Vallee Band, 1928**
Moonlight on Melody Hill...............	**Boyd Raeburn Band, 1944**
Moonlight Serenade...............	**Tex Beneke Band, 1946**
Moonlight Serenade.................	**Glenn Miller Band, 1937**
Memories of You..................	**Sonny Dunham Band, 1940**
Melancholy Lullaby.................	**Benny Carter Band, 1933**
Minnie the Moocher.................	**Cab Calloway Band, 1928**
My Shawl.......................	**Xavier Cugat Band, 1932-33**
Moon Mist, Ectasy..................	**Hal McIntyre Band, 1941**
Memories of You...................	**Memo Bernabei Band, 1958**
Midnight.........................	**Joe Haymes Band, 1932**
Music in the Moonlight.................	**Jimmy Grier Band, 1932**
My Bill..........................	**Bill Clifford Band, 1941**
My Twilight Dream..................	**Eddie Duchin Band, 1931**
My Twilight Dream..................	**Peter Duchin Band, 1962**

N

No Foolin'.......................	**Lennie Herman Band, early 1950s**
Night Train.......................	**Buddy Morrow Band, 1950**
Nightmare.......................	**Artie Shaw Band, 1936-37**
Nola...........................	**Vincent Lopez Band, 1917**
Night Must Fall.....................	**Dick Trimble Band, Oh Territory, Early 1930s**
Night Is Gone, Nice People..............	**Henry Jerome Band, early 1930s**

O

One O'Clock Jump………………… **Count Basie Band, 1935**

Oh You Beautiful Doll…………….. **Chuck Foster Band, 1938**

Oh Look At Me Now……………… **Joe Bushkin Band, 1951**

Out of the Night………………… **Ted Weems Band, 1923**

P

Piano Portrait………………….. **Jack Fina Band, 1946**

Pastoral Blossoms………………… **Tony Pastor Band, early 1930s**

Pipe Dreams…………………… **Tommy Reynolds Band, 1939**

Pagan Moon……………………. **Ted Black Band, 1929**

Polonaise, My Sentimental Heart……….. **Carmen Cavallero Band, 1939**

Pretty Little Petticoat……………… **Raymond Scott Band, 1939**

Q

Quaker City Jazz………………… **Jan Savitt Band, 1935**

R

Rippling Rhythm………………… **Shep Fields Band, 1929**

Racing With the Moon……………… **Vaughn Monroe Band, 1940**

Relaxing at the Touro……………….. **Muggsy Spanier Band, 1941**

Romance……………………… **Ray Herbeck Band, 1935**

S

Sleepy Alto…………………….. **Johnny Bothwell Band, 1946**

Slow But Sure…………………… **Charley Agnew Band, 1924**

Sunrise Serenade………………… **Frankie Carle Band, 1944**

Sometimes I'm Happy……………….. **Blue Barron Band, 1936**

Singing Wind………………… **Ralph Flanagan Band, 1949**

Sing, Sing, Sing, & Way Down Yonder In New Orleans………………… **Louie Prima Band, early 1930s**

Sunset to Sunrise……………… **Art Mooney Band, late 1930s**

Strange Cargo....................	**Freddie Slack Band, 1942**
Star Dreams.....................	**Charlie Spivak Band, 1940**
Snowfall........................	**Claude Thornhill Band, 1940**
Summertime.....................	**Bob Crosby Band, 1930s**
Song of the Islands.................	**Ben Pollack Band, 1925**
Sugar Blues.......................	**Clyde McCoy Band, 1920**
Swing Out.......................	**Erskine Hawkins Band, 1935**
Sunburst.........................	**Bob Chester Band, 1935**
Skater's Waltz.....................	**Barney Rapp Band, early 1920s**
Soft, Gravy Train....................	**Tiny Bradshaw Band, 1933**

T

Think...........................	**Will Bradley Band, 1939**
Things Aren't What They Used To Be.........	**Monk Rowe Band, 1990s**
The Chapel in the Moonlight, You Call It Madness, If I Ever Love Again..............	**Russ Carlyle Band, 1940**
Times Square Scuttle.................	**Lenny Hayton Band, 1937**
Thankful........................	**Teddy Phillips Band, 1946**
Two Clouds in the Sky.................	**Tommy Reed Band, 1946**
The Idol of the Air Lanes...............	**Jan Garber Band, 1930s**
Thinking of You.....................	**Kay Kyser Band, 1930s**
The Very Thought of You............	**Ray Noble Band, England, 1920s**
The Waltz You Saved For Me...........	**Wayne King Band, 1927**
That Old Gang of Mine, That Certain Party...	**Benny Strong Band, 1938**
Tonight We Love..................	**Freddie Martin Band, 1931**
That's What I Like About South..........	**Phil Harris Band, 1932**
Tonal Color Serenade..............	**Bob Strong Band, 1943**

Teach Me to Smile, I'm Not Forgetting…… **Don Bestor Band, 1921**

U

Up A Lazy River………………. **Si Zentner Band, 1957**

Until The Real Thing Comes Along…….. **Andy Kirk Band, 1929**

V

Vieni Su…………………… **Carl Ravazza Band, 1940**

W

What's New? Moonlight in Vermont…….. **Billie Butterfield Band, 1945**

Was I to Blame for Falling in Love With You?, Smoke Rings………………… **Glen Gray Band, 1930s**

Wailing to the Four Winds………… **Red Nichols Band, 1923**

White Star of Sigma Nu…………… **Johnny Long Band, 1932**

When the Lights Go On Again……….. **Lucky Millinder Band, 1940**

When It's Sleepy Time Down South…… **Louis Armstrong Band, 1929**

When Romance Calls…………… **Leon Belasco Band, 1936**

When My Baby Smiles At Me……….. **Ted Lewis Band, 1916**

Y

Young Man With the Horn………… **Ray Anthony Band, 1946**

You Call It Madness, I call It Love…….. **Don Glasser Band, 1938**

You Are My Lucky Star…………… **Enoch Light Band, 1929**

You Go To My Head……………. **Mitchell Ayers Band, 1935**

You're Just A Dream Come True……… **Isham Jones Band, 1919**

Themes came from various sources: Big Band Themes web site, Leo Walker's The Big Band Almanac (revised) DaCapo Press, 1989; Walker's The Wonderful Era of the Great Bance Bands (revised) DaCapo Press, 1990; Swing! The Essential Album Guide, edited by Steve Knopper, Visible Ink Press, 1999; George T. Simon's The Big Bands, MacMillan, 1971 and big band programs of the era

Who Were The Big Band Singers?

According to The Great American Big Band Data Base, there were nearly 400 male and female singers during the big band days; 178 "boy" singers and 214 "girl" singers who critics and reviewers called "thrushes," "warblers" and "canaries" to add zest to their stories.

In the early days, swing bands had more male singers but, by the 1930s, women vocalists added sex appeal and a whole range of sounds for arrangers and bandleaders who sought popularity. And who didn't in those days? From the cute, high pitched Wee Bonnie Baker to the throaty sounds of Peggy Lee, the business thrived on introducing hits and new sounds. Pearl Bailey, who went on to a great career as a single and a sometime actress, got her start with trumpeter Cootie Williams. While she sang with any number of groups during her career, she actually only sang with one band full time.

Dorothy Claire, however, started with Bobby Byrne's band, then joined Glenn Miller and finished her band singing days with Bob Crosby.

Who were some of the famed and not so famous singers of the day and who gave them their first gig? Here are some of those who had careers with several or more bands:

Mildred Bailey...*started with Paul Whiteman, also sang with Red Norvo, Glen Gray and Benny Goodman bands*

Wee Bonnie Baker...*Evelyn Nelson before she got into show business, started and ended her big band days with Orrin Tucker. In 1941, she was ranked 7th among girl singers by collegians, according to Billboard.*

Anita Boyer...*started with Artie Shaw and also sang with Jerry Wald, Leo Reisman and Tommy and Jimmy Dorsey and Harry James*

Dorothy Claire...*began her career with Bobby Byrne and later sang with Glenn Miller and Bob Crosby. A vivacious singer, popular with young or older crowds, she was ranked 9th by college students in the Billboard poll of 1941.*

June Christy...*started with Stan Kenton, recorded one of the early successes with Kenton entitled "Tampico," became Mrs. Bob Cooper (Kenton tenor sax player) and continued solo the rest of her career*

Clooney sisters, Betty and Rosemary...*both started as teenagers with WLW radio, Cincinnati, OH, singing 7 days a week for $20 each. Bandleader Barney Rapp heard them and recommended them to singer/saxophonist Tony Pastor's agent when the Pastor band did a one nighter in the river city. The Clooneys spent the next three years with the Pastor band. Rosemary continued her career as a singer and actress*

Dorothy Collins...*started singing first with bandleader Raymond Scott on the Lucky Strike Hit Parade Program and became Mrs. Scott*

Doris Day...*got her start in Cincinnati, OH with bandleader Barney Rapp who helped her change her name. She also sang for Bob Crosby before becoming a sensation with Les Brown in the early and mid-1940s where she recorded number one hits like the million seller "Sentimental Journey," "My Dreams Are Getting Better All the Time," and other top songs such as "Till the End of Time," "When the Music Plays On," "The Whole World Is Singing My Song," "Tain't Me," "You Won't Be Satisfied Until You Break My Heart," "Day By Day," "I've Got the Sun in the Morning" and "Soon Or Later." Her first song with the Brown band at 18, was "When the Music Plays On," recorded Nov. 28, 1940.*

Patti Dugan...*started with Johnny Long in 1943, continued with Gene Williams and later sang with the short term Claude Thornhill orchestra*

Dale Evans...*Roy Rogers sidekick later in life and in the movies actually started as a big band singer with Anson Weeks' popular band*

Helen Forrest...*began a singing career with Benny Goodman and then joined the Harry James' band for more money and gave Peggy Lee the chance to take her place. Helen later sang for the Artie Shaw band before doing singles*

Connie Francis...*started her career with Tommy Dorsey before doing solo work*

Ruth Gaylor...*joined Hal McIntyre and continued her career with Teddy Powell, the Hudson-DeLange band before ending with Bunny Berigan*

Jo Ann Greer...*who is perhaps best known for her singing with the Les Brown band, actually dubbed her voice for Rita Hayworth in the movie "Pal Joey." She started her career with Ray Anthony*

Connie Haines...*started with Harry James and later joined the Tommy Dorsey band before going solo*

Rita Hayworth...*her voice wasn't used in the movie Pal Joey but Rita actually started her career as a big band singer with Xavier Cugat before she became a movie actress*

Billie Holiday...*while best known for any number of singles and several movies, Billie's career with the big bands started with Count Basie, and followed on tour with Paul Whiteman, Artie Shaw and Benny Carter*

Lena Horne...*although best known for her movies and production numbers, Lena started singing with Noble Sissle and, in 1941, joined the Charley Barnet band*

Marion Hutton...*a bouncy, bubbly singer, she started her career with the sedate society band leader Vincent Lopez. She joined the popular Glenn Miller before he became Captain Miller in the Army Air Force*

Kitty Kallen...*she later became a popular TV panel show member but she started her singing career with trombonist Jack Teagarden and went on to such bands as Artie Shaw, Harry James and Jimmy Dorsey*

Paula Kelly...*while she was best known with the Glenn Miller singing group, the Modernaires, she started her career with Al Donahue before joining Miller. She later sang with Artie Shaw*

Louise, Alyce & Yvonne King...*the singing sisters started their careers together with Alvino Rey. First heard with Horace Heidt in 1937. Yvonne was best known for singing the melancholy "Nighty Night" closing number with Rey.*

Peggy Lee...*the North Dakota sultry voiced teenager was hurriedly discovered by Benny Goodman when he lost Helen Forrest. She sang with Goodman and rose quickly as a talented composer, lyricist, solo singer and actress*

Scottee Marsh...*a veteran band singer who started with Orrin Tucker and later sang and toured with Bobby Byrne, Tommy Dorsey, Shep Fields and Ralph Flanagan*

Mary Ann McCall...*she was best known for the first band she sang with, Woody Herman. She later toured and sang with Charley Barnet and Teddy Powell*

Ella Mae Morse...*Another singer who was successful with the first band she sang with, Freddy Slack. She later sang with Jimmy Dorsey*

Helen O'Connell...*very successful with her first band, Jimmy Dorsey. Later sang with Larry Funk before she began soloing*

Anita O'Day...*a talented singer with off-stage problems who was at home doing scat numbers with Roy Eldridge on the Gene Krupa Band. Later took her husky voice to Stan Kenton and Woody Herman*

Delores "Dodie" O'Neill...*started with Jack Teagarden and did tours with Bob Chester, Artie Shaw, Gene Krupa and finally, Bunny Berigan*

Lucy Ann Polk...*she started with Kay Kyser and his College of Musical Knowledge and later toured with Les Brown and Tommy Dorsey*

Ginnie Powell...*later known for her movie acting, started her career as a singer with the progressive big band of Boyd Raeburn*

Dinah Shore...*movie & tv actress and hostess, Dinah had a string of big band tours prior to her acting career. She was first with Ben Bernie, Dick Stabile and Leo Reisman and later she sang with Peter Dean, Beasley Smith and, like Rita Hayworth, she worked with the Xavier Cugat band*

Ginny Sims...*a popular singer of the day, Ginny was discovered by Tom Gerun and then spent most of her singing career with Kay Kyser*

Keely Smith...*discovered by bandleader Louis Prima, she stayed with Prima through her career although she did make some singles*

Kay Starr...*started with Charley Barnet and Joe Venuti and then went on to Glenn Miller but became a single after the Miller civilian band broke up*

Martha Tilton...*Lilting Martha was first with Benny Goodman and followed that tour with appearances with Jimmy Dorsey and Artie Shaw*

Louise Tobin...*another singer who started with Goodman, Louise also sang with Bobby Hackett and Will Bradley and later, joined Harry James and became the first Mrs. James.*

Sarah Vaughn...*while most casual music lovers remember Sarah as a soloist, she started with saxophonist Georgie Auld and later toured with Earl Hines and Billy Eckstine*

Helen Ward...*another veteran singer, Helen started with Enric Madriquera and then moved to saxophonists Hal McIntyre and Freddy Martin before joining drummer Gene Krupa. She finished her career with Harry James, Benny Goodman and Bob Crosby which demonstrated she liked singing for bandleaders who played woodwinds*

Fran Warren...*a good band singer who started with the sweet orchestra of Art Mooney, joined the progressive sounds of Claude Thornhill and finished with the hard-driving band of Charley Barnet*

Margaret Whiting...*another talented singer, discovered by bandleader Billie Butterfield, who introduced the band's top hit "Moonlight in Vermont." Went on to success as a soloist.*

Kay Weber...*although not well known, Kay sang with great bands like Jimmy Dorsey, the Dorsey Brothers band and finally, Bob Crosby*

Sister Rosetta Tharpe, *"girl" singer with Lucky Millinder big band from the 1930s which featured trumpeters Dizzy Gillespie and Charley Shavers and saxophonist Bullmoose Jackson*

Lily Ann Carol...*Trumpeter Louie Prima's first vocalist in the 1940s.*

Perri Mitchell,...*Buddy Moreno's "girl" singer when the band was broadcasting from the Casa Loma Ballroom in St. Louis in 1947*

Liza Morrow...*sang with the popular George Paxton Band of 1944 to 1949*

Mitzie Cottle...*Bob Dana of the New York World-Telegram called her the "Most refreshing band singer I believe I've ever seen" when he heard her with Benny Goodman at the Waldorf-Astoria's Empire Room in 1956*

Kay Carlton...*sang with Henry Jerome band popular in the Northeast, hotels, cruise lines*

Lynn Roberts, *joined clarinetist/arranger Jerry Jerome who did gigs in New York in between working with other major bands*

Dinah Washington...*started her singing career in the big bands with Lionel Hampton in the 1940s.*

Leah Ray...*didn't get to sing the popular "That's What I Like About the South" but was Phil Harris's first female singer when the group was in Hollywood and comedian Jack Benny's radio house band*

Nancy Read...*got her start in the majors with the Skitch Henderson Band which lasted about a year in 1948-49. In the 1950s, sang and recorded two or three numbers with the Benny Goodman band*

Betty Benson, Gloria King, Yvonne Walker, Lorraine Benson...*all sang with the popular Ray Herbeck band in the 1930s and 1940s*

Lois Costello...*sang with the Will Back band, later married bandleader Don Glasser and took over the band for a period of time when Don suffered a stroke*

Ruth Lee*...singer who introduced the popular song "Imagine" with the Earl Burnett Band at the Drake Hotel in Chicago*

Frances Hunt*...sang with Lou Bring later joined Benny Goodman and returned to the Bring band, a society group, and became Lou's wife.*

Dolly Houston*...sang with Woody Herman's 3rd Herd in 1951 handling such numbers of "Lonesome Gal" and the "The Boy Next Door"*

Betty Bonney...*Sang with the Les Brown band in the early days and recorded "Joltin' Joe DiMaggio" in August, 1941, which was the band's first hit and was number 12 on the charts*

Peggy Mann*...sang with a number of big band leaders including Ben Pollack, Benny Goodman, Teddy Powell, Gene Krupa, Larry Clinton and Enoch Light*

Eydie Gorme*...whose real name was Edith Gomezano sang with Tommy Tucker and the Tex Beneke Bands before joining husband Steve Lawrence as a duo.*

Julie London*...got her start very young with Matty Malneck in the late 1940s before becoming an actress. She recorded 40 albums as a single*

Georgia Gibbs*...she sang with Hudson-DeLange and Richard Himber bands as Fredda Lipson and then changed her name to Fredda Gibson with Artie Shaw and his Band. As a soloist, she became Georgia Gibbs.*

Ann Richards*...started with the Charley Barnet and George Redman bands and joined Stan Kenton in 1955. She was named Downbeat's best band vocalist and Mrs. Stan Kenton the same year.*

Chris Connor...spent 8 years playing clarinet prior to thinking about a big band music career as a singer and was recommended to Stan Kenton by popular Kenton vocalist, June Christy.

Lillie 'Lil' Greenword*...got her first major break singing with Duke Ellington in 1958.*

Una Mae Carlisle*...Like Rosemary and Betty Clooney, began singing on Cincinnati, OH radio and was heard by a traveling Fats Waller. She sang a style close to Fats' piano playing. Joined the Waller band, made famous the hit "I Can't Give You Anything But Love." Later sang with Benny Carter, Lester Young, John Kirby, Bob Chester, Don Redman. Recorded another hit "Walking By the River." Returned to Ohio where she died two years later at 41.*

Ann Shelton*...sang with Bert Ambrose and Glenn Miller during World War II years, toured the fronts in the European sector*

Bea Wain*...a talented singer whose claim to fame was singing and recording Larry Clinton's "The Dipsy Doodle" which was named after New York Giant pitcher Carl Hubbell's "Dipsy Doodle" pitch. Bea was named the most popular vocalist in 1939*

Jo Stafford*...sang with the Tommy Dorsey band, 1940-1943. and spent the remainder of her career singing production numbers as a soloist. Married arranger/composer Paul Weston.*

Grace Barrie*...big band singer with Abe Lyman and Dick Stabile who she later married.*

Betty Roche...*replaced Ivie Anderson with the Duke Ellington Band in 1943 and sang the very popular "Take the A Train" in the film "Reveille with Beverly" but didn't record it with the band until years later. Rejoined Ellington in 1952 for a short stay. She died at 81 in 2000.*

Linda Romay*...whose real name was Rosa Mario Almirall had to have the record number of big band stage names. A total of 6 ranging from Candy Coster to Lulu Laverne. Sang with Xavier Cugat band.*

Irene Kral...*was considered one of the best ballad singers of the big band period. Sang first with the Jay Burkhardt band and then freelanced in Chicago area before Maynard Ferguson heard her and signed her. She stayed with the Ferguson band and later joined the Herb Pomeroy band. Sadly, she died young at 46.*

Dorothy Lamour*...Her "road" movies with Bing Crosby and Bob Hope came later but Dottie Lamour started as a singer with Herbie Kay's orchestra in 1936*

Betty Grable*...There's no research to claim she sang with her husband Harry James' band but in 1933 she did sing with Ted FioRito's orchestra.*

Eileen Wilson...*sang with the popular Will Osborne and Les Brown bands in the early days and then joined Lucky Strike's TV Your Hit Parade program*

Betty Brownell...*spent her years as a big band singer with Henry "Hot Lips" Busse's band.*

Irene Day...*During the 1940s, Irene was the singer with trumpet player Charley Spivak and his band*

Edythe Wright...*Joined some of the best female vocalists like Anita Boyer, Connie Francis and Connie Haines with the Tommy Dorsey Band but had the distinction of being the first female singer with the group.*

Harold Arlen...*he was best known for his many hit songs but he got his first singing experience as "The Crooning Composer" with Leo Reisman*

Fred Astaire...*he not only was a tremendously talented dancer and later movie actor, Fred like so many others started as a singer with Leo Reisman*

Harry Babbitt...*Started and finished his singing career with Kay Kyser*

Tex Beneke...*was a tenor saxophonist who Glenn Miller heard singing to himself to stay awake while driving to a gig. Spent his career singing and playing sax with the Miller band and later his own*

Merwyn Bogue "Ishkabibble"...*became the popular comic vocalist with Kay Kyser band*

Art Carney...*better known for his role in the "Honeymooners" on TV and a number of movies, Art got his start in the business as a singer with talent finder Horace Heidt*

Perry Como...*he became a TV institution at the holidays but he got his start after barbering with the Ted Weems band*

Don Cornell...*a popular singer with the Sammy Kaye band*

Bing Crosby...*his fame came later but his beginning was thanks to the Gus Arnheim band and later Paul Whiteman*

Bob Crosby...*while he later was a popular bandleader, he was first a singer with the Dorsey Brothers band*

Vic Damone...*became a popular soloist but he started his career with Dean Hudson and his Orchestra*

Dennis Day...*well known for his radio and tv work with Jack Benny, Dennis began his singing career with Claude Thornhill's big US Navy band during World War II*

Johnny Desmond...*started with Gene Krupa and later joined Bob Crosby but his later success came from his vocals with the Glenn Miller AAF band during World War II*

Ray Eberle...*started with Gene Krupa and later worked with Glenn Miller*

Bob Eberly...*began his career with the Dorsey Brothers and later became popular as a singing duo with Helen O'Connell on the Jimmy Dorsey band*

Billy Eckstine...*joined Earl "Fatha" Hines first and then sang with his own band*

Skinnay Ennis...*launched career with Hal Kemp and became well known with his own band*

Russ Columbo...*a crooner with popularity that swept the country. Hs life ended in an accidental shooting at age 26. He sang with the Gus Arnheim band in 1928 and recorded his last songs two days before his death. Ironically, his mother was critically ill during his rise to fame and rather than break the news to her, Columbo's father wrote letters in Russ's name to his mother for 10 years. She never knew of his death.*

Kenny Gardner...*what new year's eve was ever the same after Guy Lombardo's career singer was no longer helping to usher in the year?*

Buddy Greco...*started singing career with Benny Goodman and played piano, too*

Dick Haymes...*started with Carl Hoff, jumped to Harry James, Benny Goodman and later Tommy Dorsey and a career of his own*

Woody Herman...*he was certainly best known as the clarinetist who the led the band that played the blues but he started an off and on singing career with Isham Jones. He would later take over the Jones band and begin putting together his first herd*

Eddie Howard...*a popular singer who later led his own band started with Dick Jurgens*

Red Ingle...*his singing always was involved with laughs and later with comedian Spike Jones and a band called "The City Slickers." Red actually started with Ted Weems*

"Snooky" Roy Lansen...*was remembered for his work with the Hit Parade but actually started with Ray Noble*

Carmen Lombardo...*what better place to start than with your brother Guy's band, It was a career move*

Gordon MCRae...*another popular singer who got his start with Horace Heidt*

Tony Martin...*started with Tom Gerun (then known as Al Morris in the sax section) and then joined Anson Weeks Band before soloing*

Johnny Mercer...*a talented singer, songwriter and music exec who sang with Ray Anthony, Paul Whiteman and Freddy Slack and wrote more than 200 songs as well as give the recording industry the very popular and progressive Capitol label*

Russ Morgan...*a bandleader who also sang and started with Bob Causer*

Tony Pastor...*while he gave the Clooney sisters a chance to start with his own band, his chance came with the Artie Shaw band.*

Jimmy Rushing...*considered a talent as a singer, Jimmy started with Benny Moten before he joined Count Basie and recorded*

Andy Russell...*another band singer who went on to fame as a soloist, Andy's start was with the Alvino Rey band*

Frank Sinatra...*he was an overnight success as soon as he roomed with a Harry James' trumpet player Jack Palmer and, later, Tommy Dorsey's flamboyant drummer Buddy Rich. He actually got his big start and a $50 raise when he replaced Allen DeWitt after Dorsey lost name singer Jack Leonard.*

Mel Torme...*was not only a popular singer and part-time drummer but a song writer, too. He was already on his way when he left his first and last band gig with Artie Shaw*

Harry Von Zell...*better known as a studio announcer and one of the big band remote introducers, Von Zell was first a singer with the swinging big band of Charley Barnet*

Joe Williams...*a singer with a good deep, rich voice, Joe started with the "Hey Bob-a-re-bop" band of Lionel Hampton, did a tour with Benny Moten and then became popular with the Count Basie band*

Jimmy Castle...*singer with the Dick Jurgens band during the 1940s.*

Mortin Downy...*one of the first male singers to be featured with a touring big band. He sang with the Paul Whiteman Band.*

Stan Vann...*another popular singer who sang and traveled with the Dick Jurgens Band during the 1940s*

Alan Dale...*George Paxton's male vocalist during the mid-1940s.*

Chick Bullock...*a bandleader and vocalist who became best known through his records and radio work. He was an in-house singer with the American Record Corporation and considered one of the best known singers of the 1930s. His voice was considered the most recorded male singer of the 1930s.*

Ray McKinley...*Glenn Miller's popular AAF band drummer during the war years who returned to work with trombonist Will Bradley as a drummer/singer. Later started his own band*

Russ Carlyle...*started with Blue Barron and organized his own band in later years*

Tommy Mercer...*Blue Barron's singer who led the band when Blue Barron was drafted. The band was best remembered for its hit "Cruisin' Down the River" which led the record charts for 7 weeks.*

Johnny Mercer...*composer of some of America's most whistled and sung songs of the 1930s, 1940s and 1950s like Blues In the Night, Lazy Bones, That Old Black Magic, Moon River and others, he also co-founded the pioneering record company Capitol and gave artists like Stan Kenton, Nat*

"King" Cole and the Four Freshmen their start. He sang with Paul Whiteman, the Dorsey Brothers and Benny Goodman. Died at 67 in 1976.

Henry "Butch" Stone...*He started with Larry Clinton but really spent most of his career as a saxophone player and comedy singer with the Les Brown band. One of his top hits was "Doctor, Lawyer, Indian Chief," number six on the charts in 1946. Joined the famous USO tours with Les, Bob Hope and many Hollywood celebrities from the 1940s to the 1990s*

Ralph Young...*He sang with the Les Brown band in the early 1940s and recorded the second national hit for the band "'Tis Autumn" Sept. 17, 1941.*

Jack Haskel...*Sang with the Les Brown band and recorded a number 11 hit called "I Guess I'll Get the Papers and Go Home," June, 1946. Later became a network program announcer.*

Ziggy Talent*...did the comedy songs while singing with the Vaughn Monroe Band in the 1940s.*

Herb Jeffries*...was one of Duke Ellington's early male vocalists and went on to a career as a single*

Merve Griffin*...a self-made multi millionaire because of his timing, talent and enterprise, Merve got his start before his career in television and land development with Freddie Martin and never forgot the leader or his band*

Stuart Wade*...another Freddie Martin big band singer*

Harry Prime*...spent a number of years with the Ralph Flanagan Band as a singer*

Tommy Mercer*...male singer with Ray Anthony*

(For more listings check out the Big Band Data Base www.nfo.net for the most complete listings and click on singers)

Band Leaders, Musicians, Singers' Day Jobs

Everyone, including my businessman father, had reservations about sons, daughters, nieces, nephews or any relative embarking on a "career" as a jazz or swing musician. "What in the world will you live on?" my father asked in exasperation. And few in the music business from the early 1900s to the present would disagree. I came away from a conversation with a young Stan Kenton in the late 1940s somewhat disappointed. "I want to be jazz musician and tour," I confided in him at Buckeye Lake as we unloaded his touring Greyhound. He studied my face for a full minute, smiled and said without enthusiasm "That's nice."

What do popular musicians, band leaders and singers do when they have no steady gig?

I examined a number of references, biographies and reviewed band tapes and videotapes to prepare the following partial list of part-time or full-time occupations of leaders, sidemen and singers.

Julian "Cannonball" Adderly, alto sax, composer,
High school band director

Alfred "Chico" Alvarez, trumpet player with a number of major bands such as Stan Kenton, others,
Music store owner in California

Albert Ammons, pianist,
Taxi cab driver, Chicago

Mildred Bailey, singer,
Song demonstrator

Dave Barbour, guitarist,
Actor, appeared in "Secret Fury," 1951

Ray Bauduc, drummer, leader,
Tap dancer

Billy Bauer, guitarist, big bands
Guitar school owner, author

Tony Bennett, singer
Singing waiter at 17

Milt Bernhart, trombonist, big bands
Managed a travel agency, big band promoter

Johnny Best, trumpet player, big bands
Owner, avocado orchard, CA

Barney Bigard, clarinet, saxophones, big bands
Photoengraver

Nick Brignola, saxophones, big bands
Taught jazz history at SUNY

Sonny Burke, trumpet, leader
Department store worker

Bobby Byrne, trombonist, leader
Record company producer, pilot

Buck Clayton, trumpet, arranger
Insurance agent

Ray Conniff, trombonist, leader
Highway road worker

Jack Constanzo, bongos, conga drums, big bands
Taught dancing at Beverly Hills hotel

Vinnie Dean, alto saxophone
Operated recording studio, licensed booker

Joe Dodge, drummer, Brubeck, combos
Bank clerk

Duke Ellington, pianist, leader
Sign painter

Glen Gray, band leader,
Cashier, Santa Fe Railroad

Urbie Green, trombonist, leader
Cattle farmer

Lenny Hambro, alto saxophonist, leader, big bands
Jingle producer

Bill Harris, trombonist, big bands
DJ, Miami, FL

Jon Hendricks, vocalist, songwriter
Office clerk

Milton "Judge" Hinton, bassist, big bands

Photographer

Art Hodes, pianist, big bands,
Writer, teacher

Bill Holman, tenor saxophonist, leader
Engineering

PeeWee Hunt, clarinetist, leader
Radio *DJ, Hollywood, CA*

Chubby Jackson, bassist, leader
Host, children's TV shows

Al Jarreau, vocalist
Counselor, Rehab Division, CA

J J Johnson, trombonist, leader
Blueprint inspector

Quincy Jones, trumpet, composer
A&R executive

Thomas "Red" Kelly, bassist, big bands
Restaurant owner, manager

Stan Levey, drummer, big bands
Photographer/Professional boxer

Chuck Mangione, flugelhorn, trumpet, leader
School teacher

Meade Lux Lewis, boogie woogie pianist,
Cab driver, car washer

Les McCann, keyboard, piano, arranger
Watercolorist, photographer

Susannah McCorkle, vocalist
Fiction writer

Jimmy McGriff, organist
Police officer

Lucky Millinder, leader,
Liquor salesman

Herbert and Don Mills of the Mills Brothers, vocalists,
Herbert apprentice barber; Don a shoeshine person

Charley Mingus, bassist, leader
Postal worker

Dudley Moore, pianist, leader, trio
Actor

Bill Perkins, saxophonist, big bands
Engineer, inventor

Flip Phillips, tenor saxophonist, big bands
Condo manager

Ben Pollack, drummer, leader
Restaurant owner

Boyd Raeburn, saxophone, leader
Tropical furniture business

Red Rodney, trumpet, leader
Booking agent

Bud Shank, alto saxophone, leader
TV producer, jingles

Frankie Trumbauer,
Pilot

Paul Whiteman, leader,
Farmer

Kai Winding, trombone, leader,
NYC Playboy Club music director

Pete Fountain, clarinet, leader
Pest Control Agent

Al Hirt, trumpet, leader
Pest Control Agent

Slim Gaillard, guitar, vocals
Motel Manager

Woody Herman, clarinet, leader
Sales Clerk

Anita O'Day, big band singer
Walkathon Marathon Dancer

Larry Clinton, bandleader
Pilot

Dick Jurgens, bandleader
Electronics, real estate

Buddy Rich, drums/bandleader
Dancer, actor, singer

Merv Griffin, band vocalist/TV host
Actor, Entertainment Entrepreneur

Bob Chester, Bandleader
Business executive

Bill Clifford, Bandleader
GM, radio station

Buddy Moreno, Bandleader
Radio DJ

Vaughn Monroe, Singer, Bandleader
Restaurant owner, model railroad enthusiast

Benny Strong, Bandleader
Radio station manager

Andy Kirk, Bandleader
Real estate Sales

Smith Bellow, Singer, Bandleader
Manager, missile division, Aircraft Co.

Sidney Bechtel, Clarinetist, Bandleader
Tailor

Johnny Bothwell, Bandleader
Salesman, GE

Enoch Light, Bandleader

Professor, CEO

Johnny Long, Violinist, Bandleader
English Teacher

Lyle "Skitch" Henderson, Pianist/Bandleader
Pilot/Art Gallery Owner

Billy Bishop, Bandleader
Stockbroker

Lou Levy, Piano/Bandleader
Medical Journal Publishing

Woody Allen, Clarinetist
Comedian, Actor

Xavier Cugat, Bandleader
Cartoonist

Charlie Ventura, tenor saxophonist
Hat factory worker

Sammy Kaye, bandleader
Civil Engineer

The Great Ballrooms of the Swing Era

Thanks to the National Ballroom & Entertainment Association (NBEA), there is a list of the country's top ballrooms from the swing era. Says the NBEA in its web site Archives section:

"Although ballrooms have long been associated with the Big Bands, it was the Jazz Age where many of them got their start. The '30s and '40s were undoubtedly the highpoint of the ballroom era, and ironically, it was the end of World War II that also saw the downswing in the number of ballrooms across the United States. Many ballrooms remained quite prominent through the '50s and into the '60s. But by the later '60s, changing times began to take a heavy toll on these popular dance locales. Ballrooms could be elegant or plain. They could be in the biggest cities or in the smallest rural area of the country. But they all shared a common denominator of music and dancing. For many decades the ballroom was the dominate place for social gatherings."

For more information go to the NBEA web site: www.nbea.com

California

Rendezvous Ballroom, Balboa; **Chateau Ballroom,** Los Angeles; **Ali Babi Ballroom,** Oakland; **Casino Gardens,** Ocean Park; **Mission Beach Dance Casino, Pacific Square,** San Diego; **Balconades/Wolohans, The Pergola, Shalimar, Trianon/Primalon Ballroom, Avalon Ballroom, Palamara Ballroom, El Patio,** San Francisco; **Aragon Ballroom,**
Santa Monica; **Palladium,** Hollywood;

Colorado

Elitch Gardens, Rainbow, El Patio, Trocadero Ballroom, Lakeside Amusement Park, Denver

Connecticut

Pleasure Beach Amusement Park, Ritz Ballroom, Bridgeport

Florida

Flagler Gardens Ballroom, Miami

Georgia

Tybrisa Ballroom, Tybee Island

Idaho

Miramar Ballroom, Boise

Illinois

Trianon Ballroom, Embassy Ballroom, Holiday Ballroom, Savoy Ballroom, Melody Mill, Lion's Ballroom, Paladium, Edgewater, Green Mill, Aragon, Vogue, Milford, The Blackhawk Ballroom, Pison Park Ballroom, Shutters Brothers Ballroom, Majestic Ballroom, Boulevard Ballroom, Paradise Ballroom, Boston Club Ballroom, Allegro Ballroom, Chicago; **Blue Moon**

Ballroom, Aurora; **Arcade Roof Gardens, Macomb-Roof Gardens,** Galesburg; **Melody Mill,** North Riverside; **Ingleterra Ballroom,** Peoria; **Pioneer Gardens,** Joliet

Indiana

Indiana Oasis, Michigan City;**Palais Royale Ballroom,** South Bend; **Madura's Danceland,** Whiting; **Midway Ballroom,**Cedar Lake; **Indiana Beach Ballroom**, Monticello; **Edens Ballroom,** Westchester; **Crystal Ballroom,** Bass Lake

Iowa

Warehouse, Carter Lake; **Danceland,** Cedar Rapids; **Modernistic Ballroom, German Hall, Shad Oak,** Clinton; **Aronda,** Creston; **Tromar Ballroom, Riviera Ballroom,** Des Moines;
Melody Mill, Dubuque; **Gala Ballroom,** Independence; **Riviera Ballroom,** Janesville; **Armar Ballroom,** Marion; **Coliseum Ballroom,** Oelwein; **Praire Moon,** Praireburg; **Rigadoon, Tomba, Skylon,** Sioux City; **Arnold's Park,** Spirit Lake; **Cobblestone Ballroom,** Storm Lake; **Rainbow Gardens,** Waterville

Kansas

Ritz Ballroom, Trig Ballroom, New Moon Ballroom, Wichita

Kentucky

Trocadero, Henderson; **Madrid Ballroom,** Louisville

Maryland

Famous Ballroom, Alcazar Ballroom, Baltimore

Massachusetts

The Totem Pole, Auburndale; **Butterfly Ballroom,** Springfield; **Nuttings-On-The-Charles,** Waltham; **Raynor Ballroom, Roseland State Ballroom,** Boston

Michigan

Crystal Palace Ballroom, Coloma; **Graystone Ballroom, Arcadia, Aragon, Campus, Eastwood Garden, Grand Terrace, New Danceland, Castle, Vanity Ballroom,Crystal Ballroom, Paw Paw Ballroom,** Detroit; **Manitov Beach Ballroom,** Manitov Beach;
Big Pavilion, Saugatuck; **Shadowland Pavilion,** St. Joseph; **Walled Lake Casino,** Walled Lake

Minnesota

Terp Ballroom, Austin; **Marigold Ballroom,** Minneapolis; **the Prom,** St. Paul; **the Coliseum,** Worthington

Missouri

El Torreon Ballroom, LaFiesta Ballroom, Pla Mor Ballroom, Kansas City; **Tunetown,** St. Louis

Nebraska

Owl's Roost, Arcadia; **State Ballroom,** Bee; **Turnpike Ballroom,** Lincoln; **Kings Ballroom,** Norfolk; **Royal Terrace Ballroom,** Omaha; **Oscar's Palladium,** Sargent; **Mr. Tunes,** Sioux City;**Froghop Ballroom,** St. Joseph; **Casa Loma Ballroom,**St. Louis

New Hampshire

The Arcadia, Manchester

New Jersey

Sunset Beach Ballroom, Almonesson; **Marine Ballroom, Steel Pier,** Atlantic City; **Convention Hall Ballroom,** Cape May; **Frank Dailey's Meadowbrook,** Cedar Grove; **Oaklyn Dance Ballroom,** Oaklyn; **Garden Pier Ballroom,** Ocean City; **Ivystone Ballroom,** Pennsauken; **Starlite Ballroom,**Wildwood

New York

Dellwood Ballroom, Crystal Ballroom, Buffalo; **George F. Johnson Pavilion,** Johnson City; **Stardust, Savoy Ballroom,** Harlem; **Fiesta Danceteria, Rialto Theater, Cinderella Ballroom,** New York City; **Greystone Ballroom,** Utica; **Russell's Danceland,** Sylvan Beach; **Canadaraga Park Pavillion,** Richfield Springs

Nevada

El Patio Ballroom, Reno;

Ohio

Moonlight Gardens, Canton; **Castle Farm, Moonlight Garden,** Cincinnati; **Aragon Ballroom, Trianon Ballroom, Euclid Beach Ballroom, Puritas Springs Amusement Park Ballroom, Chipawa Ballroom, Circle Ballroom, Trianon Ballroom,** Cleveland; **Columbia Ballroom,** Columbia Station; **Maples Ballroom,** Rootstown; **Cedar Point Amusement Park,** Sandusky; **Trianon Ballroom,** Toledo; **Pier and Crystal Ballrooms,** Buckeye Lake**; Valley Dale,** Columbus; **Idora Park, Elms Ballroom,** Youngstown; **Continental Gardens,** Akron; **Banater Hall,** Lorain; **Homestead Ballroom,** Lakewood

Oklahoma

White Way Ballroom, Maud; **Gibson's Ballroom,** Muskogee; **the Hippodrome, Oakmulge; the Bluebird,** Shawnee; **Cain's Ballroom,** Tulsa

Oregon

Crystal Gardens Ballroom, Salem;

Pennsylvania

Castle Rock Ballroom, Allentown; **Sunset Pavilion,** Carrolltown; **Starlight Ballroom,** Hershey; **Danceland Westview Park, Lakewood Pavilion,** Mahanoy City; **Brookline on the Boulevard, Wagner Hall Ballroom, Oakes Ballroom, Trianon Ballroom, Elite Ballroom,The Met Ballroom, Garden Ballroom, Raburn Plaza,** Philadelphia; **Aragon, Savoy, Cottage Inn, Bill Green's Casino, The Jitterbug Savoy Grotto, Garden Plantation, Syrian Mosque,** Pittsburgh; **Sommerton Springs Ballroom,** Sommerton; **Covered Wagon Ballroom,** Upper Darby; **Willowgrove Park Ballroom,** Willowgrove; **Valencia Ballroom,** York; **Bach Dance Auditorium,** Lancaster

Rhode Island

Arcadia Ballroom, Providence

Tennessee

Casino Ballroom, Memphis

Texas

Roaring 20's, San Antonio; **Pleasure Pier,** Galveston; **Rice Hotel,** Houston

Utah

Saltaire Amusement Park, Terrace Ballroom, Salt Lake City

Virginia

Tantilla Ballroom, Richmond; **Seaside Park,** Virginia Beach

Washington

Spanish Castle, Seattle/Tacoma; **Trianon Ballroom,** Seattle; **Natatorium Ballroom,** Spokane; **Century Ballroom,** Tacoma

Wisconsin

Cinderella Ballroom, Appleton; **Wisconsin Roof Ballroom,** Milwaukee; **Dutch Mill,** Lake Delaven; **Riviera Ballroom,** Lake Geneva

Hotels, Night Clubs, Cocktail Lounges, Roadhouses Where Big Bands Played

They could be the steady paychecks for bandleaders and bookers during the Big Band Era. They were the hotels, nightclubs, roadhouses, restaurants and lounges where space was so limited trombonists had to worry about their slides and drummers, bassists and piano players had to sit off the bandstand...if there was a platform. Space at a club was similar to the square footage of a NASA space capsule. At a club I once played, I spent the entire evening stooped because the ceiling was inches above my head and I was sitting on a drummer's throne! I watched Maynard Ferguson and his band in a club a couple of decades later where the trumpet players had to solo by leaving the platform over and over because of a low ceiling.

They were the one nighters, weekend gigs and, sometimes, whole summers and long term engagements that lasted years. Whether you were in a territorial band or a touring major aggregation, hotels, night clubs, cocktail lounges, roadhouses and some restaurants along with selected theaters not only kept bands working they also provided creative ways for leaders to market their music, meet customers and build reputations. In Kansas City, Count Basie and his piano were virtually sitting next to people at tables. In fact, the legend was that the Count's one fingered plinking and plunking came because he had to remain sociable while playing and he couldn't chord and talk.

Some bands never had such opportunities. A few leaders wanted to have a home life, steady local gigs and recording dates. Others limited engagements as it became more difficult to travel especially during the war years. Still a number traveled all the time; bands like Woody Herman, Ray Anthony, Stan Kenton and others had extensive road tours that included clubs and hotels.

Ballrooms, of course, were primarily for dancing and bandleaders had to have extensive chart libraries to meet such three to four hour engagements. It was different at clubs. Most lounge or club dates had to offer singers, acts and, sometimes, arrangements that met the needs of a remote broadcast from the club, hotel or restaurant. Such engagements, I remember, were also more difficult for those of us who played by ear because we frequently backed the acts, the singers and, in one instance I remember, a burlesque performer with charts and arrangements.

Listen to Willie Schwartz, saxophone/clarinet player with Miller, talking about the road tours, interspersed with the 15 minute Chesterfield radio shows, when he was on the band:

"You didn't know what day it was when you toured on one nighters. We enjoyed the radio shows though because they were added income...two or three times a week. We did them wherever we happened to be. For example, if we were in Washington DC we'd do them in the Wardman-Park Hotel. That was nice. If we were in a little town in Iowa or Virginia where there was no facility for us we'd do the show in a school auditorium or something. I even remember once we did the show in a railroad boxcar because there was no place to set up.

"We couldn't do the whole number on a show because we only had 15 minute programs so Glenn would take something from a number of our songs. We did as much music as we could. That's how Glenn came up with those medleys that were so famous; 'something old, something new, something borrowed and something blue.'"

What were some of the famous locations on many booking schedules during the 1940s and 1950s?

Here's a sample from early 1950s' Downbeat magazines:

<u>Hotels</u>

Grill Room, Roosevelt Hotel, Madhattan Room, Café Rouge, Pennsylvania Hotel, Terrace Room, New Yorker Hotel, Empire Room, Waldorf Astoria, Biltmore Hotel, Commodore Hotel, Edison Hotel, Plaza Hotel, Pierre Hotel, Piccadilly Hotel, Henry Hudson Hotel, Lexington

Hotel,Hotel Taft, St. Regis Hotel, New York City, NY;**Congress Hotel, Panther Room, Sherman Hotel, Conrad Hilton Hotel, Drake Hotel, Palmer**

House, Congress Hotel, Edgewater Beach Hotel, Chicago;**Lord Baltimore Hotel,** Baltimore; **Statler Hotel,** Buffalo; **Statler Hotel,** Dallas; **Statler Hotel,**Washington, DC;

Stallman Hotel,Spokane, WA; **Commodore Perry Hotel,** Toledo; **Radison Hotel,** Minneapolis; **Ambassador Hotel, Beverly Wilshire Hotel,** Los Angeles; **Muehlebach Hotel,** Kansas City; **Roosevelt Hotel,** New Orleans; **St. Anthony Hotel,** San Antonio, TX; **Adolphus Hotel,** Dallas;**DeSoto Hotel,** Savannah, GA; **Ivanhoe Hotel,** Miami Beach; **Syracuse Hotel,**Syracuse, NY; **Deshler Wallick Hotel,** Columbus, OH; **Hoffman Beach House,** Point

Pleasant, NJ; **Mapes Hotel, Riverside Hotel,** Reno, Nevada;**William Penn Hotel,** Pittsburgh; **Netherlands-Plaza Hotel,** Cincinnati, OH; **MiraMar Hotel,** Santa Monica, CA; **Palace Hotel,** San Francisco, CA; **Roseland State Ballroom,** Boston; **Rice Hotel,** Houston; **New Kenmore Hotel,** Albany, NY

Night Clubs, Cocktail Lounges, Roadhouses

Apache, Dayton,OH; **Charlie Johnson's,**Wildwood, NJ; **Baker's Keyboard,Roosevelt, Flame,** Detroit; **Rose Bowl,** Fremont, OH; **Rouge,** River Rouge, MI; **Tutz,** Milwaukee, WI;

Casino Royal, Washington, DC; **Backstage,** Pheonix, AZ; **Ankara, New Horizon,** Pittsburgh; **Rainbow,** York, PA; **Gleason's, Loop, Alpine Village, Pin-Wheel,** Cleveland; **Melody,Jazz City, Zardi's,** Hollywood;**Tony Pastor's, Basin Street, Metropole, Embers, Birdland, Eddie Condon's, Famous Door,** New York City;**Mocambo, Black Hawk,** San

Francisco;**Storyville,** Boston; **Blue Note, Crown Propeller, Preview, Steak House, College Inn, Chez Paree,** Chicago; **Mayfair Room,** Buckeye Lake, OH; **Ciro's,** Columbus;**Brass Rail,** London, Canada; **Terrace,** East St. Louis; **Showboat, Pep's,** Philadelphia; **Elmo,** Billings, MT;

Zanzibar, Buffalo; **Rainbow,** New Brunswick, NJ; **Cotton Club,** Rochester, NY; **Week's,** Atlantic City, NJ; **Waikika Lauyee,** Honolulu; **Carr's Beach,** Annapolis, MD; **Lagoon,** Salt Lake

City; **Palms,** Hallandale, FL; **Colonial Tavern,** Toronto, Canada; **Harrah's Stateline,** NV; **Casa Loma,** Montreal, Quebec; **Palomar Night Club,** Los Angeles; **Reno Club,** Reno, NV

Finding Swing Music on the Airwaves

Where can you find big band and jazz music on the radio these days? There are fewer stations featuring jazz than when your grandparents were listening in the 1930s and 1940s.

Sure, the times were different but your grandparents had their own problems listening to the big bands; monaural sound, station static, fading signals and, of course, it was rare that a big band or jazz program came on before 11 p.m.

Today? There are a scattering of AM stations that carry a local jazz program—normally on public service weekend times—but if you listen to National Public Radio and live near a university campus the chances are you can find jazz programming during the week throughout the country.

In the good old days, however, you heard far more live broadcasts directly from the ballroom, hotel or club which added much more excitement for the listener. You can hear swing and jazz and even special programs these days dedicated to particular artists and music and, depending upon your set, you can hear it in stereo and surround sound if you choose. The great music may be gone but technology provides us with far better sound than ever before.

Sirius Satellite Radio, a pay for play service, offers seven channels of jazz and blues which could be of interest to those who can't find a station of choice for music. For more information, contact the web site, www.siriusradio.com

Here are North American stations as compiled by NPR Jazz that broadcast swing and jazz (programming is subject to change from year to year, check out the web site www.npr.org and use the search words "jazz programming"):

Alabama Alabama Public Radio WAPR **88.3,** Selma; WQPR **88.7,** Muscle Shoals; WUAL **91.5,** Tuscaloosa; NPR Jazz—Piano Jazz, Jazz Profiles; station jazz—Evening Jazz Normal WJAB, **90.9** NPR Jazz, Jazzset, Piano Jazz, Jazz Profiles, Jazz from Lincoln Center; station jazz, Mellow Madness/Nite Moods

Arizona Tucson, KUAZ, **89.1 & 1550**, NPR—Piano Jazz, Jazz Profiles, Station Jazz Phoenix, KJZZ, **91.5** NPR Jazz—Piano Jazz; station jazz Acoustic Jazz, The Saturday Night Jazz Party

Arkansas Jonesboro KASU **91.9** NPR Jazz; Station Jazz—Jazz Tonight, Wednesdays

California San Luis Obispo, KCBX, **90.1,** NPR Jazz—Piano Jazz, Morning Cup of Jazz, Jazz Play, The Last Jazz Show, The Cutting Edge; Station Jazz—Jazz Liner Notes, Club McKenzie, Swing Cat's Ball, Riverwalk, Ritmo Latino, Freedom Jazz Dance Thousand Oaks, KCLU, **88.3, 102.3,** NPR Jazz—Jazz Profiles, Jazz From Lincoln Center, Piano Jazz, Billy Taylor, Jazz at Work, Jazz at Night, Jazz Overnight San Mateo, KCSM, **91.1,** NPR Jazz—Jazz Profiles, Jazz From Lincoln Center, Piano Jazz, JazzSet; Station Jazz—24/7 Jazz, American Jazz Countdown, Latin Jazz Long Beach, KLON, **88.1,** NPR Jazz—JazzSet, Piano Jazz, Jazz Profiles, Billy Taylor, Jazz From Lincoln Center; Station Jazz—Jazz on the Latin Side, Mostly Bop, Atomic Lounge Mendocino, KZYX, KZYZ, **90.7, 91.5, 88.3** NPR Jazz—Piano Jazz; Station Jazz—Sunday Evening Jazz, Stolen Moments, Jazz From the Wharf Sacramento, KXJZ, **88.9,** NPR Jazz—Jazz Profiles, Piano Jazz; Station Jazz—Weekday Jazz

Colorado Denver, KUVO, **89.3,** NPR Jazz—Jazz From Lincoln Center; Station Jazz—Daily Jazz Programming

Florida	Orlando, WUCF, **89.9,** NPR Jazz—Jazz Profiles, Piano Jazz, Jazz From Lincoln Center, Billy Taylor, JazzSet; Station Jazz—Weekday Jazz, Weekend Jazz Saturday, Sunday Miami, WLRN, **91.3,**NPR Jazz—JazzSet, Jazz Profiles, Jazz From Lincoln Center, Piano Jazz; Station Jazz—Weekday Jazz, Saturday Jazz
Georgia	Atlanta, WCLK, **91.9,** NPR Jazz—Piano Jazz, Jazz Profiles, Jazz From Lincoln Center; Station Jazz—Weekday Jazz
Iowa	Cedar Rapids, KCCK, **88.3,** NPR Jazz—Jazz Profiles, JazzSet, Jazz From Lincoln Center, Billy Taylor, Piano Jazz; Station Jazz—Weekday Jazz, Weekend Jazz, Saturday, Sunday
Illinois	Springfield, WUIS, **91.9;** WIPA, **89.3;** NPR Jazz—Jazz Profiles, Jazz From Lincoln Center, JazzSet; Station Jazz—Weekday Jazz, Weekend Jazz, Saturday Chicago, WBEZ, **91.5;** NPR Jazz—Piano Jazz, Station Jazz—Weekday Jazz, Weekend Jazz, Sunday Edwardsville, WSIE, **88.7;** NPR Jazz—Piano Jazz, Jazz Profiles, Billy Taylor Normal/Peoria, **89.1, 103.3,** NPR Jazz—Piano Jazz, Jazz Profiles
Indiana	Bloomington, Columbus, Kokomo, Terre Haute, WFIU, **103.7, 100.7, 106.1, 95.1;** NPR Jazz—Piano Jazz; Station Jazz—Weekday Jazz, Weekend Jazz, Friday, Saturday
Kansas	Lawrence, KANU, **91.5,** NPR Jazz—Piano Jazz; Station Jazz—Weekday Jazz
Kentucky	Louisville, WFPK, **91.9,** NPR Jazz—Jazz Profiles, Piano Jazz, Jazz From Lincoln Center JazzSet; Station Jazz—Jazz With Phil Bailey, Jazz Etc, Big Band Jump, John LaBarbera's Best Coast Jazz, Inner Ear with Dick Sesto, Jazz Folio with Dick Sesto, Gerry's Jazz
Louisiana	Baton Rouge,WWNO **90.3,** NPR Jazz—Jazz Profiles, Piano Jazz, Jazz From Lincoln Center, Billy Taylor; Station Jazz—Sunday to Friday, all jazz New Orleans, **89.9,** NPR Jazz—JazzSet; Station Jazz—Saturday
Maryland	Princess Anne, WESM, **91.3,** NPR Jazz—JazzSet, Jazz From Lincoln Center, Jazz Profiles, Piano Jazz; Station Jazz—Weekday Jazz and Weekend Jazz Baltimore, WEAA, **88.9,** NPR Jazz—JazzSet, Jazz Profiles; Station Jazz—Back Page
Massachusetts	Boston, WGBH, **89.7,** NPR Jazz—JazzSet, Jazz Profiles; Station Jazz—Weekday Jazz, Weekend Jazz, Sunday Jazz At Four, Jazz With Eric, Monday through Thursday Evening Worcester, WICN, **90.5,** NPR Jazz—Billy Taylor, Jazz Profiles, Piano Jazz; Station Jazz—Daily Jazz
Michigan	Ypsilanti, WEMU **89.1,** NPR Jazz—Piano Jazz, Jazz From Lincoln Center, Jazz Profiles JazzSet; Station Jazz—Weekday Jazz, Weekend Jazz Grand Rapids, WGVU, **88.5, 95.3,** NPR Jazz—Piano Jazz, Jazz From Lincoln Center, JazzSet, Jazz Profiles; Station Jazz—Weekday Jazz CMU Public Radio WCMU, **90.1** Grand Rapids; WCMU **89.5,** Mt. Pleasant; WUCX, **90.1,** Bay City; WCML **91.7,** Alpena; WCMB, **95.7,** Oscoda; WWCM, **96.9,** Standish; WCMZ, **98.3** Sault Ste. Marie; WCMW, **103.9,** Harbor Springs; NPR Jazz—Piano Jazz, Jazz Profiles; Station Jazz—Weekdays

Nevada Las Vegas, KUNV, **91.5,** NPR Jazz—Billy Taylor, Jazz From Lincoln Center, Piano Jazz Jazz Profiles, JazzSet; Station Jazz—Weekday

New Jersey Newark, WBGO, **88.3,** NPR Jazz—Billy Taylor, Jazz Profiles, JazzSet, Piano Jazz; Station Jazz—Weekday

New Mexico Albuquerque, KUNM, **89.9,** Station Jazz—All That Jazz, The House That Jazz Built

New York Syracuse, WAER, 88.3, NPR Jazz—Piano Jazz, Jazz Profiles; Station Jazz—Weekday Jazz, Weekend Jazz, Saturday and Sunday Buffalo, WBFO, **88.7,** NPR Jazz—Piano Jazz; Station Jazz—Overnight Jazz, Weekday Jazz, Weekend Jazz Sunday

North Carolina Durham, WNCU, **90.7,** NPR Jazz—Jazz Profiles, JazzSet, Piano Jazz, Jazz From Lincoln Center; Station Jazz—Weekday Jazz

Ohio Cleveland, WCPN, **90.3,** NPR Jazz—Jazz Profiles, Piano Jazz, Billy Taylor; Station Jazz—Weekday Jazz, Weekend Jazz, Jazz From the North Coast, Jazz Tracks Oxford, WMUB, **88.5,** NPR Jazz—Piano Jazz; Station Jazz—Weekday Jazz, Weekend Jazz Youngstown, WYSU,**88.5,** NPR Jazz—Piano Jazz; Station Jazz—Jazzscapes

Oregon Eugene, KLCC, **89.7,** Station Jazz—JazzSunday, Jazz Inside Out, Soul of Jazz, Night Jazz, Jazz Overnight

Pennsylvania Pittsburgh, WDUQ, **90.5** NPR Jazz—Billy Taylor JazzSet, Piano Jazz, Jazz Profiles Jazz From Lincoln Center; Station Jazz—Weekday Jazz, Weekend Jazz Philadelphia, WRTI, **90.1,** NPR Jazz—Jazz From Lincoln Center, Piano Jazz, Jazz Pro-Files, JazzSet; Station Jazz—Weekdays, Sundays

Tennessee Murfreesboro, WMOT, **89.5,** NPR Jazz—Jazz Profiles, Jazz at the Kennedy Center, Piano Jazz, JazzSet; Station Jazz—Weekday Jazz, Weekend Jazz Chattanooga, WUTC, **88.1,** NPR Jazz—Piano Jazz, Jazz Profiles,Jazz From the Lincoln Center; Station Jazz—Weekday Jazz, Sunday Jazz

Texas El Paso, KTEP, **88.5,** NPR Jazz—Piano Jazz, JazzSet, Jazz Profiles; Station Jazz—Weekday Jazz, Weekend Jazz

Vermont Vermont Public Radio, WVPS, **107.9** Burlington; WVPA, **88.5,** St. Johnsbury; WBTN, **94.3** Bennington; WRVT **88.7,** Rutland; WVPR, **89.5,** Windsor; NPR Jazz—Piano Jazz; Station Jazz—Tuesday to Friday

Washington Tacoma, KPLU, **88.5,** NPR Jazz—Piano Jazz, Jazz Profiles; Station Jazz—Weekday Jazz; Weekend Jazz, Saturday and Sunday

District of Columbia WAMU, **88.5** NPR Jazz—Jazz Profiles; Station Jazz—Saturday

Wyoming Laramie, Denver repeater signal, KUVO, **104.3,** NPR Jazz—Jazz From Lincoln Center, Piano Jazz, JazzSet; Station Jazz—Daily except Monday, Friday

Big Band Festivals, Celebrations, Gatherings

(Web sites, emails and telephone numbers subject to change)

January

*Miami Jazz Festival, Miami, FL Telephone 305-858-8545 www.miamijazzfestival.com Premier jazz event with top international performers. Live performances include contemporary jazz, traditional jazz, Latin jazz, blues and gospel

* Rogue Valley Blues Festival, Ashland, OR Telephone 541-482-4154

www.stclairevents.com Martin Luther King Holiday weekend. Features wide variety of blues, workshops, free performances

*Solvang Blues Festival, Solvang, CA Telephone 805-688-8000. www.solvangris.com/events/html Renown blues bands hold concerts

International Association for Jazz Education, Long Beach, CA Telephone 785-776-8744 Web site: www.iaje.org email: info@iaje.org Features Grammy Jazz Artist Forum, jazz radio symposium, over 200 concerts and workshops

*Barbados Jazz Festival, Garfield Sports Complex, Barbados, several dozen jazz artists at various venues on the island during a week. Web. www.barbadosjazzonline.com

*Jazz for Hope Concert Series, Hope House, Norfolk, VA. Telephone 757-625-6161 Concerts for a non-profit organization that provides services for developmentally disabled. Concert series January/March www.hope-house.org

*Morro Bay Jazz Festival, Morro Bay, CA Jazz from 1900 to 1940s Telephone 805-772-3361 www.morro-bay.net/jazz

February

*North Carolina International Jazz Festival, Durham, NC Telephone 919-684-4444 www.duke.edu/%7Epjeffrey/jazzfest.html Series of concerts features international jazz musicians

* Winter Dance Party, Clear Lake, IA Telephone 515-357-6151 Dance lessons, tributes to legends of pop music, bus tours

*Budweiser Lowcountry Blues Bash, Charleston, SC Telephone 843-762-9125

www.bluesbash.com From legends to moderns to post-moderns including acoustic and electric. Diverse venues

*East Coast Music Awards and Conference, Charlottetown, PE Canada Telephone 709-576-2993 www.ecma.ca/intro.html Annual celebration of East Coast Canadian Artists from Canada's five regions with weekend of concerts, seminars, workshops and awards. All live performances

*East Coast Jazz Festival, Rockville, MD Telephone 301-933-1822 www.eastcoastjazz.com/ Five days of bebop, Latin, swing and blues. Events open to the public and include jam sessions, workshops and concerts

*Melbourne Jumbalaya Jam, Melbourne, FL Telephone 407-633-4028 Good Cajun and zydeco sounds, rides, games and amusements along with music and spicy Cajun food for all ages

*Iues Blast, Mesa, AR Telephone 602-644-2560 www.phoenixblues.org

Annual festival of the Phoenix Blues Society, one of the first outdoor festivals of the season

*Lionel Hampton Jazz Festival, Moscow, ID Telephone 208-885-6765 www.jazz.uidaho.edu Leonard Feather called this the number one jazz festival which has attracted about 30,000 fans. Includes variety of performances, workshops and festival activities along with competitions and clinics

*Collegiate Showcase Invitational, Lake Buena Vista, FL Telephone 800-522-2213 Provides opportunity for college and university choirs and jazz ensembles to work with guest artists and perform on stage

*Coe College Jazz Summit, Cedar Rapids, IA Telephone 319-399-8520 www.coe.edu/~wcarson/summit.htm Jazz artists from throughout the country present clinics and workshops. High school jazz band competition and performance by Coe College Gold Jazz Ensemble

*Winterfolk Music Festival, Pagosa Springs, CO Telephone 970-731-5582 www.folkwest.com/winterfolk.htm Two day festival in new auditoroium to enjoy best singer and songwriter presentations.

*Kissimmee Festival of Rhythm and Blues, Kissimmee, FL Telephone 407-933-8368 Celebrates Black history month and offers musical entertainment

*Iuegrass Music Caribbean Cruise, Fort Lauderdale, FL Telephone 888-711-7447 www.cruise-eta.com/ Bluegrass Music Caribbean cruise with workshops, seminars, opens jam sessions

*Newport Beach Jazz Party, Newport Beach, CA Newport Beach Marriott Hotel, web: www.newportbeachjazzparty.com

*Eastern Illinois University Jazz Festival, Charleston, IL, a 2-day event featuring clinics with guest artists for high school and junior high school students. General public tickets are available. Telephone: 217-581-6628

* University of Louisville Jazz Week, Comstock Concert Hall, Louisville Campus.

Week of jazz, swing events featuring campus artists and guests. Telephone: email: miketracy@louisville.edu

*Sinfonian Dimensions in Jazz(SDIJ)/Tallcorn Jazz Festival, Performing Arts Center, University of Northern Iowa, Cedar Falls, IA. The oldest continuously running high school jazz festival in the country featuring guest artists and student talent. Telephone School of Music 319-273-6431. Web: www.uni.edu/jazzstudies.

March

*Blues Summit, York Beach, ME Telephone 207-351-3221 www.innontheblues.com/ib_home.html Blues bands play during a 3-day event

*Tribute to Bix Fest, Kenosha, WI Telephone 847-362-4016 www.geocities.com/bixfest/ live concerts, new and used record sales. Historical jazz sites bus tour, jam session, Bix Beiderbecke memorabilia email: bixguy@hotmail.com Phil Pospychala

*Music for Hunger, Fort Pierce, FL Telephone 561-489-5676 www.treasurecoastblues.com/events.html National and regional recording artists offer various events and music and workshops

*Will McLean Festival, Brooksville, FL Telephone 352-465-7208 www.willmclean.com/ Florida's best songwriters and singers perform, workshops, storytelling

*Brandon Jazz Festival, Brandon, MB Canada, Telephone 204-728-1022

http://brandonjazzfestival.com/ Features instrumental and vocal jazz groups, clinics and concerts email: bjf@brandonu.ca, Sean McManu

*River City Blues Festival, Marietta, OH Telephone 740-373-6640 www.bjfm.org/BluesFestival.html email: bjfm@bjfm.org Weekend of blues bands and music

*Tallahassee Jazz and Blues Festival, Tallahassee, FL Telephone 850-575-8684 www.tallahasseemuseum.org/ Jazz and blues festival at the museum

*Sarasota Jazz Festival, Sarasota, FL Telephone 941-366-1552 www.jazzclubsarasota.com/ email: mail@JazzClubSarasota.com A week of jazz with free events and ticketed concerts by top jazz artists

*Chantilly Invitational Jazz Festival, Chantilly, VA, Telephone 703-222-8180

http://dcfree.net/chantillybandmusic/poster.htm Features top 25 high school big bands and small combos in Virginia, Maryland and DC.

*Somers Point Jazz Fest, Somers Point, NJ Telephone 609-927-7161 ex 256

Two night event with venues

*Festival Jazz et Blues Heritage Chicoutimi, Chicoutimi, PQC, Canada, Telephone 418-549-7111 www.jazzetblues.com/ Five days of performances

*Penn State University International Assn. of Jazz Educators Jazz Festival, State College PA, Telephone 814-865-5755 www.clubs.psu.edu Festival features nightly performances by well known jazz greats and numerous clinics are held by Penn State faculty and guests.

*Tampa Bay Blues Festival, St. Petersburg, FL Telephone 727-824-6163 www.TampaBayBluesFest.com/ various groups performing

*Florida Old Time Music Championship, Dade City, FL www.dadecity.com/fotmc/ various bands play at the Sertoma Youth Ranch in Dade City

*Redwood Coast Dixeland Jazz Festival, Eureka, CA Telephone 707-445-3378 www.redwoodjazz.org/pages/dixieland/dixie.html Three days of traditional Dixie music, swing, blues, calypso, zydeco and featuring some of the best in the business.

* Blues Music Fest, Fellsmere, FL Telephone 877-637-2849 www.mesapark.com/ Various bands and events

Berks Jazz Fest, Reading/Berks, PA. Telephone 215-336-2000 Web site: www.berksjazzfest.com Weekend of jazz featuring world famous artists

Presented by the Berks Arts Council

*Annual Selmer/Big Bad Voodoo Daddy Competition, contact Selmer, PO Box 310, Elkhart, IN 46515-0310 web site: www.selmer.com

April

*Super Jazz, The Whitesboro High School Alumni Assn Jazz Fest, featuring an 18-piece band and international jazz artists. Ticket information from: The Whitesboro High School Alumni Assn, % Sound Creations, PO Box 32, Whitesboro, NY 13492-0032

*BransonFest, Branson, MO Telephone 800-897-8808 Hometown of the Lawrence Welk Orchestra, community celebrates blues, rock and roll, swing, classical, pop, soul, alternative, rap and easy listening.

*Old Settlers Music Festival, Dripping Springs, TX Telephone 512-346-1629 Bluegrass, blues, acoustic jazz in an outdoor festival near Austin.

*3 Rivers Music Festival, Columbia, SC Telephone 803-401-8990 Eight stages offer performances for rock, blues, jazz, country bluegrass and gospel.

*Natchitoches Jazz and R and B Festival, Pensacola, FL Telephone 850-433-8382 Free festival produced by the Jazz Society of Pensacola. Features Original Dixie, jazz.

*Terrif Vic Jazz Party, Victoria, BC, Canada Telephone 250-953-2011

www.terrifvic.com/ A number of international red hot jazz bands perform in seven venues throughout the city.

* French Quarter Festival, New Orleans, LA Telephone 504-522-5730 Non-stop dancing to 13 stages with jazz, Cajun and music from Caribbean, Latin America and Africa. Crowds about 300,000 enjoy the "Battle of the Bands," bartenders' competition and the world's largest jazz brunch

*Natchez Bluff Blues Fest, Natchez, MS Telephone 601-442-2988 Club performances, blues on stage.

*New York Music and Internet Expo, New York City, NY Telephone 212-965-0013 Thousands of musicians, music industry people, new media companies, performing artists, songwriters, agents and producers among others gather at Madison Square Garden's Expo Centers to network, promote their music and further careers

*Paradise Valley Jazz Party, Scottsdale, AZ Telephone 480-948-7993 The Paradise Valley Jazz Party is annually held at Merv Griffin's Scottsdale Hilton Resort.

*New Orleans Jazz and Heritage Festival, New Orleans, LA Telephone 504-941-5100 Jazz, Afro-Caribbean music, blues and gospel groups appearing on nearly a dozen stages over a two weekend period. Web: www.festivalproductions.net

*Sunbelt Jazz Festival, Carrollton, GA Telephone 770-836-4334 Unv. Of Western Georgia's Sunbelt Jazz show for high school jazz ensembles. Features a guest clinician

*Jazz in the Olympics, Port Angeles, WA Telephone 888-933-6143 features great traditional Dixie bands, dancing

*Beaufort Music Festival, Beaufort, NC Telephone 252-728-7108 Program is called Beaufort By the Sea Music Festival and features weekend of free concerts

on stages throughout the downtown. Highlights swing, jazz, pop, gospel and rock and roll.

*Buddy DeFranco Jazz Festival, University of Montana, Missoula, Montana

Telephone 406-243-5071 email irboyd@selway.umt.edu A non-competitive educational event that features high school and college jazz bands every 30 minutes during the two-day program. Clinics are also held

*Essentially Ellington High School Jazz Band Competition& Festival, Jazz at Lincoln Center New York City. For information Telephone 212-258-9812 email: ee@jazztlincolncenter.org Registration fee$50

*The Monterey Jazz Festival High School Competition Monterey, CA. Open to big bands, combos, vocal groups and individual musicians. Winners awarded scholarships, trophies, cash prizes and a two-week performance tour of Japan. Telephone 831-373-3366 email:Stella Lepine stella@montereyjazzfestival.org web site:Montereyjazzfestival.org

*Gene Harris Jazz Festival, Boise State University, Boise, ID, clinics, top jazz artists. Telephone: 208-426-JAZZ Web: www.geneharris.org/

*Annual Northwest Jazz Festival, Northwest College, Powell, WY. Top artists featured over the years such as Clark Terry, Maynard Ferguson, Lee Konitz, Woody Herman and others. Email festival chairman Neil Hansen, hansenn@nwc.cc.wy.us

*Villanova Jazz Festival, Villanova University, US Rt. 30, near Philadelphia, PA.

Week of concerts, competition which feature major jazz and big band artists.

Telephone: 610-519-7214 Web: www57.homepage.villanova.edu/jennie.dilemmo/

*Fullerton College Jazz Festival, Fullerton, CA. A two day event that features clinics, workshops and major jazz figures. Telephone: Helene Mejia, 714-525-8165 email: hmejia@fullcoll.edu

*Unv. Of Northern Colorado/Greeley Jazz Festival, a 3 day event that gathers over 6,000 college, high school and junior high musicians along with professional guest artists. For tickets call the Union Colony Civic Center, 970-356-5000 web: arts.unco.edu/uncjazz/festival/festival.html

May

*Topeka Jazz Festival, Topeka Performing Arts Center, 214 SE 8th Ave, Topeka, KS, 66603; Telephone 785-297-9000

*Newport Beach Jazz Festival, Telephone 949-721-4000, web: www.newportbeachfestival.com

*Jazz Festival, Ellicottville, NY musicians, combos playing at area restaurants, bars, Ellicottville Chamber of Commerce, Telephone 716-699-5046 800-349-9099 web site: www.ellicottvilleny.com

*Juneau Jazz & Classics Festival, Juneau, AK, a 9 to 10 day event that features everything from free noon concerts, a blues concert, 2 blues cruises, jazz concerts, non-jazz improv, workshops and includes special guests as well as Juneau's big band. Ticket information telephone: 907-463-3378 web:Juneau.com/music/ e-mail: music@juneau.com Address: PO Box 22152 Juneau, AK 99802-2152

*Annual Bakersfield Jazz Festival, California State University at Bakersfield, CA Amphitheater. Children under 12 admitted free. All proceeds go toward student Scholarships. For general information, contact www.csub.edu/jazzfest or www.vallitix.com

*Healdsburg Jazz Festival, Healdsburg, CA, Weekend jazz event, big bands, combos, Telephone: 707-433-4633 Web: www.healdsburgjazzfestival.com

*Atlanta Jazz Festival, Atlanta, GA, a week of jazz artists performing for the city's Bureau of Cultural Affairs. Telephone: 404-817-6851 email: bcamusic@mindspring.com web: www.atlantafestivals.com

*Sacramento Jazz Jubilee, Sacramento, CA, Three days of jazz venues. Telephone: 916-372-5277 Web: www.sacjazz.com

JVC Jazz Festival, Miami Beach, FL. Four days of jazz in sun. Web:www.festivalproductions.net

*Playboy Jazz at the Old Pasadena Summer Festival, Pasadena, CA. Two days of big bands and combos. Web: www.festivalproductions.net

June

*The Royal Canadian Big Band Music Festival, London, Ontario, Canada Telephone 519-663-9467 email: bigband@execulink.com

*Friehofer's Jazz Festival, Saratoga Springs, NY produced by George Wein and the Saratoga Performing Arts Center Telephone 315-587-3330 web: www.spac.org

*Glenn Miller Festival, Clarinda, IA, Telephone 712-542-2461 www.glennmiller.org email: gmbs@clarinda.heartland.net Visitors from all over the world visit Clarinda during

the second weekend in June to attend the big band concerts, lectures, panels and hear high school and college as well as professional groups play the Glenn Miller Sound.

*M&T Jazz Fest, Syracuse, NY A week long of day and evening programs featuring major headliners in outdoor arenas complete with video screens. www.syracusejazzfest.com

*Summer Jazz Camp, Schaumberg, IL Telephone 800-848-2263 web: www.bands/org Offers summer workshop experience to interested students. Hands on workshops including featured artists.

*The Dave Brubeck Institute Summer Jazz Colony, Stockton, CA week long, full scholarship program for talented and motivated musicians between their junior and senior years of high school. Telphone 209-946-3970 email: jbdyas@uop.edu web site: www.uop.edu/brubeck

*Skidmore Jazz Institute, Saratoga Springs, NY Telephone 518-580-5590 Web site: www.skidmore.edu/summer Two week intensive workshop for jazz students.

*JazzCamp West, Oakland, CA Telephone 510-287-8880 Web site: www.jazzcampwest.com A week of music, study, an all-star faculty working with vocals, music and dance.

*Mellon Jazz Festival, Pittsburgh, PA, Three days of jazz venues. Web: www.festivalproductions.net

*Playboy Jazz Festival, Hollywood Bowl, Los Angeles, CA Three days of big bands, combos in a revered California site. Web: www.festivalproductions.net

*JVC Jazz Festival, New York City,NY. Thirteen days of small combos, big bands, jazz events. Web: www.festivalproductions.net

*Mellon Jazz Festival, Philadelphia, PA. Three day jazz program. Web: www.festivalproductions.net

*Hampton Jazz Festival, Hampton Coliseum, Hampton, VA. Three day swing band program. Web: www.festivalproductions.net

*Chicago Jazz Festival, Chicago, IL Telephone: 312-744-3370 Web www.cityofchicago.org/specialevents

*Berkshire Jazz Festival, Butternut Ski Basin, Great Barrington, MA, Telephone: 413-528-4284 web www.greatbarrington.org 1st annual in 2001.

*Friday Night Jazz & Classic Films, on the Yonkers Recreation Pier at the Hudson River, free event, Jazz Forum Arts 914-631-1000 web www.jazzforumarts.org

*Dobbs Ferry Summer Music Series (June through August) free, Dobbs Ferry, NY Ten Evening Concerts at Embassy Community Center, 60 Palisade St. Dobbs Ferry, NY

*Hot Steamed Jazz, Essex, CT, 3 days at Valley R.R. Telephone 800-348-0003 web: www.hotsteamedjazz.com

*Northern Aire Jazz Festival, Wisconsin Rapids, WI, an event that features top entertainment in the jazz and swing world at the Lake Arrowhead Championship Golf Course outside Wisconsin Rapids. Telephone: 715-423-JAZZ email: info@northernairejazzfestival.com

*Stanford Jazz Workshop, June-August, Stanford University, Stanford, CA. Festival features concerts with name artists throughout the summer. Telephone 6500736-0324 email: info@stanfordjazz.org Address: Stanford Jazz Workshop, PO Box 20454, Stanford, CA 94309

*The Boston Globe Jazz & Blues Festival, FleetBoston Pavilion, Boston, MA, 7 days of big bands, jazz groups on different stages, some events free, others admission price. Telephone: 617-929-8756 web: www.boston.com/jazzfest

*Indy Jazz Fest, Indianapolis, IN, a weekend of jazz, blues, soul, gospel music.

Tickets can be purchased at ticketmaster.com Web:indyjazzfest.org

*Capital Jazz Fest, Washington, DC, World's largest contemporary jazz venue, Telephone: 301-322-8100. Tickets from ticketmaster.com Web: capitaljazz.com

*Elkhart Jazz Festival, Elkhart, IN, Bebop to classic jazz events during three days. Elkhart Centre, 227 S. Main St, Elkhart, IN 46516, Telephone: 800-597-7627

Web: www.elkhartjazzfestival.com

*Central Pennsylvania Jazz Festival, Harrisburg, PA, Hilton, a three day jazz program. Telephone: 717-540-1010 Web: www.pajazz.org

*Rochester International Jazz Festival, Rochester, NY A week long event that features 20 venues from big bands to combos and artists from all walks of music.

Telephone: 585-234-2002 Web: www.rochesterjazz.com

*Jazz-MU-Tazz, Marshall University, Huntington, WVA. A university two-day summer jazz festival. For information Telephone: 304-696-3326

July

* Patriot's Park Tarrytown Concerts, Tarrytown, NY, free held in conjunction with the Village of Tarrytown's Farmer's Market. Jazz Forum Arts Telephone 914-631-1000 web: www.jazzforumarts.org

*Columbus Jazz & RibFest, two-day event, contact Greater Columbus Convention & Visitors Bureau, Telephone 800-345-4FUN web site: www.ColumbusCVB.org

*Atlantic Jazz Festival, Halifax, Nova Scotia, a week long event with various venues. Artist information, contact Telephone 800-567-5277 or email: susan@jazzeast.com

*Essence Music Festival, Superdome, New Orleans, LA. Fourth of July jazz festival.

Web: www.festivalproductions.net

*JVC Jazz Festival, Winter Park, CO. Various jazz venues. Web: www.festivalproductions.net

*JVC Jazz Festival, Chicago,IL Two-day big band and combo event. Web: www.festivalproductions.net

*Westwood Village Jazz at the Hammer, The UCLA Hammer Museum, Los Angeles, CA. Web: www.festivalproductions.net

*Yellowstone Jazz Festival, Cody, WY, sponsored by the Yellowstone Jazz Festival and features two days of performers and concerts. Contact: email address yellowstonejazz@tritel.net

*July Jazz Getaway, Moravian College Music Institute, Bethelem, PA. No tryouts, no auditions but a period of time at a college camp playing with guest artists and learning in jam sessions and public performances. Telephone: 610-861-1650 (voice mail). Email: JJG@moravian.edu

*Iowa City Jazz Festival, Iowa City, IA, Three days of swing and jazz groups.

Telephone: 319-358-9346 (Steve Grismore) Web: www.iowacityjazzfestival.com

*North Beach Jazz Festival, San Francisco, CA, a week of combo and big band jazz. Telephone: 415-771-2061 Web: www.nbjazzfest.org

*Hawaii International Jazz Festival, Honolulu, HI, Hawaii's longest running major jazz festival offering big band, Latin, Hawaiian jazz. Telephone: 808-943-0224
Web: www.hawaiijazz.com email: aewjazz1@aol.com

August

*Telluride Jazz Celebration, telephone 970-728-7009 email: paul@telluridejazz.com web: telluridejazz.com

*Lander Jazz Festival, Lander, WY, Labor Weekend jazz events in a scenic area.
PO Box 413, Lander, and WY 82520 Telephone: 800-433-0662 Email: shallam@rmisp.com Web: www.landerjazz.com

*Annual Great River Jazz Fest, LaCrosse, WI. All-star groups from Dixie to big band. Web: www.centurytel.net/jazzfest

* J&R Downtown Jazzfest, New York City, web: www.jazzfest.com

*JVC Jazz Festival, Fort Adams State Park, Newport, RI The George Wein traditional event that features a large billing of major jazz stars. Web: www.festivalproductions.net

*Sleepy Hollow Concert Series, free, at the Kingsland Point Park at the Hudson River, NY

*Peekskill Celebration @Riverfront Green, Peekskill, NY Jazz Forum All Stars
Telephone 914-736-2000 web: www.peekskillcelebration.com

*Annual Berkshire Jazz Festival, Butternut Ski Basin, Great Barrington, MA
Telephone: 914-631-1000 web www.jazzforumarts.org

*Long Beach Jazz Festival, Long Beach, CA., Premier artist list for 3 day event.
Telephone: 562-424-0013 Web: www.longbeachjazzfestival.com

*Idyllwild Jazz In The Pines, two day of jazz combos and bands. Telephone:
909-659-4885 Web:www.idyllwildjazz.com

*Costa Mesa/Orange County Classic Jazz Festival, Orange County, CA. Four days of jazz programs. 1520 West Yale Ave, Orange, CA 92867 Telephone:888-215-6222 Email: jdieball@jadtec.com Web: www.oc-classicjazz.org

*Fidelity Investment Park City International Jazz, Park City, UT Web:www.festivalproductions.net

*JVC Jazz Festival, Concord, CA A one-day jazz concert at the Chronicle Pavilion Web: www.festivalproductions.net

*JVC Jazz Festival, Los Angeles, CA Hollywood Bowl. Web: www.festivalproductions.net

* Litchfield Jazz Festival, Goshen Fairgrounds, CT, A three-day event with featured performers. Telephone: 860-567-4162 Web: www.litchfieldjazzfest.com

September

*The Monterey Jazz Festival, considered the world's longest running jazz festival, has featured more than 500 artists performing in non-stop jazz entertainment on 7 stages during two days and three evenings. The festival is held on 20 acres of the Monterey Fairgrounds in Monterey, CA Telephone 925-275-9255 www.montereyjazzfestival.org

*Traditional Jazz Series, University of New Hampshire, Durham, NH, begins in September. Offers programs monthly featuring international and national artists. Telephone 603-862-2404 Web: www.unh.edu/music

*Jazz at the Lincoln Center (Fall Series) Wynton Marsalis, artistic director, Telephone 212-721-6500 web site: www.jazzatlincolncenter.org

*Ford Detroit International Jazz Festival, North America's largest free music event. Music Hall, Hart Plaza, Detroit, MI

*Jazz on the Water Festival, Hood River, OR. Combines celebrated jazz artists and awe-inspiring Columbia Gorge together with sandy beaches in three day event. Telephone: Hood River Chamber, 800-366-3530 web: www.jazzonthewater.com

*Annual Sunnyside Jazz Festival, at Washington Irving's Hudson River Estate, NY Telephone 914-631-1000 web: www.jazzforumarts.org

*Vail Jazz Festival Labor Day Weekend, Vail, CO. Showcases big band and combo musicians for Vail Jazz Foundation. Telephone: 888-VAILJAM for tickets.

Web: www.vailjazz.org

*Ziegler Kettle MoraineJazz Festival, Riverside Park, West Bend, WI, international & domestic jazz headliners in two-day event. Telephone: 877-271-6903

Web: www.kmjazz.com

Verizon Music Festival, New York City, NY Four days of a variety of venues.

Web: www.festivalsproduction.net

October

*Verizon Music Festival, Los Angeles, CA Web: www.festivalproductions.net

*Kennedy Center Jazz, John F. Kennedy Center for the Performing Arts, Washington, DC. Celebrates special guests during Fall season. Offers visiting artists program, individual programs. Telephone 800-444-1324 Web: kennedy-center.org/jazz

*Lake Ozark Annual Dixieland Jazz Festival, Lake Ozark, MO Telephone 800-964-6698 Weekend Dixie jazz sessions at the Country Club Hotel & Spa

*The Santa Fe Jazz & Festival, Santa Fe, NM A month long event with various venues and jazz artists. Telephone: 505-989-8442 Web: www.santafejazzfestival.com

November

*Hollywood Jazz Festival, Hollywood, FL web site: www.southfloridajazz.org

*San Francisco Jazz Festival, San Francisco, CA Telephone 800-850-SFJF

Web site: www.sfjazz.org

*Verizon Jazz Festival, Tampa Bay, FL, Week of small combo and big band jazz. Web: www.festivalproductions.net

December

*The JazzTimes Tour, Havana International Jazz Festival, Telephone 800-380-4777 web: www.jazztimes.com

Big Band Internet Sources

(Internet and web sites change from time to time. These sites were available mid-2002)

www.jldeanorchestra.com…………	James Dean Big Band 40s swing to rock with musicians from era Haledon, NJ
www.gapmangione.com	Gap Mangione bio and schedule
www.maynardferguson.com	Maynard Ferguson bio and schedule
www.npr.org/programs/specials	NPR 100 most important American Musical Works In 20th Century
www.jazzsteps.com	Jazz Newsletter online published by and for Seattle jazz enthusiasts
www.bigbandjump.com/newshome.html	Newsletter published 6 times a year by Hagen Williams about big bands of yesterday and today
www.bolewis.org	Bo Lewis/Big Band Dance Party
www.rexfoundation.org/gleason.html	Rex Foundation—Ralph Gleason Awards
www.montereyjazzfestival/.org/press/factsheet.html	Monterey Jazz Festival Annual
www.jaybeckenstein.com/biography.html	Spyro Gyra leader from Buffalo, NY, top adult contemporary band
www.jazzwest.com www3.uop.edu/brubeck/	Monterey Jazz Festival The Brubeck Institute at Unv. Of Pacific
www.glennmiller.org email: gmbs@clarinda.heartland.net	Glenn Miller Birthplace Society, Program, Plans
www.bigbandsinternational.org	Big Band International Society membership, newsletter

www.manciniinstitute.org/hmi.html	Henry Mancini Institute, CA
www.musicians.com	free membership; owned by Virtual Countries, a Seattle web site
www.bigband.com	The Great American Big Band in Silicon Valley, CA
www.nfo.net	The American Big Bands Data Base (outstanding archive for Big band devotees) Murray L. Pfeffer
http://library.thinkquest.org	Swing Era, 1932-1944
www.JimmyScalia.com	Jimmy Scalia, official archivist for Bobby Darin
www.stevegood.com/	The sounds of Swing & Romance A CA band of 5,7 or 11 pieces
www.woodyherman.com	Woody Herman Society, supports Woody Herman's music and musicians. Al Julian, director
www.bigband-era.com	David Miller, host, Swingin' Down the Lane on NPR
woodyou@tele-net.net	Frank Wood, big band player studio musician, CA
swingorch@earthlink.net	(Bill Elliott) 15 piece band plays music from 30s, 40s,50s West Coast
www.allmusic.com	Music guide for big bands
www.headsup.com	Spyro Gyra band
www.bigbandjazz.com	online source for big band music
www.chuckmangione.com	Chuck Mangione profile, schedule
www.bigbandmusic.com	Big band music store site in St. Louis, MO
www.culturekiosque.com/jazz/features	jazz features
www.jazz-clubs-worldwide.com	site, type of jazz clubs

www.americanjazzmuseum.com	American Jazz Museum, Kansas City, MO
http://people.a2000.n//ahbone/Lionel Hampton1937-1989.html	Lionel Hampton story, photos
www.geocities.com/Bourbon Street/Square/2077/page/.html	Tribute to Louis Prima, photos
www.btinternet.com/~dreklind/whtmnbio.htm	Paul Whiteman biography
www.nfo.net/.HITS/1940.html	Your Hit Parade
www.monkrowe.com	Monk Rowe, biography, resume, director Hamilton College Archives
www.nprjazz.org/stations	National Public Radio jazz stations
www.dukeellington.com	biography of Duke Ellington
http://members.tripod.com/hardbop/rumsey.html	Howard Rumsey, bassist, founder of the Lighthouse All-Stars
www.redhotjazz.com/	A History of Jazz Before 1930
www.jazzonweb.com	A jazz portal, reviews, resources
www.allabout jazz.com	Jazz talk site, free monthly newsletter
www.Jazz.About.com	Generic music site
www.JazzReview.com	Jazz reviews, CD reviews, book reviews, articles, biographies
www.jazzcorner.com	Generic music site
www.concordrecords.com	major jazz recording company
www.zildjian.com/vintage	Cymbal manufacturer for major drum stars of past
www.anitaoday.com	former big band singer with Krupa, Newport Jazz Festival
www.dorisday.com	big band singer with Barney Rapp, Les Brown; actress, Pillow Talk, Calamity Jane, others

www.tuxjunction.net	George Spink's jazz and big band cd collections
www.sierramusic.com	Bob Curnow's music publishing Site, Sierra Music
www.bigbandmusic.com	Listings of great dance bands and vocalists. Takes orders. Email:
bigbandbil@mindspring.com	
www.gibson.com	Slingerland, one of the nation's oldest drum maker and Gibson instrument sites
www.mannheimsteamroller.com	One of the country's most popular New Age touring bands, Chip Davis & Mannheim Steamroller
www.asoundinvestment.com	Mobile DJ entertainer with extensive listings of songs from 1930s, 1940s, 1950s
www.readio.com/clubs/newyorkclubs1.html	Celebrated New York clubs
www.bigbandworld.com	Big Band World, a Canadian big band magazine
www.geocities.com/gkiiorchestra	Gene Krupa bio, Krupa fan club
www.gkrp.net	Gene Krupa story
www.drummerman.net	Gene Krupa
www.Jazzlegends.com	Dr. Bruce Klauber, home page, features
www.kingstontrio.com	Folk singing collegians who were popular in late 1950s
www.grovemusic.com	Comprehensive music dictionary
www.sonymusic.com/artists	Brief descriptions of performers, records
www.selmer.com	Excellent instrument site to locate top college, high school jazz bands
www.bigbandjazz.com	Virtual music store and CD catalog

	listing
www.bigband-era.com	Swingin' Down the Lane with David Miller, host on NPR's radio jazz Program
www.brittannica.com	music biographies
www.clevelandjazz.org	jazz history by Joe Mosbrook of one the country's outstanding concert jazz orchestras
www.allmusic.com	Claude Thornhill bio
www.dickjurgens.com	Popular sweet/swing band during 1930s to 1950s; excellent site for photos, nostalgic moments of past To talk to Jurgens' son, contact him at dick@hawaii.rr.com
www.downbeat.com	professional magazine for all musicians
www.neptune.com	Movies of the period
www.moviediva.com	Movies of the period
www.eonline.com/facts/movies	Information about movies
www.prairienet.org/ejahiel	Movie reviews
www.swingfever.com	San Francisco Bay area's swing band with musicians from top groups; Brubeck, Basie, Goodman, others
www.ludwig-drums.com	Drum manufacturer site
email: jamtimes@aol.com	World Jazz Network, international group that promotes jazz Bob Washington, director 701 Boliver St. Lady Lake, FL 32159
www.jazztimes.com	monthly jazz magazine
www.jazzimprov.com	JazzImprov magazine, source for everything jazz
www.swingsouthflorida.com	dedicated to South Florida

Swing Dance Society, swing Music, events, reviews

www.cmjo.com — Chicago Metropolitan Jazz Orchestra, the newest Midwest Big band with 20 veterans of Such bands as Kenton, Rich, Herman, Ferguson and others. Plays original Kenton arrangements.

www.jazzprofessional.com — One of the best and easy to use sites on big bands. Covers the spectrum; big bands, events, recordings, musicians, biographies. It's a cyberspace treat for those who love the era.

www.davehanlonscookbook.com — Central New York drummer, bandleader, Sammy Award winner

www.museum.media.org/duke/duke.html — The Duke Ellington Society, Duke Ellington Appreciation Page

www.library.ucla.edu/libraries/music — Register of the collection of big Band photographs, ca. 1930-1945 UCLA

WWW.zootsuitstore.com — Here's the place to find what to wear from a bygone era

www.tri-c.cc.oh.us/jazz — Cuyahoga Community College Jazz Studies Program

Yellowstonejazz@tritel.net — Annual Yellowstone Jazz Festival at Cody, WY

www.iaje.org — International Association for Jazz Education

info@stanfordjazz.org — Stanford Jazz Workshop, Stanford Unv.

hmejia@fullcoll.edu — Fullerton College Jazz Festival, Fullerton, CA

www.pyramidband.com — The Pyramid Dance Bands, professional ensembles from Northeastern US and Southern Canada

www.winternet.com/~trmpts/	Mike Vax, big band leader, trumpeter Educator
www.jazzreview.com/corners96.html	Big Band...What's Big? Viewpoint by Richard V. Duffy
music@sl.directabout.com	What you need to know about bands, blues, swing with Editor Bob Timm
arrangers@lushlifemusic.com	Arrangements for the big bands by bandleaders and arrangers
www.littlebigband.com	A creative home page for those interested in helping children find out more the big band sound
www.jazzhall.org/bbjhf.html	The Big Band & Jazz Hall of Fame explanation
www.jazzeast.com	Nova Scotia's online source for jazz
www.teorecords.com	Teo Macero, one of the major producers of big band albums for Maynard Ferguson, Woody Herman and others; about big bands
www.AnySwingGoes.com	Offers features, auction items, history William Ransom Hogan Archive Of New Orleans Jazz email:raeburn@tulane.edu Collection covers King Oliver's Creole Jazz Band days to later jazz & big Band. Dr. Bruce Boyd Raeburn, Curator
www.drummerman.net/biography.html	The biography of late, great drummer, Gene Krupa (with photos)
www.jazzprofessional.com/Summit/RichParnell FergusonSummit_1htm.	Part 1 of a conversation in a London Hotel which included Buddy Rich, Maynard Ferguson and Jack Parnell
www.tritonejazzfantasycamp.com	One of those once in a lifetime experiences designed for adult players (21 and over) to spend a week immersed in listening and playing great music with outstanding players of today
www.oscarpeterson.com	Canadian jazz pianist

www.bigbandsand www.bignames.com	Craig's site for big band, singer reviews
www.jangarber.com	site for the Garber band with Howie Schneider
www.jazztimes.com	solid jazz magazine with features

Where Jazz 101 Is Taught

The first contemporary jazz music education program started at North Texas State University in 1947 by Gene Hall and continues today, thanks to the pioneering efforts of Leonard Breeden who took over in 1959 and remained through 1981. In fact, North Texas is one of the few universities that offers bachelor's and master's degrees in jazz.

I spent nearly four months examining college and university web sites searching for jazz education programs. While a number of magazines had lists, I frequently found that such rosters included all campuses that had music schools, not those that offered jazz courses. As you will read, there is a difference.

While prohibited from majoring in music during my college days by my parents, I found it difficult to practice jazz even as a member of an ROTC Marching Band that played among popular numbers at the time, the St. Louis Blues March. Music practice rooms, I was told on more than one encounter with a music instructor, were "off limits" to jazz players.

The enclosed list of jazz and big band education programs is certainly not complete but I caution those seeking such a compendium to note the inconsistencies caused frequently by colleges and universities that permit graphic designers to become so creative their web sites don't include telephone numbers, addresses and other pertinent educational information. The roster below includes the information about schools with jazz web sites and their program features. My thanks to JazzTimes which offered a compendium in its 2001 directory issue. It led me to college catalogs, music instructors and more web sites about colleges than I want to visit again!

Once again, don't forget that web sites change from time to time. Some colleges allowed jazz programs to be listed under the personal site of the program director but they were not included in the search engine of the institutional site.

Alabama

University of Alabama, School of Music, Jazz Dept., PO Box 870366 Tuscaloosa, AL 35487, Telephone: 205-348-7110 web site: www.bama.ua.edu/~twolfe/ Jazz Studies Program, ensembles, seminars, degree, guest artists

Arizona

Arizona State University, School of Music, Box 870405, Tempe, AZ 85287-0405 Telephone: 480-965-3371 web site: www.asu.edu Jazz Studies uses Ravenscroft Jazz Complex

Northern Arizona University, School of Performing Arts, PO Box 6040, Flagstaff, AZ 86011-6040 Telephone: 928-523-3779 web site: www.nau.edu Jazz Studies, College of Fine Arts, 3 big bands, 4 combos, 4 jazz improv, 6 jazz history sections

California

University of Pacific, The Brubeck Institute, 3601 Pacific Ave., Stockton, CA 95211 Telephone: 209-946-3970 web site: uop.edu/brubeck BA in Jazz Studies (under development) Institute of Jazz Studies, Interdisciplinary Education

Cal State Fullerton, Music Dept, Box 6850, Fullerton, CA 92834-6850 Telephone: 714-278-5523 web site: www.fullerton.edu Jazz Studies, Jazz Ensemble, Combos

Cal Poly State University, Music Dept, San Luis Obispo, CA 93407 Telephone: 805-756-6699 web site: www.calpoly.edu Jazz Studies Program, Jazz Bands, Combos, Vocal Jazz

Cal State University at Bakersfield, 9001 Stockdale Highway, Bakersfield, CA 93304 Telephone: 661-664-3093 web site: www.csubak.edu/jazzfest Jazz Program, Jazz Albums, Festival, Ensembles, Jazz Singers

Cal State University at Northridge, 18111 Nordhoff St., Northridge, CA 91330-8314 Telephone: 818-677-3169 web site: www.csun.edu Jazz Studies, Guest Artists, Jazz Band

Diablo Valley College, 321 Golf Club Road, Pleasant Hill, CA 94523 Telephone: 925-605-1230, ext 452 web site: www.dvc.edu/music Jazz Studies

El Camino College, 16007 Crenshaw Boulevard, Torrance, CA 90506 Telephone: 310-532-3670 web site: www.elcaminocollege.org Jazz Course

The Jazzschool, 2375 Shattuck Ave., Berkeley, CA 94704 Telephone: 510-845-5373 web site: www.jazzschool.com Jazz Ensembles, Ear Training, Computers in Music, Jazz Movement, Big Band, Recording

Los Angeles Music Academy, 370 Fair Oaks Ave., Pasadena, CA 91105 Telephone: 626-568-8850 web site: www.lamusicacademy.com Performance, Fundamental Skills, Certificate of Completion

Los Medanos College, 2700 E. Leland Road, Pittsburg, CA 94565 Telephone: 925-439-2185 web site: www.losmedanos.net Guest Artists, Jazz Concerts

Musicians Institute, 1655 McCadden Place, Hollywood, CA 90028 Telephone: 323-462-1384 web site: www.mi.edu Recording Artist Program, Guest Artists

San Diego State University, School of Music and Dance, 5500 Campanie Drive, San Diego, CA 92182-7902 web site: sdsu.edu Bachelor and Master's in Jazz Studies, Ensemble, Big Band, Guest Artist

San Francisco State University, 1600 Holloway Ave., San Francisco, CA 94132 Telephone: 415-338-1344 web site: www.sfsu.edu/~music Bachelor in Jazz & World Music Studies, Guest Artists, Blues/R&B Ensemble, Bop Ensemble, Fusion Ensemble, Afro-Cuban, Creative World Ensembles

Sonoma State University, 1801 E. Cotati Ave., Rohnert Park, CA 94928 Telephone: 707-664-2324 web site: www.sonoma.edu/depts/performing Arts Jazz Studies Program, Degrees, Big Band Ensemble, Latin Jazz Ensemble,

Stanford Jazz Workshop, PO Box 20454, Stanford, CA 94309 Telephone: 650-736-0324 web site: www.stanfordjazz.org Jazz Camps, Jazz Residency, Guest Artists

University of Southern California, Thelonious Monk Institute of Jazz, 3443 Watt Way, Los Angeles, CA 90089-1102 Telephone 213-821-1500 web site: www.monkinstitute.com Institute Jazz Programs, International Jazz Competition, International Jazz Programs

University of California at Berkeley, 91 Cesar Chavez Centre, Berkeley, CA 94720 Telephone: 510-642-0212 web site: www.ucjazz.berkeley.edu Jazz Ensembles, Big Band, Guest Artists

University of Southern California, Thornton School of Music, 840 West 34th St. Los Angeles, CA 90089-0851 Telephone: 213-740-6935 web site: www.usc.edu/music/ Jazz Studies Program

Colorado

University of Colorado at Boulder, College of Music, Imig Bldg, 18th and Euclid, 301 UCB, Boulder, CO 80309-0301 Telephone: 303-492-6352 web site: www.colorado.edu/music Jazz Studies Program, Certificate in Undergraduate Jazz Studies, clinics, guest artists, ensembles, 3 big bands, 7 jazz combos

University of Denver, Lamont School of Music, 7111 Montview Blvd, Denver, CO 80220 Telephone: 303-871-6973 web site: www.du.edu/lamont Bachelor's in Jazz Studies, combos, African-American musics, guest artists, Bachelor's in Commercial Music

University of Northern Colorado, Jazz Studies Program, 501 20th Street, Greeley, CO 80639 Telephone: 970-351-2577 web site: www.arts.unco.edu/uncjazz Guest Artists, Jazz Studies, combos

Connecticut

Fairfield University, 1073 North Benson Rd., Fairfield, CT, 06430 Telephone: 203-254-4000 ext 2458 web site: www.briantorff.com University Jazz Company, University World Music Ensemble, Guest Artists, Minor in Jazz/Popular Performance

District of Columbia

Howard University, College of Arts & Sciences, Jazz Studies Division, 2400 6th St., NW, Washington, DC, 2005 Telephone: 202-806-7137-7082 web site: www.howard.edu

Florida

Florida State University, School of Music, Tallahassee, FL, 32306-1180 Telephone: 850-644-3424 web site: www.music.fsu.edu Bachelor of Arts in Jazz, Master of Music in Jazz, Jazz Vocal Ensemble, Guest Artists

Georgia

Idaho

University of Idaho, Lionel Hampton School of Music, Music Bldg, Room 206, Moscow, ID 83844-4015 Telephone: 208-885-6231 web site: www.uidaho.edu/LS.music email: music@uidaho.edu Music Camps, bachelor's degrees, master's degrees, festival Boise State University, School of Music, Clinics, Gene Harris Jazz Festival, big band

Illinois

Augustana College, 639 38th St, Rock Island, IL 61201, Telephone: 309-794-7233; 800-798-8100 ext 7239 Web site: www.augustana.edu, minor in Jazz Studies, Jazz ensembles, Guest Artists, combos

Bloom School of Jazz, 218 Wabash Ave, Suite 600, Chicago, IL 60604 Telephone: 312-957-9300

Chicago College of Performing Arts, Roosevelt University, 430 S. Michigan Ave, Chicago, IL 60605 Telephone: 312-341-3789 web site: www.roosevelt.edu Bachelor of Music, Jazz Studies; Jazz Studies, Composition; Guest Artists, Combo

Columbia College Chicago, 600 S. Michigan Ave., Chicago, IL 60605 Telephone: 312-344-6322 web site: www.colum.edu

DePaul University, School of Music, 804 W. Belden Ave., Chicago, IL 60614 Telephone: 773-325-7444 web site: www.music.depaul.edu Jazz Studies Program, ensembles, combos, guest artists

Eastern Illinois University, 600 Lincoln Ave, Charleston, IL 61920 Telephone: 217-581-6628 web site: www.eiu.edu/~eiujazzJazz Email: cfswf@eiu.edu Jazz Studies Program, Festival, Guest Artists,

Northern Illinois University, School of Music, 310 Carol Ave, DeKalb, IL 60115 Telephone: 815-753-1551 web site: www.vpa.niu.edu/music

Northwestern University, School of Music, 711 Elgin Road, Evanston, IL 60208-1200 Telephone: 847-491-3141 web site: www.northwestern.edu/musicschool Jazz Studies, Commercial Music Certificates

Southern Illinois University at Carbondale, School of Music, Carbondale, IL 62901 Telephone: 618-536-8742 web site:www.siue.edu/MUSIC/index.html

Southern Illinois University at Edwardsville, Music Department, Box 1771, Edwardsville, IL 62026-1771 Telephone: 618-650-2026 web site: www.siue.edu/Bachelor's in Music Specializing in Jazz Performance, Ensembles

Indiana

Indiana University, School of Music, 1201 East 3rd St., MU 101, Bloomington, IN 47405 Telephone: 812-855-7998 web site: www.music.indiana.edu/som/jazz Jazz Studies Department, 4 Ensembles, Guest Artists

Iowa

University of Iowa, Jazz Studies, Voxman Music Building, Iowa City, IA 50614-0246 Telephone 319-335-1604 web site: www.uiowa.edu

University of Northern Iowa, School of Music, Cedar Falls, IA 50614-0246 Telephone: 319-273-6431 web site: www.uni.edu/jazzstudies Division of Jazz Studies, Bachelor's in Jazz

Studies, Jazz Specialization, Minor in Jazz Studies, Master's in Jazz Pedagogy, 3 jazz bands, combos, guest artists, Scholarships

Kansas

Kentucky

University of Louisville, Jamey Aebersold Jazz Studies Program, School of Music Louisville, KY 40292 Telephone: 502-852-6907; 800-334-UofL Web site: www.louisville.edu/music/jazz Bachelor of Arts in Jazz, Bachelor of Arts in Music Industry, Master of Music/concentration in Jazz, Jazz Ensemble, Jazz Combos, Vocal Jazz Ensemble

Louisiana

Loyola University New Orleans, College of Music, 6363 St. Charles Ave, Box 8, New Orleans, LA 70118 Telephone: 504-865-3037 web site: www.loyno.edu/music. Bachelor of Music Jazz Studies, Guest Artists, Jazz Band

University of New Orleans, Dept. of Music, New Orleans, 70148 Telephone: 504-286-6381 web site: www.uno.edu/~music, Bachelor of Arts, Music/Jazz Performance, Guest Artists, Ensembles

Maine

University of Maine at Augusta, 46 University Drive, Augusta, ME 04330-9410 Telephone: 207-621-3274, 877-UMA-1234 web site: www.uma.maine.edu, Jazz and Contemporary Music Program, Jazz Week, Guest Artists, Ensembles

Maryland

Towson University, Music Dept., 8000 York Road, Towson, MD 21252 Telephone: 410-704-2839 web site: www.towson.edu/music, Vocal Jazz Ensemble, Guest Artists, Combos, Latin Jazz Ensemble, Jazz Guitar Ensemble

University of Maryland, School of Music, 2116 Clarice Smith Performing Arts Center College Park, MD 20742-1211 Telephone: 301-405-1313 Web site: www.umd.edu, Bachelor's with Jazz Studies Emphasis, Master's in Jazz Studies, Ensembles, Guest Artists

Massachusetts

Berklee College of Music, 1140 Bolyston St, Boston, MA 02215 Telephone: 800-BERKLEE web site: www.berklee.edu

Longy School of Music, 1 Follen St., Cambridge, MA 02138 Telephone: 617-876-0956 web site: www.longy.edu

New England Conservatory of Music, 290 Huntington Ave., Boston, MA 02115 Telephone: 617-585-1100 web site: www.newenglandconservatory.edu, Jazz & Improvisation, Ensembles, Guest Artists

University of Massachusetts at Amherst, Dept. of Music & Dance, Fine Arts Center Box 32520, Umass-Amherst, MA 01003 Telephone: 413-545-6046 Web site: www.umass.edu/music-dance, Jazz & Afro-American music

University of Massachusetts at Lowell, College of Fine Arts, Durgin Hall, 35 Wilder St., Lowell, MA 01854 Telephone: 978-934-3850 web site:www.uml.edu

Michigan

Michigan State University, School of Music, 102 Music Building, East Lansing, MI 48824 Telephone: 517-355-2140 web site: www.music.msu.edu

University of Michigan, School of Music, 1100 Baits Drive, Moore Building, Ann Arbor, MI 48109-2085 Telephone: 734-764-0583 web site: www.music.umich.edu Jazz & Improvisation Studies, Bachelor's in Jazz & Contemporary Improvisation, Bachelor's in Jazz Studies, Bachelor's in Jazz & Contemplative Studies, Master's In Improvisation, Ensembles, Big Bands

Wayne State University, Dept. of Music, 1321 Old Main, Detroit, MI 48202 Telephone: 313-577-1795 web site: www.music.wayne.edu, Jazz Division, Jazztet, 2 big bands, Ensembles, Guest Artists, Vocal Jazz, Bachelor's with Concentration in Jazz Studies

Western Michigan University, School of Music, 1201 Oliver, Kalamazoo, MI 49008 Telephone: 616-387-4667 web site: www.wmich.edu/music/, Bachelor's in Jazz Studies, Master's in Jazz Performance, Jazz Scholarships, Vocal Jazz, Ensembles

Minnesota

Music Tech, Musicians Technical Training Center, 304 North Washington, Minneapolis, MN 55401 Telephone: 800-594-9500 web site: www.musictech.com, Associate Of Applied Science Degree, Experiential Music, Mentoring Education programs, 9,000 Square foot Music Recording Complex

University of Minnesota at Duluth, Dept. of Music, School of Fine Arts, 231 Humanities Building, 10 University Drive, Duluth, MN 55812 Telephone: 218-726-8212 web site: www.d.unn.ed/music

Mississippi

Jackson State University, Dept. of Music, PO Box 17055, Jackson, MS 39217 Telephone: 601-979-2141 web site: www.jsums.edu

University of Southern Mississippi, School of Music, Box 5081, Hattiesburg, MS 39406-5081 Telephone: 601-266-4047 web site" www.arts.usm.edu Jazz Studies Program, 2 big bands, 8 combos of various sizes, Guest Artists, Jazz Scholarship,

Missouri

Central Missouri State University, Dept. of Music, Warrensburg, MO 64093, Telephone: 816-543-4530 web site: www.cmsu.edu/music

University of Missouri at Kansas City, Conservatory of Music, 4949 Cherry St, Kansas City, MO 64110-2229 Telephone: 816-235-2900 Web site: www.umkc.edu/conservatory

Webster University, 470 East Lockwood Ave, St. Louis, MO 63119 Telephone: 314-968-7032 web site: www.webster.edu, Bachelor's Of Music in Composition, Jazz Performance, Jazz/Music Technology Combos, Big Bands, Jazz Singers, Guest Artists

Montana

Nebraska

University of Nebraska at Kearney, 905 West 25th St., Kearney, NE 68847 Telephone: 308-865-8616 web site: www.unk.edu

Nevada

University of Nevada, Las Vegas, 4505 Maryland Parkway, Las Vegas NV 89154-5025 Telephone: 702-895-4992 web site: www.univ.edu/colleges/fine_arts/music/jazz/html

University of Nevada, Reno, Music Dept, Reno, NV 89557 Telephone: 702-784-6145 web site: www.unr.edu/unr/

New Hampshire

University of New Hampshire, Dept. of Music, 30 College Road, Paul Creative Arts Center Durham, NH 03824-3538 Telephone: 603-862-2404 Web site: www.unh.edu Ensembles, Jazz Graduate Assistantship

New Jersey

Rowan University, Maynard Ferguson Institute of Jazz Studies, Wilson Hall, Music Dept Glassboro, NJ 08028 Telephone: 856-256-4000 web site: www.rowan.edu Bachelor's in Jazz/Performance, Jazz/Music Education, Master's in Jazz Studies, Dixieland Band, Big Band, Ensembles, Jazz Voice

New Jersey City University, 2039 Kennedy Blvd, Jersey City, NJ 07305-1597 Telephone: 201-200-3091 web site: www.njcu.edu, Jazz Studies Track 2 Ensembles

Princeton University, Woolworth Center of Musical Studies, Princeton, NJ 08544-1007 Telephone: 609-258-4241 web site: www.princeton.edu/~puje, Ensembles, Big Band

Rutgers-The State University of New Jersey, Dept. of Music, 100 Clifton Ave, Douglass Campus, New Brunswick, NJ08901-1568 Telephone: 732-932-9302 web site: www.musicweb.rutgers.edu, Ensembles, Jazz Graduate Assistantship, Guest Artists

William Paterson University, Music Dept, Shea Center for the Performing Arts, 300 Pompton Road, Wayne, NJ 0747 Telephone: 973-720-2268 web site: www.wpunj.edu Bachelor's in Jazz Studies & Performance, Bachelor's Music Management Jazz Performance, Combos, New York Internships

New York

Aaron Copland School of Music, Queens College/CUNY, Flushing, NY 11367-1597 Telephone: 718-997-3800 web site: www.qc.edu, Jazz Ensemble, Big Bands, Combos

Brooklyn Conservatory of Music, 587th Ave, Brooklyn, NY 11217 Telephone: 718-622-3300 web site: www.brooklynconservatory.com

The Brooklyn-Queens Conservatory of Music, 42-76 Main St, Flushing, NY 11355 Telephone: 718-461-8910 web site: www.brooklynconservatory.com, Jazz Division, Professional Diploma, Graduate Diploma, Jazz Ensembles

The Collective, Jazz Studies, 541 Avenue of the Americas, 4th Floor, New York, NY 10011 Telephone: 212-741-0091 web site: www.thecoll.com, The Jazz Workshop, Octette, R&B Blues Band,

The College of Saint Rose, 432 Western Ave., Albany, NY 12203 Telephone: 518-454-5178 web site: www.strose.edu, Jazz Studies, Concentration, Music Industry Concentration

Eastman School of Music, 26 Gibbs St, Rochester, NY 14604 Telephone: 800-388-9695 web site: www.rochester.edu/Eastman, Jazz Studies, Guest Artists

Hamilton College, Clinton, NY 13323-1411, Jazz Archive Telephone: 315-859-5914 web site: www.monkrowe.com

Ithaca College, School of Music, 3322 Whalen Center, Ithaca, NY 14850 Telephone: 607-274-3366 web site: www.ithaca.edu, Bachelor's of Music in Jazz Studies, Big Bands, Ensembles, Guest Artists

New School Jazz & Contemporary Music Program, 55 West 13th St, New York, NY 10011, Telephone: 212-229-5896 web site: www.newschool.edu/jazz, Jazz Performance, Jazz Vocals, Guest Artists

New York University, 35 West 4th St, Room 777, New York, NY 10012 Telephone: 212-998-5424 web site: www.nyu.edu/education/music/mjazz, Bachelor's with Sequence in Jazz, Master's in Jazz Performance/Jazz Composition, Doctor Philosophy, Jazz Performance/Jazz Composition, Ensembles, Guest Artists

School for Improvisational Music, 28-15 Steinway St, Astoria, NY 11103 Telephone: 212-631-5882 web site: www.schoolforimprov.org. guest artists, Ensembles

Skidmore Jazz Institute, Skidmore College, Office of the Dean of Special Programs, 815 North Broadway, Saratoga Springs, NY 12866 Telephone: 518-580-5590 web site: www.skidmore.edu

SUNY College at Fredonia, Mason Hall, School of Music, Fredonia, NY 14063 Telephone: 716-673-3151 web site: www.fredonia.edu, Concentration in Jazz Studies,

Syracuse University, School of Music, 402 Crouse College, Syracuse, NY 13244-1010 Telephone: 315-443-2191 web: www.syracuse.edu

North Carolina

Brevard College, 400 North Broad St., Brevard, NC 28712 Telephone 828-883-8292, 800-527-9090 web site: www.brevard.edu, Music With Jazz Studies Emphasis

East Carolina University, School of Music, Greenville, NC 27858 Telephone: 252-328-6851 web site: www.music.ecu.edu, Jazz Major, Ensembles Elon College, Campus Box 2800,

Elon College, NC 27244 Telephone: 336-278-5600 web site: www.elon.edu, Guest Artist, Jazz Studies

University of North Carolina at Asheville, Dept. of Music, CPO 2290 One University Heights, Asheville, NC 28804-8510 Telephone: 828-251-6432 web site: www.unca.edu, Bachelor's in Music With Jazz Studies Emphasis, Ensembles

University of North Carolina at Chapel Hill, Dept. of Music, Hill Hall CB#3320 Chapel Hill, NC 28804-8510 Telephone: 919-962-7560 Web site: www.unc.edu.depts/music/index.html

University of North Carolina at Greensboro, Miles Davis Jazz Studies Program, School of Music, PO Box 26167, Greensboro, NC 17402-6167 Telephone: 336-334-5789 web site: www.uncg.edu/mus, Jazz Studies Program, West African Ensemble, Guest Artists,

Ohio

Bowling Green State University, College of Musical Arts, Moore Musical Arts Center, Bowling Green, OH 43403-0290 Telephone: 419-372-2181 web site: www.bgsu.edu/colleges/music, Jazz Studies, Bachelor's of Music in Jazz Studies, Ensembles

Capital University, 2199 East Main St, Columbus, OH 43209-2394 Telephone: 614-236-6411, 800-289-6289 web site: www.capital.edu, Bachelor's of Music in Jazz Studies, Ensembles

Cleveland State University, Black Studies Program, African-American Cultural Center, University Center Room 103, Cleveland, OH 4415-2214 Telephone: 216-687-3655 web site: www.csuohio.edu

Oberlin Conservatory of Music, 77 West College St., Oberlin, OH 44074 Telephone: 440-775-8413 web site: www.oberlin.edu, Guest Artists, Jazz Performance Major Jazz Composition Major, Jazz Ensemble, Jazz Trios, Jazz Octet

Ohio State University, School of Music, 1866 North College Road, Columbus, OH 43210 Telephone: 614-292-2870 web site: www.arts.ohio-state.edu/Music/ Tri-C Jazz

Studies at Cuyahoga Community College, 2900 Community College Ave,' Cleveland, OH 44115 Telephone: 216-987-4254 web site: www.tri-c.cc.oh.us/jazz, Ensembles, Guest Artists

University of Akron, School of Music, Guzzetta Hall, Akron, OH 44325-1002 Telephone: 330-972-6910 web site: www.uakron.edu/music_welcome.html

University of Cincinnati, College of Conservatory of Music, Cincinnati, OH 45221-0003 Telephone: 513-556-5463 web site: www.ccm.uc.edu, Jazz Studies Program, Guest Artists, Ensembles, Bachelor's of Music in Jazz Studies

Youngstown State University Dana School of Music, One University Plaza, Youngstown, OH 44555 Telephone: 330-742-3636 web site: www.fpa.ysu.edu

Oregon

University of Oregon, School of Music/Jazz Studies, 1225 University of Oregon, Eugene, OR 97403-1225 Telephone: 541-346-2107 Web site: www.uoregon.edu, Bachelor's of Music in Jazz Studies, Chamber Jazz, Big Bands, Vocal Jazz Ensemble, Jazz Combos

Pennsylvania

Duquesne University, Mary Pappert School of Music, 600 Forbes Ave, Pittsburgh, PA 15282 Telephone: 412-396-5983 web site: www.duq.edu

East Stroudsburg, University of Pennsylvania, Fine & Performing Arts Center, Music Dept., 200 Prospect St, East Stroudsburg, PA 18301-2999 Web site: www.esu.edu/, Music Minor in Jazz Studies, Pop/Jazz Singers, Jazz Ensemble

Lehigh University, College of Arts & Sciences, Dept of Music, Zoellner Arts Center, 420 East Packer Ave, Bethlehem, PA 18018 Telephone: 610-758-3835 web site: www.lehigh.edu/~inmsc

Millersville University, Music Dept, PO Box 1002, Millersville, PA 17551-0302 Telephone: 717-872-3460 web site: www.millersv.edu, Jazz Studies, Jazz Ensemble, JazzLab Band,

Moravian College, Music Dept, 1200 Main St, Bethlehem, PA 18018 610-861-1650 web site: www.moravian.edu, Bachelor's of Music in Jazz Performance, Jazz Vocals, Guest Artists, Ensembles

Slippery Rock University of Pennsylvania, 225 Swope Music Hall, Slippery Rock, PA 16057 Telephone: 724-738-2444 web site: www.sru.edu

Temple University, Esther Boyer College of Music, 2001 North 13th St. Philadelphia, PA 19122 Telephone: 215-204-8301 web site: www.temple.edu/music Bachelor's of Music in Jazz Arranging, Jazz Performance, Guest Artists, Jazz Band, Lab Band, Fusion Ensemble, Percussion Ensemble, Guitar Ensemble, Vocal Ensemble,

University of the Arts, School of Music, 320 South Broad St, Philadelphia, PA 19102 Telephone: 215-717-6340 web site: www.uarts.edu

Rhode Island

University of Rhode Island, Dept. of Music, Fine Arts Center, 105 Upper College Rd, Kingston, RI 02881-0820 Telephone: 401-874-2765 Web site: www.uri.edu Jazz Ensembles, Big Band,

South Carolina

College of Charleston, Music Dept, 54 St. Philips St, Charleston, SC 29424
Telephone: 843-953-4991 web site: www.cofc.edu, Jazz Program, Jazz Concentration

University of South Carolina, School of Music, Columbia, SC 29208 Telephone: 803-777-4280 web site: www.music.sc.edu, Bachelor's with Emphasis in Jazz Studies, Master's with emphasis in Jazz Studies, Jazz Combos, Guest Artists

Winthrop University, Dept of Music, Rock Hill, SC 29733 Telephone: 803-323-2255 web site: www.winthrop.edu/music, Jazz Ensemble, Jazz Voices, Jazz Combos,

Tennessee

University of Memphis, Rudi E. Scheidt School of Music, Jazz & Studio Music Division, Memphis, TN 38152 Telephone: 901-678-2541 web site: www.music.memphis.edu, Bachelor's in Jazz and Studio Music, Master's In Jazz and Studio Music, Guest Artists, Ensembles

Texas

Collin County Community College, 2800 East Spring Creek Parkway, Plano, TX 75074 Telephone: 972-881-5108 web site: www.ccccd.edu, Jazz & Instrumental Studies, Big Band, Jazz Combos, Vocal Jazz

Lamar University, Dept. of Music, Theatre & Dance, PO Box 10044, Beaumont, TX 77710 Telephone: 409-880-8144 web site: www.lamar.edu

Southwest Texas State University, School of Music, 601 University Drive, San Marcos, TX 78666-4616 Telephone: 512-245-2651 web site:www.swt.edu, Bachelor's Of Music in Jazz Studies, Ensembles,

Texas Christian University, School of Music, Box 297500, Fort Worth, TX 76129 Telephone: 817-257-7640 web site: www.tcu.edu, Jazz Festival, Guest Artists, Jazz Ensembles, Studio Jazz Orchestra

University of North Texas, Jazz Studies, PO Box 305040, Denton, TX 76203 Telephone: 940-565-3743 web site: www.music.unt.edu/jazz, Bachelor's In Jazz Performance Arranging, Jazz Performance Instrumental, Jazz Performance Vocal, Master's Jazz Studio, Master's in Music Education for Jazz, One O'Clock Band, Two O'Clock Band, Jazz

Repertory Band, Zebras Keyboard, Jazz Guitar, Jazz Singers, 7 lab bands, Jazz small groups, NT Jazz Septet, Jazz Strings

Utah

Virginia

James Madison University, 800 South Main St, MSC 7301, Harrisonburg, VA 22807 Telephone: 540-568-6197 web site: www.jmu.edu, Bachelor's in Jazz Performance, Ensembles, Guest Artists

Shenandoah University, 1460 University Drive, Winchester, VA 2260 Telephone: 540-665-4581 web site: www.su.edu, Bachelor's in Jazz Studies,

Virginia Commonwealth University, 922 Park Avenue, Box 842004 Richmond, VA 23284-2004 Telephone: 804-828-1166 Web site: www.vcu.edu, Jazz Studies, Bachelor's in Jazz Studies, Ensembles, Guest Artists, Jazz Orchestra

Virginia Tech University, Music Dept, Jazz Studies, 242 Q Squires Blacksburg, VA 24061 Telephone: 540-231-4719 Web site: www.music.vt.edu

Virginia Union University, Dept of Music & Fine Arts, 1500 North Lombardy Richmond, VA 23220 Telephone: 804-257-5665 Web site: www.vuu.edu, Bachelor's in Commercial Music/Jazz Studies, Ensembles

Washington

Cornish College of the Arts, 710 East Roy St, Seattle, WA 98102 Telephone: 206-323-1400 web site: www.cornish.edu, Jazz Courses, Guest Artists, Ensembles

Shoreline Community College, 16101 Greenwood Ave North, Seattle, WA 98133 Telephone 206-5464759 web site: www.ctc.edu

Washington State University, Music Program, PO Box 645300, Pullman, WA 99164-5300 Telephone: 509-335-4244 web site: www.wsu.edu/music_and_theatre, Jazz Studies, Minor in Jazz Studies, Jazz Big Band, Vocal Jazz Ensemble, combos

Whitworth College, 300 West Hawthorne Road, Spokane, WA 99251 Telephone: 509-777-3280 web site: www.whitworth.edu

West Virginia

West Virginia University, Division of Music, PO Box 6111, Morgantown, WVA 26506 Telephone: 304-293-4617 web site: www.wvu.edu/~music, Bachelor's in Jazz Studies, Master's, Doctorate in Jazz Pedagogy

Wisconsin

Lawrence University, Conservatory of Music, Appleton, WI 54912-0599 Telephone: 800-227-0982 web site: www.Lawrence.edu, jazz studies & Improvisational Music, Guest Artists, Big Bands, Ensembles, Jazz Vocals. Scholarships

University of Wisconsin-Indianhead, Indianhead Arts & Education Center, PO Box 315 Shell Lake, WI 54871 Telephone: 715-468-2414 Web site: www.swt.edu

University of Wisconsin-Stevens Point, Dept of Music, Stevens Point, WI 54481-3897 Telephone: 715-346-4054 web site: www.uwsp-edu/music/jazzstudies.htm

Wyoming

Northwest College, Music Dept, 231 West 6th St, Powell, WY 82435 Telephone: 307-754-6301 web site: www.nwc.whecn.edu

Canada

The Banff Centre for the Arts, Box 1020, Station 23, Banff, Alberta TOL OCO Telephone: 403-762-6188 web site: www.banffcentre.ca/music, Jazz Orchestra, Vocal Jazz Workshop, International Jazz Workshop

The Hamilton College Jazz Archive

The Jazz Archive contains a rich, extensive videotape collection of the leaders, musicians, arrangers of the swing, big band days. To access the tapes and archive material contact Monk Rowe, director at www.monkrowe.com.

Below are the players in the collection (7/2002) by instrument or category:

Piano

Toshiko Akiyoshi, Steve Allen, Joanne Brackeen, Dave Brubeck, Ray Bryant, John Bunch, Joe Bushkin, Jeannie Cheatham, Herbie Hancock, Dick Hyman, Keith Ingram, Jane Jarvis, Pete Jolly, Dick Katz, Roy Kral, Pete Levin, Junior Mance (parts I & II) Dave McKenna, Marian McPartland, Jay McShann, Marty Napoleon, Oscar Peterson, George Shearing, Ray Sherman, Norman Simmons, Derek Smith, Paul Smith, Frank Strazzeri, Ralph Sutton, Billy Taylor, Ross Tompkins, Johnny Varro, Dan Wall, Gerald Wiggins, Mike Wofford, Richard Wyands

Bass

Keter Betts, Walter Booker, Ron Carter, Bob Cranshaw, Bill Crow, Phil Flanigan, Steve Gilmore, Bob Haggart, John Heard, Milt Hinton, Chubby Jackson, Jay Leonhart, Jack Lesberg, Jimmy Lewis, Bob Magnusson, Christian McBride, Michael Moore, Genevieve Rose, Frank Tate, Buster Williams

Flute

Holly Hoffmann, Sam Most (clarinet & tenor), Dave Valentin, Frank Wess (& tenor)

Guitar

Howard Alden, John Abercrombie, Billy Bauer, Gene Bertoncini, Cal Collins, Herb Ellis (parts I & II), Marty Grosz, Henry Johnson, Bucky Pizzarelli, John Pizzarelli Jr.

Clarinet

Kenny Davern, Buddy DeFranco, Bob Gordon, Eiji Kitamura, Abe Most, Ken Peplowski (alto saxophone), Allen Vache, Bob Wilber (& saxophone)

Drums

Don Alias, Joe Ascione, Louie Bellson, Frank Capp, Greg Caputo, Jimmy Cobb, Panama Francis, Chico Hamilton, Jake Hanna, Duffy Jackson, Eddie Locke, Sherri Maricle, Roy McCurdy, Butch Miles, Adam Nussbaum, Alvin Queen, Mickey Roker, Bob Rosengarden, Ed Shaughnessy (parts I & II), Hal Smith, Jackie Williams, Jimmy Wormsworth

Vocalists

Ruth Brown, Jackie Cain, Jeannie Cheatham, Jon Hendricks (Part I & II), Joanne "Pug" Horton (Wilber), Etta Jones, Sheila Jordan, Rebecca Kilgore, Roy Kral, Diannne Reeves, Annie Ross, Joe Williams, Nancy Wilson, Jimmy Witherspoon

Saxophone

Harry Allen, Tom Baker, Jane Ira Bloom, Nick Brignola, Buddy Colette, Charles Davis, Jerry Dodgion, Frank Foster (Parts I & II), Al Gallodoro, Jim Galloway, Scott Hamilton, Bob Hardaway, Red Holloway, Jerry Jerome, Plas Johnson, John LaPorta, Carmen Leggio, Charles McPherson, Don Menza, Billy Mitchell, James Moody, Lanny Morgan, Sam Most, Tommy Newsom, Harold Ousley, Dave Pell, Houston Person (Parts I & II), Flip Phillips, Vi Redd, Jerome Richardson, Scott Robinson, Ray Shiner, Lew Tabackin, Buddy Tate, Joe Temperley, Norris Turney, Benny Waters, Bobby Watson, Frank Wess, Phil Woods

Trombone

Wayne Andre, Dan Barrett, Eddie Bert, Jimmy Cheatham, Buster Cooper, Urbie Green, Al Grey, Bob Havens, Bill Hughes, George Masso, Grover Mitchell, Benny Powell (Parts I &II), Alan Raph, Roswell Rudd, Bill Watrous, Spiegle Willcox

Vibraphone

Lionel Hampton, Terry Gibbs

Violin

Claude "Fiddler" Williams

Trumpet

Nat Adderly, Bill Berry, Johnny Best, Wendell Brunious (Parts I & II), Conte Condoli, Pete Condoli, Doc Cheatham, Rusty Dedrick, Peter Eckland, Harry "Sweets" Edison, Bobby Johnson Jr, Jon Erik Kellso, Sam Noto, Jack Palmer, Ed Polcer, Randy Sandke, Bob Schultz, Jack Sheldon, Lew Soloff, Bryon Stripling, Clark Terry, Warren Vache, Joe Wilder (Parts I & II), Gerald Wilson, Snooky Young

Arrangers, Composers, Authors, Etc

Manny Album, Steve Allen, George Anakin, Jean Bach, John Budd, Ray Connive, Helen Oakley Dance, Stanley Dance, Milt Fillius Jr., Ira Gentler, Leslie Gorse, Skitch Henderson, Mona Hinton (Mrs. Milt), Bill Holman, Stanley Kay, Ruth Lion (Mrs. Alfred), John Levy, Albert Murray, Maria Schneider, Peter Vacherie, Jillian Williams (Mrs. Joe) Don Wolff

Big Band Music Live In Concert

There was nothing more exciting, adrenalin-pumping or important to me while growing up than a date to see a big band. Unlike the electronic umbilical today that can make virtual performances from digital, videotape and a number of cyberspace links, you either were among the eager crowds in the 1940s and '50s or you missed a performance never to be heard again.

Fortunately, some bandleaders, sound engineers and record company producers intuitively decided that particular events were too good to pass up. Consequently, some 33 1/3 vinyls began showing up on the music racks in the 1950s from audio recordings of remote locations at hotels, restaurants and ballrooms.

What made live performances so memorable?

Virtually everybody you ask who was there has a different take on the evening. Some women remember it as the special night with a special date, the playing of a special number, an eventful high school or college, fraternity or sorority evening or the night that special someone got pinned or popped the question.

Musicians normally offered a different perspective. It was the night a great soloist failed to meet high standards that locals set for his performance. It was the night you heard Woody Herman's Four Brothers sax section demonstrate how different and exciting it was. Or it was the night you heard the power of Stan Kenton brass section. Maybe it was the evening you heard the subtle tones and artistry of outstanding soloists and leaders like Tommy Dorsey or Benny Goodman. You listened to them on records but you never saw them up close and personal from the space you spent hours protecting near the bandstand. You knew what you wanted to hear if you went to listen to Count Basie, Duke Ellington, Kenton, Gene Krupa and, in later years, Buddy Rich. Krupa and Rich represented totally different eras of drumming and their bands offered totally different sounds but to say one was better than the other was to say you really didn't understand the fun the two had in drum battles while a part of Jazz at the Philharmonic. A brash Buddy Rich was the Rush Limbaugh of music at the time. Krupa was the "shucks, gee whiz" Jimmy Stewart type on and off the stand. Both gave performances right up until the end of their lives that required sweat towels to accompany drumsticks.

Technology played a dominant role in the live performances of the period, too. Crude monaural single track, bulky equipment recorded the concerts in the early 1950s.

But music engineers were always trying to perfect their craft. At the Hollywood Palladium, Gerry Macdonald built a stereo sound system to record big band events and he persuaded Les Brown to let him tape a Band of Renown's appearance. Larry Elgart and Harry James followed the Brown orchestra at the Palladium and both were also recorded. Les took the tapes home and forgot about them. Like the famous Benny Goodman Carnegie Hall tapes discovered in the closet years later, Les discovered the recordings in the early 1990s, said Malcolm Laycock of the BBC Radio in the Big Band International Newsletter, August, 2001, and they were issued on CD.

What were some of the outstanding live performances of the Big Band era? Here are a few that I believe stand out although they are merely representative of the period and not selected to be the best of the breed.

Les Brown at the Hollywood Palladium, Coral Records, 1953

Certain locations told leaders they could produce a good live recording. Having a good book of charts and great musicians to play it could rarely be overlooked either. Both contributed to Les Brown's decision just before Labor Day early in the 1950s to record his Band of Renown's three week stint at the Hollywood Palladium. He made sure all his radio broadcasts were taped and, with the help of Bob Thiele, the edited tapes were examined to include, not exclude, long solos of importance. Nothing worse than hearing a swinging band building to a climax with a soloist and have the transcription shortened so the recording meets a prescribed length. That's what made Les Brown at the Hollywood Palladium such a powerful album. And a surprising one, too.

Most people associated Les and his band to background sound for comedian Bob Hope and his many USO tours, introducing stars and vocalists.

The Palladium album demonstrated the energy and creativeness of the Brown band.

Said the late Leonard Feather of Les and his music: "Though unwilling to feature himself as a soloist, Les is neither the figurehead nor the 'businessman-only' bandleader type; he is the musical guide and mentor of everything that happens in the band." Listen carefully to his 33 1/3 album and you hear Les exhorting guys to "walk it," "play it" and "kick it." The album demonstrated clearly how the Brown band could swing when given the chance. Listen to Wes Hensel's trumpet on his own composition Montoona Clipper. Follow Dave Pell's rapidly building tenor sax as the band takes the chart from 1st to overdrive without deviating from the chart.

The band at the time was composed of solid West Coast players you might find at Howard Rumsey's Lighthouse sitting in any night. Ronnie Lang and Sal Libero were on alto saxophones, Rolly Bundock on bass, Geof Clarkson on piano, Don Fagerquist and Hensel of trumpets, Dick Noel and Ray Sims on trombones, Butch Stone on tenor and vocals and one of the smoothest, talented percussionists of the day, Jack Sperling on drums.

One Night Stand At The Aragon Ballroom, Chicago, Harry James, Columbia, Fall, 1952

Like one night stands by any of the major bands—Goodman, Ellington, Basie, Kenton and others—Harry James knew how to market a band of talent but no real star performers besides himself. He also knew that the era of the big band was becoming more difficult to sell as ballrooms closed and club dates became fewer and farther between. James and Columbia pop album director George Avakian thought that a live performance of the band might rekindle the flame that had existed in the 1940s. When the band was due in to play at one of the historic ballroom of ballrooms in the Midwest, the Aragon, the CBS engineering department put a line in to tape the band's late broadcasts. The sound was great and James and CBS got permission from the American Federation of Musicians to produce an album of live music.

These two sides of vinyl were carefully arranged to simulate a typical James ballroom set for dancing and listening. To make it more actual, there are bars of the band's sign off signature on one side. The album plays to the strength of Harry James, somewhat similar to an album by Maynard Ferguson and his band at Jimmy's in New York City. Both are powerful trumpet players and their bands focused on spotlighting their leaders and their talents with the instrument.

You won't find featured stars in the James' sections but you do hear solid musicianship. Bob Poland on sax, Nick Buono on trumpet, Bruce MacDonald on piano and Jackie Mills on drums...you'll even hear Harry pull out all the stops and play bongos on "Mom Bongo." Lots of unison chorusing and shorter solos but every number featured solid beats.

The final sentence from the Harry James album jacket liner says it all:

"The one night stand is clearly one of the most effective ways to bring live popular music and its audiences together, and stands such as this one indicates that the tradition has plenty of life left in it—at least as long as Harry James is etching out the lead with his unforgettable trumpet."

Jazz At Oberlin, The Dave Brubeck Quartet, 1953, Fantasy Jazz

We traveled from Bowling Green State Unv, Bowling Green, OH to hear a big sound not a big band that night, March 2, 1953. Brubeck wasn't a household word in the music business at the time. He was a 33-year-old pianist with some progressive thoughts about composition and chording. He was a jazz revolutionary who studied with French composer Darius Milhaud at Mills College, formed an octet of Milhaud students in 1946 and played his first off-campus concert two years later.

"Counterpoint, which had become almost dormant in the Swing Era and is now a commonly accepted in modern jazz, was the distinguishing feature of the Octet," Dave wrote in 1956. If you listen to such numbers as "These Foolish Things," "Perdido," "How High the Moon," "The Way You Look Tonight," with sidemen Paul Desmond on alto sax, Ron Crotty on bass and Lloyd Davis on drums you'll have a better understanding why a year later, Dave Brubeck was selected the man of the year by Time Magazine, edging out his good friend Duke Ellington who, incidentally, brought the issue to Dave's door to congratulate him.

If you listen even more carefully you'll hear me among the enthusiastic audience in Finney Chapel at Oberlin College that cold Monday night in northern Ohio. You'll also hear a great drummer, overlooked by the passage of time, who played the gig and carefully balanced a solid beat with creative brush and stick work while sick with the flu and a temperature of 103. Oberlin, a distinguished Conservatory campus, was typical of many institutions at the time. It had a mainstream classical music program with no courses on jazz or innovative contemporary music. The evening with Dave Brubeck changed all that. "The success of the concert had an immediate effect," says James Newman of Oberlin, in his liner notes. "Students organized the Oberlin College Jazz Club, with plans for three concerts during the following year, including a return performance by the Quartet...The concert was the force which gave birth to jazz at Oberlin."

Benny Goodman Carnegie Hall Jazz Concert, Vol I & II, Columbia, 1950

It may have been the first jazz concert recorded by a single mike for 24 players and a singer on a concert stage. It was definitely the shot heard around the world in jazz. Benny Goodman's celebrated Jazz Concert at Carnegie Hall, Jan. 16, 1938, was a milestone for everyone; audience, promoters, Carnegie Hall staffers and, above all, the musicians. And it might have been lost to posterity had it not been for Benny's daughter Rachel who found the obscure recording 12 years later in a closet in the Goodman home. At the time of the recording, CBS relayed the monaural sound from the overhead mike to a production site. One copy was sent to the Library of Congress. Benny didn't remember he had the other copy until his daughter found it. It was a concert that few thought would record any history, really. It was a cold night in the city, a packed house and seats erected on the stage to handle the overflow. The applause was polite in the beginning as Benny, in tails, entered, bowed, and stepped off the tempo for "Don't Be That Way." Some believe that the program really ignited where the first 12 inch recording ended. "Sing, Sing, Sing," the number written by Louie Prima which was fused with Fletcher Henderson's "Christopher Columbus" by Jimmy Mundy, was the catalyst.

Drummer Gene Krupa's heavy tom-toms, together with Benny's clarinet and Harry James' trumpet excited this previously reserved crowd. It lifted the audience and the performers, most believe. Irving Kolodin wrote later that the musicians," in this kind of music, were the thing and so it would remain...it brought out that family feeling that all good jazz musicians have for their celebrated predecessors, permitting a backward look at such landmarks at the popular music field as the Original Dixieland Band, Bix Beiderbecke, Ted Lewis, Louis Armstrong and the perennial Duke Ellington."

Ted Heath at the London Palladium, Vol. 3, London, 1955

He was England's Glenn Miller. His sound was similar in an era when many tried to copy the immensely popular Miller. But Ted Heath was a versatile musician, also a trombonist, who knew how to use arrangements, talented sidemen and good connections to make his own success. The London Palladium series, which began in 1945 as the war against Japan ended, was a gamble. Heath was struggling to make his band a paying proposition. Worse, it meant finding more creative arrangements to entertain a different kind of crowd. Playing dance music was one thing but pulling together production numbers for a 16 piece band was another. This Feb. 20th, 1955, concert demonstrates his success. "The precision of the section work, the full impact of the ensemble and the general taste in presentation…set a high standard. A standard which still places Heath before any other British bandleader," said Ray Horricks in the liner notes. Count Basie fully concurred. Heath "scared Basie death," Horricks added.

Good reason. He took standards like" Skylark," "Flying Home," "Crazy Rhythm," "Lover" and "Sweet Georgia Brown," and featured American sound alikes such Don Lusher on trombone (listen to Kenton's Frank Rosolino) and drummer Ronnie Verrell (a sound alike for Woody Herman's Don Lamond) and surrounded them with talent like clarinetist Henry Mackenzie, trumpeter Eddie Blair, bassist Johnny Hawksworth and pianist Frank Horrox and gave it that distinctly special big band swing feel and beat.

Yet, the arrangements were also distinctly Heath, too.

Duke Ellington and his Orchestra Festival Session, Columbia, 1959

Here's Duke and an assortment of some of best sidemen coming off the road from the Poconos to Newport, RI, offering some of the Ellington music that made him so famous. "Perdido," "Things Ain't What They Used To Be," "Duael Fuel," "Launching Pad" and "Idiom '59" are great reminders of the sound Duke used to create on those grinding road tours from Boston to Monterey. That all-star Ellington sax section of Johnny Hodges, Harry Carney, Jimmy Hamilton, Russell Procope and Paul Gonzalves is here along with trumpeters Clark Terry, Ray Nance and Cat Anderson. Gonzalves creates a postscript to his 1957 marathon solo on "Copout." "Duael Fuel," shows the work of two Ellington drummers, Sam Woodyard and Jimmy Johnson. It's the first stereophonic drum festival with a drum battle at the end.

Woody Herman Live at Monterey, Atlantic, 1959

Nothing like Woody the way many fans want to remember his herd. It started with a Woody trademark, "Four Brothers," the Jimmy Giuffre original composition for Stan Getz, Zoot Sims, Woody and Serge Shaloff. This particular Saturday afternoon, the sax section was Zoot, Bill Perkins and Richie Kamuca on tenor saxes, Woody on clarinet and alto and Med Flory on baritone. Said jazz critic Ralph Gleason, the number had been in the book for more than 10 years but ironically it was only the second time it had been recorded. While the weather turned cold and foggy by the evening set, Woody was telling everyone he wished he could take this herd on the road again. The band rehearsed most of the week and the results were outstanding, said reviewers like Gene Lees of Down Beat and that's with a few newcomers in the band like Mel Lewis on drums.

Claude Thornhill and his Orchestra, Hindsight Records, 1947

A band that was thoroughly enjoyed by critics, musicians and insiders but never really scored popularity with the public was the Claude Thornhill big band. With bop influenced arrangements by Gil Evans and Gerry Mulligan and Claude's beautiful scene-setting theme "Snowfall," many believed it was just a matter of time for the band to take off. Claude's band received praise from unexpected places. "The only really good big band I've heard in years," said Thelonious Monk. If there were commercial victims of World War II, Claude was one of them. His band attracted attention in an appearance at Glen Island Casino in 1941. The exposure was short-lived. Claude was soon in the US Navy leading a great band and distinguishing himself with commendations for his personal valor under enemy fire. While he was to attract 12 of his sidemen to join him after the war, more and more musicians didn't want to go on the road. Fortunately, this compilation of Claude's best 16 were the first to be pressed thanks to one the big bands most loyal fans, Wally Heider. What made Thornhill so great? No question he had some talented sidemen like Red Rodney on trumpet and alto saxophonist Lee Konitz and vocalist Gene Williams. But most were infatuated with a person Duke Ellington called a "beautiful man." He was, said George Simon, who wrote The Big Bands, a leader with taste, and a piano style that offered a range of ideas yet gave sparkle to ballads and added wit to jazz.

Stan Kenton and his Orchestra, June Christy, Four Freshmen "Road Show," in Concert at Purdue University, Fall, 1959, Capitol Records

Whether you like the excitement that a Stan Kenton Band could generate, he played this particular concert with special guests June Christy, the former Kenton singer, and the Four Freshmen, the quartet Stan found in nearby Dayton and helped push to stardom, at Purdue's Edward C. Elliott Hall of Music and made it an electrifying evening for the capacity crowd. Or maybe it was because Purdue had beaten Wisconsin the first time since 1945 that afternoon before the show. This was a good band midway through a typical road tour that started Sept. 28 at Murray State in Kentucky and would end up in Boston, Nov. 4. It was a "hit and run" tour as such one-nighters were called. Tired musicians trying to grab what sleep they could, miserable weather which may have given Miss Christy the cold that caused her voice to be much more husky than normal. But what you come away with whether you were among the 6,000 listeners that October night in Lafayette or you've heard it for the umpteenth time as I have on record, is a true Kenton performance with all the fanfare, talent and power such shows produce. Listen to the crowd reaction BEFORE Stan introduced June and later, the Four Freshmen. Thirty-eight shows in 38 days and the amazing thing is that, even with an occasional clam (sour note for the outsiders), this concert demonstrates the power of the big band at the end of the era.

Stan Kenton Live at the Hollywood Palladium, 1951 Jazz Band Release

Ten years after he started his Balboa Beach-on-the-Pacific experiment for dancers, this concert represents the quality Stan Kenton always knew he could project with 18 outstanding musicians. And he did it in the fabled Palladium no less.

The band at the time featured Canadian Maynard Ferguson, the young Montreal trumpet player who remembers playing with pianist Oscar Peterson in the same high school band a decade or so earlier, drummer Shelly Manne, a creative saxophonist, Bud Shank, and the inventive trumpeter and arranger Shorty Rogers who played his uptempo number "Jolly Rogers." The orchestra shows its range and musicianship when it shifts from the soft ballad "Laura" to smooth but louder "Easy Go" and then puts the pedal to the metal with "Lover." Kentonites know the excitement that rises when the tingling cymbal sound becomes a pronounced sizzle and crashes as the band heralds the familiar "Artistry in Rhythm" whether it was a calypso, waltz, fox trot or rumba tempo. Stan told an audience once he used every beat imaginable for his theme. At the Palladium that night the crowd didn't really care. It was pure Kenton for the home team.

Create Your Own Big Band Quiz Show

Everybody loves to one up someone else with special knowledge about history, old songs, the bands who played them, the musicians and singers who performed them and general trivia about an earlier era.

I could usually do my best on the sounds of the big bands and combos. How about you?

Here's a chance to demonstrate your skills on a period you either lived through, slept through or read about. Taking such a test certainly helps you gain status among your peers and, if you're over 50, makes you proud your mind hasn't been invaded by creeping dementia. It should cause you to be more interested in the old party games that flourished in the 1940s and 1950s. It beats Scrabble if you can just remember the names of the songs you used to hum.

Below are 50 questions that require short answers. 45 to 50 right gives you a big band of your own and a contract to play the Hollywood Palladium; 39 to 44 correct lets you know that you could be a Musicians' Union member; 29 to 38 right puts you in a territorial band playing the only bar in Sitka, Alaska; 28 and below right answers and you may want to rethink your plans to leave your day gig for the bandstand.

Let's get started.

1. Some music historians believe he was the first white big bandleader. He had a handle bar mustache and he was a portly gentleman violinist who took over the baton by accident. He was called "Pops." Who was he?
2. It was the place in New York City to be seen and heard. Some called it the Carnegie Hall of Jazz Clubs; others called it "The Mecca of the Hip." It was opened in 1935 by an intellectual bohemian named Max Gordon. What was the name of this famous club that continues in New York City today?
3. Frank Sinatra was well-known for his musical numbers with the Tommy Dorsey band. However, the crooner actually got his start as a "boy" band singer out of Hoboken, NJ with what big band leader?
4. Singer Anita O'Day was discovered in the early 1940s by drummer Gene Krupa. She joined the band and within months recorded a very popular ditty with trumpeter Roy Eldridge. It became a $1 million hit overnight. What was the number called?
5. Unlike a good number of bandleaders of the swing era who had any number of singers, Ray Anthony had only four. One was a songwriter who later became the president of Capitol Records. Who was he?
6. He arranged 100 numbers for Stan Kenton between 1945-1949 and was credited with helping to create the Kenton sound. He also arranged for Nat "King" Cole, Mel Torme, and Peggy Lee among others. Later, he wrote and arranged the music for the TV series "The Fugitive," "Felony Squad" and the very popular movie, M*A*S*H. What was his name?
7. Glenn Miller scored movie hits with two films before he entered the service in October, 1942. One was called "Sun Valley Serenade." What was the other movie?
8. It was 1948 and a famous group started at Fort Wayne, IN. The group included Bob Flanigan, Ross Barbour, Dave Barbour and Hal Kratzsch. They called themselves what?
9. They called it the band that played the blues and it could also swing. It opened at the Roseland Ballroom, Brooklyn, in 1936. What was the band?
10. 1944 turned out to be a year for singers and popular songs. Jo Stafford and Perry Como recorded "Long Ago and Far Away." The Ink Spots sang the hit "I'll Get By" and a man critics called "der bingle" sang "I'll Be Seeing You." Who was the singer?
11. A popular bandleader from the early days he used to always add "yousah," "yousah" to every radio broadcast or personal appearance. Who was he?

12. In Hollywood, CA this was THE place to play because it had radio time and it was extremely popular with West Coast audiences. What was it called?
13. Buddy DeFranco, Artie Shaw and Woody Herman all were known because of one particular instrument they played. What was it?
14. He was born in Texas, played with his dad in a circus band and later joined the Benny Goodman before he started his own band. Who was he?
15. He could have been a successful cartoonist but he loved to lead Latin bands. Who was he?
16. Two brothers from Rochester, NY were introduced into the band business in the 1950s by their father who brought touring musicians home for spaghetti dinners. One became a Grammy winner and composer of an Olympic theme song. Who were they?
17. When he began in the band business, he organized a group of collegians and they called themselves the Duke Blue Devils. His band later went on to renown. He was?
18. Johnny Mercer was a great song writer and singer who wrote such pieces as "Blues In the Night," "Jeepers Creepers," "That Old Black Magic." What many didn't know is that Mercer was president of what recording company?
19. Legendary bandleader Glenn Miller actually didn't like to fly but he felt compelled to make a short hop on the morning of Dec. 15, 1944 to make arrangements for his band's visit. Where was he headed and what happened?
20. It was called Jazz at the Philharmonic and it made one nighters across the country on its first tour. The founder of the successful jazz tour that featured so many popular artists was who?
21. Chick Webb, a popular young drummer at the Cotton Club, New York City, introduced a singer whose first claim to fame was taking over his band when he died prematurely at age 30. Who was the singer?
22. In 1952, two arrangers put together their own sounds with a band that featured An odd assortment of instruments. They briefly toured the country but people found it difficult to dance to one of the group's great hits, Doodletown Fifers. The leaders of the band were?
23. He didn't play the drums and he wasn't with the Benny Goodman band at Carnegie Hall when "Sing, Sing, Sing" aroused an elite Concert Hall crowd. But he is credited with writing the number and using it as his theme during the early 1930s. Who was he?
24. During the war years, he decided to start a band with a theme he had written called "Sunrise Serenade." He played the piano. His name was?
25. "Holiday Inn," filmed in 1942, became a traditional yuletide favorite and continues to be a TV rerun hit today. It starred Bing Crosby, Fred Astaire and introduced Irving Berlin's White Christmas. The band that backs the musical numbers is a brother to one of the stars of the show. What was the bandleader's name?
26. Occasionally, the movie "Wintertime" is seen during the late night reruns. The story was about Norwegian skating star, Sonja Henie, but it had actors such as Cesar Romero, Carol Landis and Cornell Wilde in leading roles. The band in this 1943 movie was a swinging herd. Whose band backed the musical numbers?
27. It was among the last of the stories about big band leaders. It followed movies like the Benny Goodman Story, The Glenn Miller Story, the Eddie Duchin Story and the Fabulous Dorseys. It was produced in 1959 and featured Sal Mineo. The name of the show was?
28. He was named Anthony Dominick Benedetto but he became much more popular as a singing waiter. He took what name to launch his career?

29. Her name was Doris Mary Anne Kappelhoff and she sang with the Barry Rapp band in Cincinnati, OH. Barry told her to drop the last name and recommended her to bandleader Les Brown. What did she call herself when she went with Les and his band?
30. His mother was with the Phil Spitalny All-Girl Orchestra, his father was a music teacher. He was trained as a bassoonist but became a drummer and arranged some of the most innovative Christmas music of the late 20th century. Who is he and what's the name of his group?
31. He had a deep rich voice and he was tall and handsome. He launched his own band in 1940 and he added a vocal group called the "Moon Maids" and gained popularity singing "Racing With the Moon." Who was this singing bandleader?
32. Two musicians roomed with Frank Sinatra when the Harry James and the Tommy Dorsey bands featured the singer. One was a trumpet player and the other a drummer. Who were Frank's roommates?
33. A number of presidents played musical instruments. Harry Truman and Richard Nixon, for example, were piano players. This president played the saxophone and actually went on the Arsenio Hall television show to play "Heartbreak Hotel." Who was he?
34. It was the first movie to show the dark side of the music business. It was a 1950 film about the life of trumpet player Bix Biederbecke. The movie featured Doris Day and some great songs by Hoagy Carmichael still remembered today like "Too Marvelous For Words," and "With A Song In My Heart." The name of this 1950 film was what?
35. Frank Dailey was a bandleader on the East Coast but his real claim to fame was operating a ballroom in New Jersey that frequently brought fame to a big band because of radio network hookups. The name of this famous ballroom was?
36. Harry James' band was known as the Music Makers, Stan Kenton had the Artistry in Rhythm band and Les Brown had the "Band of Renown." What was the slogan used for the Shep Fields band?
37. Musical families were also found in the big bands of the 1940s and 1950s. The Lombardos were prominent, the two Dorseys, Tommy and Jimmy; Ray and Leo Anthony among many. Who were the members of the bandleading Elgart family?
38. She was Roy Rogers' wife but she started as a big band singer with Anson Weeks. Her name was?
39. The Wild One was a 1954 film that featured Marlon Brando and Lee Marvin in the first biker movie at a time when rebels like James Dean were popular. The sound track for the movie was written by a former Stan Kenton trumpeter and composer/arranger. Who was this musician?
40. They were known as "Mr. and Mrs. Swing" and they became one of the first inter-racial marriages among big band personalities. Both had famous but separate careers in the music field. Who were they?
41. It was not an elite eastern college but it had dynamic people like Gene Hall and Leonard Breeden to steer the first jazz studies academic program in an American college or university. It now has advanced degrees in the subject. Name the college that started jazz education.
42. George Wein produced the country's first celebration of jazz in 1953. What was it called and where was it held?
43. He started with an octet, organized a popular trio in 1951 and by 1954 was named the Time Man of the Year. During World War II, he was a member of Gen. George Patton's 5th Army Band. Who was this piano player?
44. It was nominated for three musical Oscars thanks to songs like Chattanooga Choo Choo, In the Mood and Moonlight Serenade. This 1941 musical story featured singers, a big band and skater Sonia Henie who even sang a few bars. There was a young Dorothy

Dandridge singing and dancing and even Uncle Miltie—Milton Berle—with a small part in this famous movie. What was the name of this wartime hit?

45. Lionel Hampton started his first band in 1940 after working for such famous bands as Benny Goodman and others. His excitement as a vibraphonist and drummer and his humorous mumbling and singing along with his solos made him one of the popular bands of the 20th century. His theme was easily identifiable. What was it?
46. He started in Detroit in the 1930s, entered the military service during the war and came back to start another of the number of Glenn Miller-styled bands in the late 1940s. His theme was "Sunset to Sunrise" but it certainly wasn't his most famous hit. He recorded "I'm Looking Over a Four-Leaf Clover" as a novelty in 1948 and it became a tremendous pop number for the band. Who was this bandleader?
47. She is perhaps best remembered along with Danny Kaye and Bing Crosby in Irving Berlin's great seasonal movie in 1954, White Christmas. But she began her career, as many young singers of that era did as a big band singer. She got her big break in Cincinnati when bandleader Barney Rapp put she and her sister in touch with Tony Pastor. Who was this great singer of the big band era?
48. If you smoked in the 1930s, '40s, '50s and hadn't given it up by the 1960s you probably remember a famous radio show that later became a television show of the top weekly musical hits. It's original theme in 1935 was "Happy Days Are Here Again." What was the name of this show?
49. He was famous as a society pianist and popular bandleader especially on the East Coast. At the peak of his career he was diagnosed with leukemia. Hollywood gave his life the personal drama that so many other celebrity movies lack. Although it was more than two hours long, actors Ty Power, Kim Novak and James Whitmore helped the film receive four Academy nominations and pianist Carmen Cavallaro's soundtrack added to the realism of the story. What was the name of the film?
50. He actually was a big band musician who decided in the early 1940s that the field was so crowded he'd be better off looking for a novelty band. He made cowbells, washboards, idiotic sounds from all kinds of homemade instruments his identity. What was the name of this band and what was its unlikely theme song?

The answers to the Big Band Test:

1. *Paul Whiteman*
2. *Village Vanguard*
3. *Harry James*
4. *Let Me Off Uptown*
5. *Johnny Mercer*
6. *Pete Rugolo*
7. *Orchestra Wives*
8. *The Four Freshmen*
9. *Woody Herman*
10. *Bing Crosby*
11. *Ben Bernie*
12. *The Hollywood Palladium*
13. *The clarinet*
14. *Harry James*
15. *Xavier Cugat*
16. *Chuck and Gap Mangione*
17. *Les Brown*

18. *Capitol Records*
19. *He was headed for France and his single engine plane went down in the channel and his body was not recovered*
20. *Norman Granz*
21. *Ella Fitzgerald*
22. *Eddie Sauter and Bill Finegan*
23. *Louie Prima*
24. *Frankie Carle*
25. *Bob Crosby*
26. *Woody Herman*
27. *The Gene Krupa Story*
28. *Tony Bennett*
29. *Doris Day*
30. *Chip Davis and the Mannheim Steamrollers*
31. *Vaughn Monroe*
32. *Jack Palmer, the trumpet player, and drummer Buddy Rich*
33. *President Bill Clinton*
34. *The Young Man With the Horn*
35. *The Meadowbrook*
36. *Rippling Rhythm*
37. *Les and Larry Elgart*
38. *Dale Evans*
39. *Shorty Rogers*
40. *Mildred Bailey and Red Norvo*
41. *North Texas State*
42. *The Newport Jazz Festival, Newport, RI*
43. *Dave Brubeck*
44. *Sun Valley Serenade*
45. *Flying Home*
46. *Art Mooney*
47. *Rosemary Clooney*
48. *Lucky Strike Cigarettes Hit Parade (later known as Your Hit Parade)*
49. *The Eddie Duchin Story (1956)*
50. *Spike Jones and his City Slickers; Cocktails For Two*

The Big Band Days Bibliography

My two-year research for materials about the Big Band Days ranged from newspapers, magazines, books, web sites, emails, radio and television program tapes, personal and telephone interviews.

What started out in late 1999 as a book about a Central Ohio bandleader blossomed as I discovered that a good book with sources about the actual days and lives of the nationally recognized as well as territorial and lesser known big band musicians, leaders and vocalists wasn't available. Furthermore, there wasn't a central listing of information about jazz radio programs, jazz festivals and other details concerning swing and dance music. As a former player and a devotee of the period, the concept of a memoir and source book intrigued me. While certainly not complete, the citations listed here were valuable in my research and reference work.

Some excellent sources that you can find without much assistance on the web are: the Big Band Data Base, the work of Murray L. Pfeffer, www.nfo.net, truly one of the most comprehensive repositories of big band information one can find anywhere. If you're nostalgic for old ballrooms and dance pavilions check out www.nbea.com and its many links that bring back memories. In fact, if you know of a ballroom that's not listed...contact the web site and let the organization know.

Don't forget that any number of traveling bands simply use their names.com. Finally, while I tried to be complete and up-to-date, remember web sites change as fast as emails and cell phone addresses these days.

Personal or Telephone Interviews

Stan Kenton, Buckeye Lake Crystal Ballroom,OH Summer, 1948, 1950
Gene Krupa, Buckeye Lake Pier Ballroom,OH Summer, 1949
Don Fagerquist, Buckeye Lake Pier Ballroom, OH summer, 1949
Lenny Dee, Buckeye Lake Mayfair Room,OH Summers, 1949, 1950, and 1951
Les Brown, Rolly Bundock, Jack Sperling, Stumpy Brown, USO Tour, Tokyo, Japan-Seoul, Korea, winter, 1957-1958
J.R. Monterose, Utica College, NY, Spring, 1983
Jack Palmer Jr., Rome, NY April, 2002
Johnny Vincent, Ray Anthony Band, Buckeye Lake, OH Summer, 1950
Ray Brown, Seattle, WA, June 19, 2001

Web Site Sources

Dates indicate day site was available

Bassist Ray Brown Welcomes Recognition As Pittsburgh Jazz Legend, by Bob Karlovits, Tribune-Review Music Writer, www.pittsburghlive.com/x/tribune-review/entertainment/s_21056.html 7/21/2002
Rob McConnell www.concordrecords.com/bios.mcconell/bio.html 11/29/2001
Ron Kolber www.ameritech.net 11/14/2001
Spyro Gyra, Jay Beckenstein www.headsup.com/albums 10/6/2001
The Bob Norval Orchestra www.bobnorval.com 11/15/2001
Bo Lewis Big Band Dance Party www.bolewis.org 1/12/2002
The LittleBigBand www.littlebigband.com 6/18/2002
The Big Band Jazz & Hall of Fame www.jazzhall.org 5/4/2002
Zoot Suits www.zootsuitstores.com 4/7/2002
New Vintage Big Band www.bigbandjazz.com 4/7/2002
Retro Bands www.pennsylvania 6500.com 4/7/2002

Big Band Theme Songs www.bigbandmusic.com 2/14/2002
Big Band Websites www.thesjo.com/pages/lislink 01.html. 2/22/2002
Jazz Radio Stations. www.jazz.com/tpl/radio_stations2.html 4/27/2002
Paul Whiteman Bio www.btinternet.com/~dreklind/whtmanbio.htm 11/14/2001
New York City's Famous Jazz Clubs, www.readio.com/clubs/newyorkclubs6.html 2/4/2002
How Women In Jazz Developed www.hartbeat07/womeninjazz/tex/about.html 5/6/2002
Ken Watters Group KenWattersgroup@aol.com 1/5/2002
Mike Vax: Big Band Leader www.winternet.com/~trmpts 5/4/2002
Big Band...What's Big? Review by Richard Duffy, www.jazzrew.com/corners96.html 5/14/2002
The Fabulous Four Freshmen www.fourfreshmen.com/index.htm 8/11/2001
KUAZ Online www.kuaz.org 3/10/2002
WCPN Cleveland Radio www.wcpn.org 1/27/2002
Teo Macero www.teorecords.com 4/26/2002
Frank Woods woodyou@tele-net.net 12/27/2001
Jazz in the NPR 100 www.nprjazz.org/programs/npr100.html 4/27/2002
Bobby Darin Biography www.biography.com/tv/listings/darin_b.html 11/29/2001
Al Porcino Big Band 'Live' www.btinternet.com/~j.r.Killoch/porcino.html 11/29/2001
Iridium Jazz Club NYC www.iridiumjazzclub.com 7/7/2001
Tritone Jazz Fantasy Camps www.tritonejazzfantasycamp.com 5/17/2002
Gene Krupa Biography www.drummerman.net/biography.html 4/29/2002
Welcome to Mainly Big Bands www.j.r.killoch.btinternet.co.uk 5/12/2002
Steve Good Band www.stevegood.com 12/23/2001
Horace Heidt Band www.bigbands.com/hhsr.htm 7/3/2001
Dick Jurgens Orchestra After WWII www.dickjurgens.com 2/5/200
Dick Jurgens Orchestra-Road Stories www.dickjurgens.com 2/8/2002
Les Brown www.delafont.com/music_acts/Les-Brown.htm 11/14/2001
Find A Grave (obituaries of musicians) www.findagrave.com 6/21/2002
Big Bands Live www.bigbandlive.org 6/21/2002
Ken & Harry Waters Group Kenwatt@aol.com 10/20/2001
Pyramid Dance & Swing Bands www.pyramidband.com 5/4/2002
Mark Buselli & Brent Wallarob Band www.bwjo.org 5/4/2002
Bob Rogers audiobob@rogers.com 2/ 25/ 26/ 2002
WAER Radio Music Page, www.waer.org/jazz 4/27/2002
WCPN Cleveland Radio www.wcpn.org 4/27/2002
JazzOnline www.jazzonline.com/jazz101 11/29/2001
Wage & Recording Scale2001-02 www.local802afm.org/wage/phono.htm 1/26/2002
American Big Bands Database www.nfo.net 11/13/2001, 1/26/2002
Craig's BigBands&Big Names www.bigbands&bignames.com 7/8/2001
Jazz Vocalists '30s-'50s www.ddg.com/LIS/InfoDesignF961/Ismael/jazz/930s.html 2/4/2002
Big bands www.barberusa.com/orchest.htm 2/14/2002
Popular Songs, 1950-1959 www.asoundinvestment.com/50.-59.htm 2/4/2002
Neil Hansen, Yellowstone 862@hotmail.com Jazz Festival 5.26/2002
Rayo Nulsen, Barney Rapp grandson, rayo@fuse.net 3/8/2002
Milt Bernhart On the Road www.professional.com/humour/bernhart.html 2/12/2002
Neal Hefti by Kent Lungberg www.mit.edu/people/klund/hefti/hefti.ftml 2/3/2002
Ray Anthony Biography www.rayanthony.net/RABiography.html 11/14/2001
Glossary of Common Musical Terms www.64.33.34.112/.www/glossary.html 1/12 2001
Swing Era www.64.33.34.112/www.slang.html 11/12/2001
Music Educators www.iaje.org 5/5/2002
Dave's Top 40 Big Bands www.letsdanceradio.com/top40.html 6/23/2002

New York Big Band www.bobjanuary.com 6/23/2002
Sammy Kaye www.sammykayeorchestra.com/sammy.htm 2/22/2002
Bands, recordings www.bigbandmusic.com
Gap Mangione www.gapmangione.com
Chuck Mangione www.chuckmangione.com
Well known Recording Radio Studio Bands www.64.33.34.112/.www/storks.html
Hit Parade www.64.33.34.112/.HITS/index.html
Peggy Lee's Death www.startribune.com/stories/457/1114874.html 1/23/2002
Maynard Ferguson www.gr8music.com/Ferguson_Maynard/maynard.html 10/01/2001
Melodies www.64.33.34.112/.WWW/melodyb.html 11/12/2001
Society Bands www.64.33.34.112/.www/society.html 10/2/2001
Jazz site www.jazzwest.com 10/1/2001
Monk Rowe, musician www.monkrowe.com/man/bio.html 7/16/1999
Rosemary Clooney www.rosemaryclooney.com/biography.html 1/29/2002
Ella Fitzgerald www.ellafitzgerald.com 1/29/2002
Connie Haines www.conniehaines.com/Connie/index.html 1/29/2001
San Francisco big band www.swingfever.com 12/24/2001
Great Bandleaders, Singers www.americanmusicclassics.com/artist/i.htm
Jazz Radio Stations www.npr.org/stations/index.html 12/31/2000
Praise Big Band Christian Music www.pe.net/~musicl/schedule.htm 1/1/2002
Big Band stock arrangements, www.loc.gov/rr/perform/bigbandstocks.html 2/22/2002
Big Band Leader Remembers the Real Sinatra, www.breezypointresort.com/breezypointer/carlile/html 2/22/2002
Doris Day, singer, www.dorisday.com 1/24/2002
www.afterhoursbigband.com
Musicians' site www.musicians.com 2/4/2002
Musicians' site www.jazzprofessional.com 2/12/2002
Kingston Trio www.kingstontrio.com 2/4/2002
Johnny Ray, singer www.tsimon.com/ray.htm 2/4/2002
Tommy Dorsey www.redhotjazz.com/tommy.html 2/4/2002
Anita O'Day, singer www.anitaoday.com 1/24/2002
Cleveland, OH Jazz History www.clevelandjazz.org/history.htm 12/24/2001
Swing Music Discussion www.64.33.34.112/.www/swing.html 11/12/2001
Songs of World War II www.64.33.34.112/.www/ww2/html
Trumpeter Red Rodney www.fantasyjazz.com/catalog/rodney 11/15/2001
Trumpeter Buddy Childers www.candidrecords.com/79749.html
Between the Wars www.chnm.gmu.edu/courses/hist409/swing/html 12/24/2001
21st Gene Krupa www.geocities.com/gliiorchestra/ 2/4/2002
Jazz Scene, Seattle, WA www.jazzsteps.com/newsletter 12/4/2001
Big Band & Jazz Hall of Fame, www.jazzhall.org.bbjhf.html 12/24/2001
American Jazz Museum, www.americanjazzmuseum.com 2/9/2001
NYC Jazz Club, Village Vanguard, www.villagevanguard.net 7/7/2001
NBEA History, www.nbea.com/archives.htm 1/1/2002
Rhythm Nation: A Guide to American Jazz www.brittanica.com/bcom/orginal/article/0.5744.16612.html 12/13/2001
Origins of Big Band Music, Bob Thomas, 1994 www.redhotjazz.com/bigband.html 12/13/2001
The Swing Era-Bring It Back! www.e46.com/swingEra/home.shtml 12/24/2001
The Monterey Jazz Festival www.montereyjazzfestival/.org
Drummer Buddy Rich www.buddyrich.com 7/8/2001
Buddy Morrow, official site of Tommy Dorsey Band www.buddymorrow.com 7/11/2001

NYC Jazz Club, Birdland, www.birdlandjazz.com/history.html 7/7/2001
NYC Jazz Club, Blue Note, www.bluenote.net/newyork/index.html 7/7/2001
Dave's Top 40 Big Bands, Carmel, CA www.letsdanceradio.com/top40.html email: dave@letsdanceradio.com
Dave Hanlon Band www.davehanlonscookbook.com 7/25/2001
Pianist Oscar Peterson www.oscarpeterson.com
Stan Kenton Alumni www.52ndstreet.com/kenton/sidemen.htm
Ballroom Rules www.nbea/com/archives5.htm
Register of the Collection of Big Band Photos ca. 1930s, ca. 1945, Unv. of California, Los Angeles, CA
www.library.ucla.edu/libraries/music/mlsc/ead/bigband_htm
Glenn Miller Orchestra Itinerary www.glennmillerorchestra.com/itinerary/html 6/21/2002
All About jazz www.allaboutjazz.com 2/5/2002

Letters, Memorabilia, E-Mails

Lou DiSario, Philadelphia, PA, letters, materials, March 27, 2002; Feb. 13, 2002; Feb. 19, 2002; Feb. 27, 2002
Harold Whittemore, Aug.22, 1989
Jim Booker, letters, March 16, 2000; April 7, 2001
Jimmy Scalia, archivist, Bobby Darin, e-mail April 4, 2002; April 13, 2002; January 9/2002' February 25, 2002
Charles "Chuz" Alfred, letters, Oct. 16, 1987; Oct. 30, 2000; 7/24/2000
David Dudajek, e-mails, March 30, 2002; April 4, 2002
Steve Early, e-mails December 16, 2001; December 17, 2001; December 20,2001
Paul R. Kumler, letter July 27, 2000
Jimmy Sain, letters, July 2, 2000; July 19,2000; Aug. 2, 2000
Howard Schneider, letter, materials, March 14, 2002
David Miller, NPR, e-mail December 24, 2001
Neil Hansen, Yellowstone Jazz Festival, e-mail May 26, 2002
Audree Coke Kenton, letters, July 18,1989: Sept. 2, 14, 1989
Al Julian, notes, June 10, 2000; June 20, 2001
Frank Woods e-mail December 27, 2001
Bob Derosa, e-mail May 15, 2002; June 25, 2002
Bob Rogers, audiobob@rogers.com Feb. 25, 26, 2002
Rayo Rapp, grandson bandleader Barney Rapp, rayo@fuse.net March 8, 2002
Dr. Bruce Boyd Raeburn, emails May 3, 2002; May 15, 2002
Gary Greenfelder, email OneBeatBack.com March 13, 2002
Chip Davis, Dan Wieberg, American Gramaphone, February 8, 2002; packet
Dick Jurgens Jr, emails, February 7, 2002; February 20, 2002
Mrs. David James, letters, emails, June 9, Dec. 4, 2000; Feb. 19, 2002; March 7, 2002
Anthony J. Agostinelli, editor, Network,letters, Aug. 4, 1994; March 9, 2000 ajagostinelli@worldnet.att.net
John Matter, NBEA, emails, January 2, 2002; March 6, 2002 www.nbea.com
Chris Riddle, email, 8/12/2001 www.epluri.com/TSA/AMHall/AMHFFiles/NelsonRiddleBio.html
Bill Elliott, Swing Orchestra, email, swingorch@earthlink.net November 14, 2001
Arlene Leonard, secretary, Glenn Miller Birthplace Society, letter, materials, www.glennmiller.org February 1, 2001
Robert J. Robbins, email,secretary, Big Bands International, September 20, 2001

Newspaper, Magazine Articles

A Mohawk Valley 'Family Man & 'Music Man', Vinnie Garco, Life & Times of Utica (NY) March 8-14, 2001
Crowd Enjoys Show Despite Rain, Ball State Daily News (IN), July 2, 2001
PBS 'Jazz' Deserves Audience, North Texas Daily (TX), Jan. 25, 2001
Jazz Chronicles Dodging Sour Notes, Utica Observer-Dispatch (NY), Sept. 3, 2000
Experience Jazz World at Hamilton College's Jazz Archive Utica Observer-Dispatch (NY) Jan. 27, 2000
Jazz Program Sets High Bar With Students, Annual Festival, North Texas Daily (TX) April 6, 2000
Some Notes Are Absent From Jazz, Albany Times-Union (NY) Feb. 11, 2001
Arts Center to Showcase Swing City Jazz Series, Kansas State Collegian(KS) May 10, 2002
Sounds of Denton, North Texas Daily (TX) March 8, 2002
A Look Back by Frank Tomaino, Utica Observer-Dispatch (NY)Jan. 1, 1990
Battle of the Hollywood Bowl, New York Times, Sept. 4, 2001
John Ashcroft, Parade, May 4, 2002
Les Brown, Swing Bandleader, Dies At 88, New York Times, Jan 6, 2001
Jazz in the Catbird Seat; It Wasn't Always So, New York Times, Jan. 6, 2001
Fox Chase Entertainer Remembers Old Pal Frank Sinatra, Breeze Newspapers, March 7, 1991
Bandleader Woody Herman Has Jazz To Thank, The Daily Campus, Sept. 9, 1987
Woody Herman Played It All, Utica Observer-Dispatch (NY) Oct. 30, 1987
Woody Remembered, editorial, Christian Science Monitor, Nov. 1, 1987
Herman It Tune With All Times, USA Today, Oct. 30, 1987
The Long, Some Times Rocky Road of Jazz Great Woody Herman, USA Today, Oct. 30, 1987
Buddy Rich, USA Today, June 25, 1986
Popular Musicians Left Their Mark on Central Ohio, Sporting Lines (OH) May 18, 1994
June Christy Singer 64, Is Dead, New York Times, June 24, 1991
Energy Level of Rich Band 'Up" Arizona Daily Wildcat (AZ), Aug. 30, 1983
Mangione Discusses 'Life, Music, Future,' Ball State Daily News (IN), Dec. 4, 1981
Saxist Steve Marcus Still Burns, Arizona Daily Wildcat (AZ) Aug. 26, 1983
All That Jazz, by Ken Burns, USA Weekend, Jan 5-7, 2001
Dick Trimble Story Brought Back Memories, Lancaster Eagle-Gazette (OH) letter to editor, 7/25/1993
Young Players A Big Hit At Jazz Fest, Syracuse Herald-American (NY) June 24, 2001
Jazz Legend Gives 'Good Feeling, Syracuse Herald American (NY) June 24, 2001
50 Years of UNI Jazz: Underground to Downbeat, Northern Iowan (IA) Feb. 13, 2001
Swing Dance Makes Comeback, Ball State Daily News (IN) June 27, 2001
Peggy Lee Dies at 81, New York Times, Jan. 25, 2002
6,000 Elbows, One Long Party, New York times, Nov. 12, 2001
Jazz Clubs Swing Back to Life, New York Times, Oct. 19, 2001
Bad Rap: Is Foul Language A Staple of Hip Hop? Albany Times-Union (NY) Jan 6, 2002
These Four Friends Go to A Few Bars to Sing a Few Bars, Albany Times-Union (NY) Jan 27, 2002
Artie Shaw's Address to IAJRC Convention, Aug, 15, 1998, IAJRC Journal, Winter, 1999
Sax Player Brignola Dies, Utica Observer-Dispatch (NY) Feb. 8, 2002
Play It Again, Bill, Gannett News Service, circa 1998
Count Basie, 79, Bandleader and Master of Swing, Dead, John Wilson, New York Times, April 27, 1984
Jazz Fest Supplement, Syracuse Herald American (NY) June 18, 2000
Al Julian: Promo Seltzer, LA Jazz Scene (CA) April, 1999

Stan Kenton's Artistry In Rhythm and Sound,Jack Behrens, Home Newspapers (NY) NY Aug. 21, 1989
Romans Mourn 'Dynamite trumpet player;' share fond memories, David Dudajek, Utica Observer-Dispatch (NY) Jan.8, 2000
Swing and Sway Started Right Here, Lakewood, OH Sun Post, Dec. 21, 1989
Tex Beneke, 86, Saxophonist Who Sang Miller's Hits, Dies, New York Times, June 1, 2000
Norris Turney, 79, Saxophonist Who Recorded With Ellington, New York Times, June 22, 2001
Lou Levy, 72, Versatile Pianist For Top Singers in Jazz World, New York Times, Jan. 31, 2001
Burns' 'Jazz' Heats Up Winter, Daily Nebraskan (NE) Jan. 8, 2001
Swinging to the Tunes of the Dick Trimble Band, Lancaster (OH) Eagle-Gazette, July 7, 1993
Milton Gabler, Storekeeper of the Jazz World, Dies at 90, New York Times, July 25, 2001
Billy Mitchell, 74, Saxophonist Who Played in Top Jazz Bands, New York Times, May 2, 2001
USO Nostalgia Returns to Muncie, Ball State Daily News (IN) July 5, 2001
Jazz Legend Set to Lecture on Musical Expertise, North Texas Daily (TX) Feb. 7, 2001
All That Jazz, Ball State Daily News (IN) March 20, 2001
Ray Brown Trio, Unv. Of Washington Summer Daily (WA) undated
How Did Benny Goodman Get to Carnegie Hall, American History, April 2001
World Famous Sounds: One O'Clock Band, North Texas Daily (TX) Nov. 1, 2000
A Busy Harry Connick Jr. Kicks Off a Tour At the Landmark, Syracuse Post-Standard(NY) Nov. 4, 2001
Joe Henderson, Saxophonist and Composer, Dies at 64, New York Times, July 3, 2001
Nick Fatool, 85, Drummer Who Kept the Beat for Swing Era Bands, New York Times, Oct, 2000
Ralph Burns, 79, Arranger, Composer From Big Bands to Broadway, New York Times, Nov. 28, 2001
Empty Field Contains Whispers of Laughter, Lancaster (Oh) Eagle-Gazette, July 30,1991
Trombonist Fred Zito, Big Band Player, Dies, Utica Observer-Dispatch (NY) Aug. 4, 1994
Norman Granz Dies at 83, New York Times, Nov. 27, 2001
The Herds: The Woody Herman Society, A.J. Julian, editor, Winter, 1999/Spring, 2000; Summer, 2000;Fall, 2000;Winter, 2000/Spring, 2001; Summer, 2001;Fall, 2001; Winter, 2001/Spring, 2002
The Big Bands International Magazine, August, 2001; November, 2001; February, 2002; May, 2002
Bob Cooper: A Shaper of West Coast Jazz, The Network, XVII, September, 1993
25-Year-Old Band To Spread Word, Ball State Daily News (NY) April 12, 2002
Dixieland Jazz Visits Taiwan, by Nancy Kobryn, Home News (NY), February 5, 1995

Books

The Gigography: Reflections Of 'The Road,' Charles "Chuz" Alfred, (unpublished manuscript, 1994)
50th Anniversary NBEA Directory, 1997
The Movies, Richard Griffith and Arthur Mayer, Simon and Schuster, 1970
Recensio Yearbook, 1953, Miami University, OH
The Biographical Encyclopedia of Jazz, Leonard Feather and Ira Gitler, Oxford University Press, 1999
The Swing Era, Gunther Schuller, Oxford University Press, 1989
The Trumpet Blues: The Life of Harry James, Peter J. Levinson, Oxford University Press, 1999
Jazz: The Rough Guide, Ian Carr, Digby Fairweather and Brian Priestley, (2nd ed) The Rough Guides, 2000
The Wonderful Era of the Great Dance Bands, Leo Walker, Da Capo, 1990
The World of Swing: An Oral History of Big Band Jazz, Stanley Dance, 2001
Leader of the Band: The Life of Woody Herman, Gene Lees, Oxford University Press, 1995

The Swing Book, Degen Pener, Back Bay Books, 1999
Music Hound: Swing, The Essential Album Guide, Steve Knopper, editor, Visible Ink Press, 1999
The Big Bands, George T. Simon, Macmillan, 1971
The Big Band Almanac, Leo Walker (rev. ed) Da Capo, 1989
Jazz: History, Instruments, Musicians, Recordings, John Fordham, Dorling Kindersley, 1993
Swing! The New Retro Renaissance, V.Vale, V/Search Publications, 1998
Eddie Condon's Scrapbook of Jazz, Eddie Condon, Hank O'Neal, Galahad Books, 1973
Stan Kenton: The Early Years, 1941-1947, Edward F. Gabel, Balboa Books, 1993
Jazz Anecdotes, Bill Crow, Oxford University Press, 1990
Music, Popular, Folk and Jazz, Collier's Yearbook, 1965

Audio

Newport Beach Hyatt, CA—Woody Herman Alumni Gathering, September, 1993 (courtesy Sherman Wilkinson, Largo, FL)
Birdland, NYC—Stan Kenton, July 1958; Hollywood Palladium, Interview with Bud Shank, 1951 (courtesy of Sherman Wilkinson, Largo, FL)

Television Programs

ReInventing Dave Brubeck, WCNY-TV, PBS, December 27, 2001
Jazz, Ken Burns PBS Television Series, WCNY-TV January, 2001
Glenn Miller's Greatest Hits, Public Television with Kathy Lee Gifford, 1995
Glenn Miller Band Reunion with Original Band Members, Public Broadcasting Station Special
Buddy Rich At the Top, Feb. 6, 1973, Rochester, NY Hudson Music Classic Performance Series Video
Woody Herman Remembered, Leisure Video, 1991

Radio Shows

WIBX (NY)—Composers & Arrangers of Big Band Era, Monk Rowe, June 4, June 11, June 18, 2000
WIBX (NY)—Big Bands At Holiday Time, Monk Rowe and Don Cantwell, Dec. 7, 14, 21, 2001
WIBX (NY)—A Swinging Time, Don Cantwell and Dick Robinson, March 15, 2001
WIBX (NY)—Chuz Alfred and Friends, August, 2000
WIBX(NY)—Swing Music's Like Fine Wine, Dick Robinson and Don Cantwell, March 3, 10, 2002
WHOK(OH)—Dick Trimble Band, Lancaster, OH 1949

For The Folks Who Made This Book A Reality

I read acknowledgement pages out of curiosity. They give me faith in humankind, actually. In a day when some don't take time to say thank you, many could care less about digging out old photographs or spending a few minutes trying to be thoughtful. At the same time, I found some truly tried to help although their searches were fruitless.

Authors (and door to door sales people) know what it's like to experience days and weeks of rejection soliciting information to find a kernel, a nugget or that diamond...After writing and editing 16 books and more than 11,000 magazine pieces, I've heard about every excuse imaginable and suffered my share of rudeness that surprisingly came from normally nice people as well as those considered gruff and insensitive.

"Oh yes, I'll help you but NOT now...not next year in fact."

"I realized I promised you but something came up and I can't."

"I really don't want to be interviewed if you've included him."

And those were from people I finally tracked down. A number never returned repeated emails or calls.

I was fortunate, however. High school and college friends, big band connections on the East and West Coasts and six months of compiling nearly 2,500 web sites about the big bands, swing era, musicians and that all too vague term, "Jazz" helped me flesh out my memories for this story of the big band days and the sources you can tap to entertain or educate yourself.

Some folks stand out for their support and their efforts. And while I've tried to keep a log of everyone, I apologize here to any I've missed. It wasn't intentional...it was the scope of a two-year search and the pages of bibliography you'll find attached that clouded a normally clear mind as I finished this labor of love.

Chuz Alfred and Jim Booker, both of Columbus, OH, brought me into the world of music. We had the kind of youthful experiences during the tense Cold War years that I wish my children and grandchildren could have experienced. The uncertainty and fears we feel today we felt then. No generation can escape it, it seems. Chuz introduced me to corn silk cigarettes (the fun was rolling them, not smoking them I discovered but I wanted to be cool), harmony, chording (not exactly in that order) and how to make a snare drum and hi-hat cymbal provide the beat for the Alfred musical gatherings at the family cottage on Buckeye Lake, OH. We both summered at the resort, had outboard runabouts which took us all over the seven mile body of water and frequently deposited us at the Buckeye Lake Park where the big bands would come and go weekly. It was idyllic; it would start each Memorial Day and end every Labor Day.

Jim and I, by contrast, have been friends since grade school and, once again, music was the catalyst for both of us. We followed musicians, bandleaders, band tours in Downbeat like youngsters track baseball, hockey and football players today. We both were in marching band and Jim, a good reader as a reed man, became my high school connection to the band business for two important reasons. He had a car and he had talent. Drummers, I was told many times, could be found everywhere. When I got my first set, I had to practice elsewhere because my parents absolutely opposed the instrument and my playing it. My practice time was at the bandleader's music store where I put in more hours on the drums than my homework. It was Jim, the good friend, who took his high school buddy, the drummer and his bulky instrument to gigs. Though military service, college and careers separated us, we've stayed in touch...and we continue to do so today.

Lou DiSario of Philadelphia, PA is another integral part of this book. An entertainer, singer and a ballroom announcer at major East Coast sites, he contacted me when he first heard about the book and offered his help. Lou had a front row seat to the big bands. He was invaluable as you'll find as you read the book.

Central New York musicians and big band enthusiasts Don Cantwell, Monk Rowe, Dick Robinson, Dave Dudajek, Jack Palmer Jr. and Bob DeRosa of Rochester offered their contributions about the times as well as their own experiences a few hundred miles from the Big Apple. Too often, upstate New York was considered not "hip" when it came to jazz and big bands. I hope this book sets the record straight; there were and are outstanding players and music north of the New York State Thruway.

Others offered their views of something they enjoyed at another time in their lives.

Mrs. David "Doe" James talks about her days singing with big bands while in college. She creates an up close and personal contrast of the excitement of the gig and the drudgery of the road that every musician felt then and continues to feel today. Jimmy Sain, a longtime DJ in Central Ohio, tracked down musicians for me and recalled for us the difficulties engineers had taping performances in the old days and former Dick Trimble saxophone player, Paul Kumler, told about his years as a sideman.

Gannett Op-Ed Page Editor and part-time trumpet player, David Dudajek, provided his interviews with big band players like Jack Palmer and the talented Zito family. Palmer's son Jack Jr. gave me an interesting account of his life growing up in the big bands on the road and why he didn't follow his dad's footsteps as a trumpet player.

Down South, Tulane's Dr. Bruce Boyd Raeburn, son of two important big band icons, bandleader Boyd Raeburn and singer Ginny Powell, talked to me about what he believes is the future of the band business. So did National Public Radio's veteran disk jockey David Miller and Big Band International Secretary, Robert Robbins.

People like Dick Jurgens Jr, son of bandleader Dick Jurgens, and an ageless singer who I remember seeing in person, Connie Haines, offered their thoughts about the days when the bandstand was the place to be. Al Julian, the hard-working director of the Woody Herman Society, gave me names and addresses and Chip Davis and his pr person, Dan Frieberg, of the innovative sound, the Mannheim Steamrollers, talked about the changes in the music business since his mother was with Phil Spitalny and his All-Girl Orchestra. Bandleader Howie Schneider gave me an interesting look at a musical name of the past, the Jan Garber Band, and how it continues today.

A sound engineer and longtime Utica College friend, Bill Parker, provided the technological assistance that reproduced interview tapes and helped me get material important to this book. High school friends John Imhoff and Ken Nihiser put in their two cents and Bobby Darin's archivist, Jimmy Scalia, provided an interesting assessment of one of America's talented composers and arrangers Torrie Zito, another Central New Yorker.

And there were others along the way who took the time to offer their thoughts and efforts; genial bassist Ray Brown at a Far West appearance who took time to take a phone call, John Matter of the NBEA, and Audree Coke Kenton were among those I remember.

The graphic pictorial wouldn't have been included had it not been for the excellent work of Valerie Sorrells of Rochester.

My family contributed the support that I've been so fortunate to have throughout my career, too. Son Mark. for example, helped me find one of Duke Ellington's rhythm section and interview him. Steve Early, Duke's drummer in the 1960s, offers a somewhat different view of the era, the people and the changes that occurred.

Of course, there's no question this manuscript received the much needed criticism that an author can only get from a spouse who cares (even if she didn't really appreciate the music). Without my wife Patty this project would merely be another dream under the pile of yearbooks somewhere in the basement.

Finally, a tribute to a group of men who made me a musician. Without Dick Trimble, Dano Estell, Webb Ricketts and Jimmy Claar, Lancaster, OH, musicians and mentors, there probably wouldn't have been a musical interlude in my life. Dick offered me my first paying gig, a place to practice from time to time and experiences that I never really found again during my playing years. It was a lifetime of six years that I will never forget.

Jack Behrens Clinton, NY

Index

ABOUT THE AUTHOR

A nationally known and award-winning columnist, editor and writer, Jack Behrens founded the journalism program at Utica College of Syracuse University New York in 1972 and continues to teach as a *Reader's Digest* Foundation Magazine Professor at several eastern universities. Columbia Scholastic Press Association awarded him the coveted Gold Key Award in 2000 for his efforts and devotion to student press issues.

He has authored or edited fifteen books and written more than 11,000 magazine articles for national and international publications. His popular public affairs radio program is broadcast weekly in Central New York.

His work with *Roots* author, Alex Haley, in the 1970s produced three books on writing including a popular *text, The Writing Business* (Steffen, 1991). An earlier book, *Typewriter Guerrillas* (Nelson-Hall, 1976-77) was chosen and *Editor & Publisher* best seller.

His big band days, however, were a special six years in the late 1940s and early 1950s when he played and met bandleaders and musicians he never forgot. And he never forgot hauling a Slingerland drum set through Midwest towns and cities.

This book is dedicated to the more than eighty musicians, bandleaders, dancers, entertainers and music lovers who participated by remembering their involvement in the "swing era" and playing music that has never died.

CPSIA information can be obtained
at www.ICGtesting.com
Printed in the USA
LVHW100813190520
656015LV00003B/15

9 781403 368584